T0041548

Samatha, Jhāna, and Vipassana

Samatha, Jhāna, and Vipassanā

Practice at the Pa-Auk Monastery: A Meditator's Experience

Hyunsoo Jeon, MD, PhD

Translated by HaNul Jun

Foreword by Sayadaw Revata

Wisdom

Wisdom Publications
199 Elm Street
Somerville, MA 02144 USA
wisdompubs.org

© 2018 Hyunsoo Jeon
All rights reserved.

No part of this book may be reproduced in any form or by any means,
electronic or mechanical, including photography, recording, or by any
information storage and retrieval system or technologies now known or
later developed, without permission in writing from the publisher.

Library of Congress Cataloging-in-Publication Data is available.

ISBN 978-1-61429-357-6   ebook ISBN 978-1-61429-374-3

22 21 20 19 18
5 4 3 2 1

Despite diligent efforts, the photographer of the cover image is
unknown. We're grateful for the use of this material. Cover design by
Gopa & Ted 2, Inc. Set in Diacritical Garamond Pro 11/15.

Wisdom Publications' books are printed on acid-free paper and meet the
guidelines for permanence and durability of the Production Guidelines
for Book Longevity of the Council on Library Resources.

♻ This book was produced with environmental mindfulness.
For more information, please visit wisdompubs.org/
wisdom-environment.

Printed in the United States of America.

MIX
Paper from
responsible sources
FSC
www.fsc.org
FSC® C011935

Please visit fscus.org.

Contents

List of Tables

Foreword

The purpose of practicing meditation is to know and to see the truth. The Buddha said:

> Bhikkhus, develop concentration. One who is concentrated knows and sees the four noble truths as they really are.
>
> *The Discourse on Concentration*, SN 56.1

The author of this book has successfully developed concentration, and he shares his personal experience of samatha and vipassanā practice through this book. With the help of the light of concentration, he was able to see what is beyond the naked eye.

The Buddha, through the omniscient knowledge he attained by means of concentration, was able to know the existence of beings living in other realms, such as the brahma, deva, ghost, and hell beings, as well as the corresponding causes of rebirth in these realms. As a perfectly self-enlightened one, he taught about these realms when he expounded the Dhamma.

The author of the present work practiced the Dhamma as it was taught by the Buddha, so that, with the help of the light of concentration, which can illumine one to see what is beyond the naked eye, the author himself was also able to see such beings. He was able to see tree gods, hungry ghosts, heavenly beings, and hell beings. He knew for himself that these beings exist. With the help of the light of concentration, he was also able to see his various internal organs such as the heart, the liver, the spleen, and the kidneys very clearly through the practice of meditation on the thirty-two constituent parts of the body. He could see the five aggregates of clinging in the form of ultimate materiality and mentality, which is the first noble truth. He was also able to see his past lives and future lives, and understand the causes and effects of these existences. This means he was able to see and understand the second noble truth, which is the truth of dependent origination.

The Bodhisatta gained supreme enlightenment under the bodhi tree because he had penetrated the first noble truth, the second noble truth, the third noble truth, and the fourth noble truth. Anyone who wants to gain enlightenment needs to see the four noble truths.

As one who got the opportunity to practice meditation according to the way taught by the omniscient Buddha, the author could practically experience and see the teachings for himself, according to his concentration and capability. He then describes them for aspiring practitioners who would also like to see for themselves such deep and profound reality, which is beyond the naked eye.

Anyone who wishes to see things directly, as they really are, needs to develop concentration. If you have developed concentration, you too, with the help of the light of concentration, or the light of wisdom, will know and see things you have never seen before in your life. Through seeing them, you will be enlightened.

This is a book that conveys a profound message to those who would like to know and see the truths as they really are. But this book cannot serve as a stand-alone manual. Whoever would like to practice needs to find a qualified teacher to practice systematically in more detail.

As the Buddha said:

This Dhamma that I have attained is profound, hard to see and hard to understand...unattainable by mere reasoning, subtle, to be experienced by the wise.... It is hard for this generation to see this truth, namely, specific conditionality, Dependent Origination.

The Discourse on the Noble Search, MN 26.19

When the author of the present book writes about causality and causal relationships—about dependent origination—his explanation will be difficult to understand just by reasoning. As the Buddha says in the above quote, seeing the truth of dependent origination is unattainable by such methods. One can realize this truth only through direct knowledge, which can be attained with the help of the light of concentration. So if the reader encounters difficulty in understanding these parts of the book, it is only to be expected.

Without concentration, the Dhamma is hard to see and hard to understand. Unless we understand it, however, our liberation is utterly impossible. As the Buddha said to Ānanda:

> This dependent origination is deep and appears deep. It is because of not understanding and not penetrating this Dhamma, Ānanda, that this generation, which delights in sensuality... like a knotted ball of thread... does not pass beyond the plane of misery, the bad destinations, the nether world, saṃsāra.
>
> *The Discourse on Causation*, SN 12.60

Both you and I wander in saṃsāra because we do not know dependent origination. It is deep and profound—but it is possible for us to realize it. Those who would like to realize this truth need to see it directly. It is difficult to see, but as the Buddha said, one who is concentrated will know and will see the truths as they really are. So one who has developed concentration will know and see them, unlike one who just reads but has not developed concentration.

The Buddha does not urge anyone to come and believe but to come and see. In other words, the four noble truths are not articles of faith; they are not something we hear or read and then simply believe. They are "to be known by the wise"—that is, the wise can know and see these truths for themselves. One who develops right concentration will know and see them with absolute certainty.

May this book be a motivation for those who would like to attain enlightenment.

May this book inspire those who would like to be free from all suffering. Sādhu! Sādhu! Sādhu!

Much mettā,
Bhikkhu Revata
Pa-Auk Meditation Centre, Singapore

A Few Words from the Translator

Any work of translation requires a delicate balance between adhering closely to the original language and making sure that the proper meanings are conveyed. This project has involved a series of exchanges between the author and translator to achieve this difficult goal.

As the translator, I would like to clarify a few decisions I have made during the process, all of which I have discussed with the author.

First, since this is a book on Buddhist meditation, many concepts have been expressed in Pāli. We have provided working English definitions whenever it was deemed necessary and offered a comprehensive glossary to aid the reader.

Secondly, there are many instances in which the words *consciousness* and *mental factors* appear in combination as "consciousness + mental factors." This is because consciousness is counted separately when calculating the total number of things to be discerned. Therefore, when it is said that there are "thirty-four consciousness + mental factors," it means that there is one consciousness and thirty-three mental factors, for a total of thirty-four.

Lastly, excerpts from Pāli Buddhist texts are quoted throughout the book. Whenever possible, we have used translations of the Nikāyas from Wisdom Publications' *Teachings of the Buddha* series as well as Bhikkhu Bodhi's rendition of relevant terms from *A Comprehensive Manual of Abhidhamma*. We have also used both Bhikkhu Ñāṇamoli's and Pe Maung Tin's translations of the *Visuddhimagga*. There may be some differences in translation of terms, as we have generally retained direct quotations. In the few cases where English translations were not available, I have translated directly from Korean while referring to the original Pāli text.

While this is certainly not the only book on Buddhist practice translated into English, nor is it the only book about *samatha* and *vipassanā* meditation in the Pa-Auk tradition, I hope that the broad scope of the work combined with the attention to detail and the personal experience of the author will provide practitioners with a new perspective on meditation.

May all beings be happy and peaceful.

Preface

This book is a detailed and comprehensive personal narrative and account of my experiences of practicing meditation in the Pa-Auk samatha and vipassanā tradition from November 2013 to September 2014. Its main contents are my experiences of samatha meditation and meditation on materiality, mentality, and dependent origination, as well as vipassanā meditation, on the basis of the practice of samatha. Based on my experiences, I put forth in detail how we can practice these meditations, as well as what samatha is and what it means.

Although these are my own experiences, I am not the only one to have experienced them. Since first beginning my practice of samatha and vipassanā in the Pa-Auk tradition around the year 2006, I have received guidance from the Burmese monks Pa-Auk Sayadaw, Sayadaw U Sīla, Sayadaw U Revata, and the Korean monk Venerable Dhammadāyāda. The latter three are all disciples of Pa-Auk Sayadaw.

Although Pa-Auk Sayadaw revived a lost tradition of meditation on his own, he did so with the help of the Nikāyas, the commentaries (aṭṭhakathā), and the subcommentaries (ṭīkā). Though he didn't directly receive instructions from a living teacher, he received guidance from the writers of these commentaries and subcommentaries, which transcend both time and space. The commentators who helped Pa-Auk Sayadaw themselves had teachers. And so, if we continue following the line of teachers' teachers, we eventually arrive at the Buddha. Therefore the root of the meditation that I practiced is the Buddha. I am thus connected to a pulse that flows from the Buddha and through Pa-Auk Sayadaw, Sayadaw U Sīla, Sayadaw U Revata, and Venerable Dhammadāyāda.

I experienced the first *jhāna* (or absorption concentration) by receiving guidance on practicing *ānāpānasati* (mindfulness of breathing) from Pa-Auk Sayadaw. I experienced the second, third, and fourth jhānas of ānāpānasati under the guidance of Sayadaw U Revata; with him, I also practiced meditation on the thirty-two constituent parts of the body and meditation on the white *kasiṇa* (literally meaning "totality," kasiṇas are objects of varying colors and characteristics that can be expanded and that serve as focal points for meditation). I received partial guidance on kasiṇa meditation and the four elements meditation (*catudhātuvavatthāna*) from Venerable Dhammadāyāda. Most recently, I experienced the kasiṇas; the four immaterial jhānas (*arūpajhāna*); the four sublime abidings (*brahmavihāra*); the four protective meditations (*caturārakkha bhāvanā*); the four elements meditation; meditation on materiality, mentality, and dependent origination; and vipassanā meditation while receiving the guidance of Sayadaw U Sīla.

This book is organized into six chapters. In the first chapter, I present an account of undertaking the challenge of practice. It contains the process from my first encounter with Buddhism to my practice of Pa-Auk meditation. I also explain what Pa-Auk meditation is, what the heart of the practice is, and what experiences it sets as its goal. The remaining chapters are about the practice of Pa-Auk meditation. Based on my experiences, I explain thoroughly and in detail the practice of samatha, materiality, mentality, dependent origination, and vipassanā. I have also made an effort to search for the implications inherent in each practice concerning mental health and psychotherapy.

While my teacher Sayadaw U Sīla was in Seoul in the fall of 2014 giving a talk on samatha and vipassanā meditation, he requested that I speak about my experiences during his Dhamma talks. So after each of Sayadaw U Sīla's twelve talks, I would tell people about my experiences for about forty minutes. This not only allowed me to clearly outline Pa-Auk meditation for others, but it also helped my practice. In addition, I had the opportunity to talk about my experience of meditation several times with the steering committee members of the Korean Association of Buddhism and Psychotherapy (KABP) and others, and to engage in meaningful discussion with all the participants in the association. Through these two experiences, I discovered that a detailed account of meditation experience had been helpful to people, and so I decided to publish a book to share my experiences with even more people.

The practice of samatha and vipassanā in the Pa-Auk tradition is not yet widespread in my country, and there aren't very many people who can teach this practice. Many people who want to receive guidance are unable to do so. Therefore I have tried to write a detailed account of experiences in a way that is easy and clear, in order to help readers examine their own practice. Even so, I definitely recommend confirming your own experiences by receiving direct guidance from a teacher.

All of the contents of this book are my own experiences. I have tried to write about my experiences as plainly as possible. In the Book of Eights of the Aṅguttara Nikāya, the Buddha said:

> (1) Saying that one has not seen what one has not seen; (2) saying that one has not heard what one has not heard; (3) saying that one has not sensed what one has not sensed; (4) saying that one has not cognized what one has not cognized; (5) saying that one has seen what one has actually seen; (6) saying that one has heard what one has actually heard; (7) saying that one has sensed what one has actually sensed; (8) saying that one has cognized what one has actually cognized. These are the eight noble declarations.
>
> AN 8:68; trans. Bhikkhu Bodhi

As a disciple of the Buddha, I have tried to follow his teachings as closely as possible.

Though I have tried my best in my own way to confirm the things I am unsure about with Sayadaw U Sīla, I believe there may still be some things that are lacking or mistaken due to the limitations of my experience and knowledge. These are entirely my own limitations. If you find them, I would be grateful if you were understanding toward them.

Sayadaw U Sīla played a big role in being able to compile even these small achievements into a book. Even under difficult circumstances, Sayadaw U Sīla consistently came to Korea for several years in order to teach practitioners.

I learned and experienced much while supporting Sayadaw U Sīla by his side and receiving his teachings. In particular, through him I was able to see directly how Buddhists in Myanmar live nowadays and how they protect the Dhamma. As a practitioner myself, I have always felt that I was receiving Sayadaw U Sīla's protection. He has helped me experience difficult practices such as meditation on materiality and mentality without difficulty. He always brought out people's positive sides as much as possible and gave them courage. I was able to learn much about how to see the world as a Buddhist and how to protect the Dhamma while living with him and receiving his instructions. I was lucky to have been able to receive guidance from Sayadaw U Sīla.

I have received the help of many people while practicing. First of all, I am thankful to the people who provided a place for me to practice: various temples in Korea as well as in the Pa-Auk Forest Monastery in Myanmar. I would like to give my thanks to those who provide those meditation centers.

I don't know how I can express my gratitude toward my wife, who took care of my family while I was gone for nearly a year and supported me so that I could focus on my practice. Being able to get at least this far in my practice was most certainly due to my wife's help. I am not sure if I will be able to completely repay this debt.

This is a specialized topic and one that people may not be very interested in, and so I'd like to express my gratitude to the people who decided to publish this book. I'd particularly like to express my thanks to the editing staff, who worked hard to make this book presentable and easy to read. Among them I want to give my thanks to two people, Josh Bartok and Laura Cunningham. Josh showed kindness to me and interest in my manuscript when I first contacted Wisdom Publications. Laura is my editor who always showed her kindness to me; I felt she tried to do her best to make a good book, and she raised good and keen, revealing questions.

Finally I want to give special thanks to Sayadaw U Revata who wrote the foreword and gave invaluable suggestions and comments for my book, making up for my lackings and limitations and refining my book in the midst of his very busy schedule.

Although I can't list everyone individually, I feel grateful and will remember the countless beings who have helped me. I wish to share my experiences with all of them. May all beings be happy and peaceful.

1. What Is Pa-Auk Meditation?

I walk on two paths: psychotherapy and Buddhism. Within the field of psychiatry, there are treatments through medicine, and treatments through dialogue and analysis; I primarily engage in the latter, psychotherapy, although I combine it with medication when needed.

I have walked the second path, Buddhism, ever since 1985, when by chance I encountered my first Buddhist teacher, the late professor Ko Ikjin. Professor Ko was a major scholar within the Buddhist community in Korea and was also a practitioner who had deep meditation experiences. At that time, I was a thirty-year-old second-year resident majoring in psychiatry. When Professor Ko heard of my major, he said, "Buddhism is a complete system for resolving suffering, and psychiatry is also a system for resolving mental suffering. If we just change the terminology of Buddhism's system, it could become a great system of psychiatry." This struck me close to my heart and I thought that I should study with Professor Ko if I had the chance. And so when the opportunity came, I did.

Not long after I started learning from Professor Ko, I heard a lecture on "the doctrine of *kamma*," which concerns what the world is composed of and the principles by which it operates. After hearing about this I came to understand, "Ah! This is how the world works." I felt that my eyes were opened, that I could really see the world. I gained confidence in Buddhism as truth. As I became convinced that the doctrine of kamma was the truth and that it could help both me and my mental health patients, I decided, "I need to study Buddhism and meditation for the rest of my life, for the sake of both my own life and my study of psychiatry and psychotherapy."

At first I thought to integrate Buddhism and psychotherapy. After my eyes were opened to Buddhism through studying and practicing meditation, however, I realized that Buddhism itself was a great form of psychotherapy— that Buddhism and psychotherapy aren't two different things. Buddhism shows us the world's true form, including human existence, and the world's composition and the principles it operates on. And it helps us choose the best path on the basis of that knowledge. Psychotherapy is also a profession that enables us to overcome psychological suffering or problems through self-change, after helping us know our own minds and the minds of others as they actually are. The world operates by its own principles; it doesn't operate according to our thoughts and hopes. The thoughts and hopes we have that differ from the way the world works are the cause of our own suffering. It is for this reason that both Buddhism and psychotherapy try to know the form of things as they truly are.

Having discovered this truth, I am now setting up a system of Buddhist psychotherapy. The experiences I had by studying Buddhism and practicing meditation have helped me in my life, and I share my experiences with my patients when I am convinced that they are universal truths.

My process of studying Buddhism, practicing meditation, and practicing psychotherapy from 1985 until now can be largely divided into four stages. The first stage was the period during which I gained confidence in Buddhism while learning and understanding the doctrine of kamma from my first teacher, Ko Ikjin. At this time, I established the base for being able to study Buddhism in depth by learning Sanskrit and Pāli, the original languages of Buddhist scriptures.

The second stage was understanding the characteristics of the body and the mind by observing them moment-to-moment. During this period I came to know clearly the "three marks of existence" within Buddhist doctrine— impermanence (*anicca*), suffering (*dukkha*), and nonself (*anattā*). This knowledge helped me greatly in resolving my own suffering and in treating my patients.

The third stage was a period of two years starting in 2006, during which I understood clearly what Buddhism was by reading the Nikāyas: Buddhist scriptures recorded in the Pāli language that can be taken as historical accounts of the events that occurred between the Buddha and his disciples. There are five Nikāyas, but the main contents are in four of them. I read these four Nikāyas for two years in a reading group with other Buddhist scholars and practitioners. We read the Nikāyas on our own and then we met once a week to share our thoughts. While I was reading, I made it a goal to look for the following two things: First, what were the teachings of the Buddha, and among them what were the ones I had experienced and the ones I hadn't?

Second, can Buddhism become psychotherapy? In a way I was able to satisfactorily answer both of these questions. Within the Nikāyas the Buddha thoroughly investigated whether the things he had experienced were universal truths, and he taught them to his disciples once he was convinced that they were. Then his disciples themselves also experienced what the Buddha had experienced, though there have been differences in depth. Just as an experiment in a lab is deemed successful if we get the same results when we set it up with the same principles and the same conditions, the fact that the Buddha's disciples were able to experience the same things as the Buddha indicates that the teachings are universal truths. Thus the Nikāyas can be seen as records in which the disciples prove that the Buddha's teachings are the truth.

At that time I had experienced many things through my practice, and thankfully many parts of the Buddha's teachings that I had experienced and understood were in accordance with the Buddha's teachings. Although there were many important things among the Buddha's teachings that I had not yet experienced at that time, including the jhānas and the mechanism of *saṃsāra*, I became convinced through the four Nikāyas that Buddhism itself had a complete system of psychotherapy and that the Buddha and even the *arahants* (or perfected ones) were extraordinary psychotherapists.

The fourth stage was the period during which I practiced samatha and vipassanā meditation in the Pa-Auk tradition. I had heard that I could experience the jhānas, and see and know or understand the process and mechanism of *saṃsāra* by practicing in this tradition, which teaches forms of meditation used during the Buddha's time, which Pa-Auk Sayadaw had worked throughout his entire lifetime to restore.

According to what I have heard, Pa-Auk Sayadaw was born in Myanmar, ordained as a novice Buddhist monk at the age of ten, became a fully ordained *bhikkhu* (monk) at the age of twenty, and one year after his higher ordination passed the *dhammācariya* (Dhamma teacher) examination. He began to practice forest dwelling during his tenth *vassa*, or rains retreat. From then, he received instructions from Burmese meditation teachers for several years. But having felt that there was something lacking in those practices, he continued to practice on his own in the forest while referring to the Nikāyas, commentaries, and subcommentaries. Pa-Auk Sayadaw was seeking to rediscover the method of meditation that the Buddha and his disciples practiced in order to attain *nibbāna* (the unconditioned state; complete cessation of suffering). He tried and tried again to find this method.

It is said that Pa-Auk Sayadaw laid out the Nikāyas, commentaries, and subcommentaries in his room and discovered today's Pa-Auk meditation method by repeating the practice according to what was written. After practicing like this for thirteen years in Ah-sin Forest, Ye Township, the second abbot of the Pa-Auk centre called Pa-Auk Sayadaw to him one day and requested that he become the third abbot of the center after he died. It was in the year 1981. Pa-Auk Sayadaw consented, and a few days later the second abbot passed away. This is when he became known as Pa-Auk Sayadaw, which means "the abbot of Pa-Auk monastery." Even after becoming the abbot of the Pa-Auk center in his late forties, Pa-Auk Sayadaw continued to practice meditation in the forest, and he started teaching this way of practice to yogis in 1983. The task of restoring the traditional meditation method continued until he was sixty-three years old, when he completed the restoration by publishing *Way of Practice Leading to Nibbāna*, a work of five massive volumes in Burmese.

To this day, hundreds of practitioners have been able to have the same experiences that Pa-Auk Sayadaw had by practicing this restored method of meditation. Of course, there are probably some differences in the degree of their experiences.

I have closed down my clinic twice in order to practice the Pa-Auk meditation method; the method is too intense for me to practice and treat patients at the same time. The first time was in 2009, when I received teachings from Pa-Auk Sayadaw. Extraordinary things occurred while I was practicing; as I was about to enter jhāna, my bones and spine would align themselves as if a giant being were setting my bones, and afterward I would automatically sit in a very straight and proper posture. However, I wasn't able to maintain this state as time passed. I stopped practicing after six months, as I had decided that the depth of my experience of jhāna was not strong and that it would not be easy to enter into a deep state of jhāna. I reopened the doors to my clinic and started treating patients again, and I continued to do that and read the Khuddaka Nikāya and the *Milinda Pañha* for several years.

In 2013, I experimented with going to temple once a month and practicing for a week. Over the course of three months, I continuously had extraordinary experiences. During the first month, my breath decreased continuously while I observed it until it disappeared entirely, and then I felt a massive energy come up from the lower part of my belly. I felt like my body was going to go straight up and bump into the ceiling of the meditation hall. During that time I also often burst into tears. There was intense joy and delight. Although there had always been light while I observed my breath, during this time it was especially bright, and I was in a focused state. All these things in that month happened for the first time since I started practicing meditation. After this experience, the rotating energy revolved from top to bottom in my belly. The energy continues to revolve even now. After having this experience, my posture automatically became straight whenever I sat down.

During the second month of practice in 2013, a smooth and warm energy wrapped itself around my spine and descended while I was practicing sitting meditation. The month after that, there were two kinds of energy flowing while I was practicing sitting meditation. There was the energy in my belly from the first month and there was energy that formed around my nose. At first as energy formed around my nose, I was worried that it would go upward. Before long, however, the energy around my nose and the energy in my belly became one. When I breathed through my nose, it went deep into the lower part of my belly. I thought of the hypogastric breathing that I had previously only heard about. I thought, "Ah! This must be hypogastric breathing."

For these three months, changes continued to occur in this way. I'm not exactly sure what sort of things were occurring inside of me. I have never done any qi practices, nor have I ever read any books on that subject, and to be honest I wasn't very interested. The only thing I did before having that experience was not losing track of my natural breath and observing it moment-to-moment. Through this experience, I learned that observing the breath can bring about significant changes in the body. After this experience, sitting down wasn't very difficult and I didn't need to pay much attention to my posture. In some way, I felt like I had established a stepping-stone for practicing samatha, as it is necessary to be able to sit for a long time in order to practice samatha meditation.

Not long after I had these experiences, I met a fellow practitioner who had completed the Pa-Auk meditation course. After hearing about this person's meditation experience, I came to know that the Pa-Auk meditation method follows the Nikāyas as they are. The Pa-Auk meditation method begins with the practice of samatha, after which practitioners use the strength of the jhānas to see the ultimate realities of materiality and mentality. After experiencing the twelve links of dependent origination (*paṭiccasamuppāda*) on that foundation, practitioners engage in vipassanā meditation, taking ultimate materiality, ultimate mentality, and dependent origination as objects. This particular practitioner said that she saw countless past lives when she practiced meditation on the twelve links of dependent origination. I asked this person, "Would I be able to experience what you did?" After her reply of "Yes," I decided to practice meditation intensively one last time, since at that point I was approaching the age of sixty. Since I had read the Nikāyas and I was able to sit for a long time due to the proper flow of energy, I wanted to confirm the things I had not yet experienced through practice and establish a system of Buddhist psychotherapy. And so in November 2013, I again closed down my clinic and embarked solely on the path of meditation. From then until September 2014, I practiced meditation at temples in both Myanmar and Korea. This time, after having briefly received guidance from Venerable Dhammadāyāda, I received most of my instruction from Sayadaw U Sīla and experienced the jhānas, ultimate materiality, ultimate mentality, dependent origination, and vipassanā.

Pa-Auk Meditation and the Four Noble Truths

The samatha and vipassanā meditation in the Pa-Auk tradition focuses on truly knowing and seeing the four noble truths.

The four noble truths are the most important of the teachings of the Buddha. After the Buddha attained enlightenment, he said the following:

> When my knowledge and vision, in three phases and twelve aspects, was thoroughly purified in this way regarding these Four Noble Truths, then I claimed to have awakened to the unsurpassed perfect enlightenment in this world with its devas, Māra, and Brahmā, in this generation with its ascetics and brahmins, its devas and humans.
>
> *Dhammacakkappavattana Sutta*, SN 56:11; trans. Bhikkhu Bodhi

In addition, Sāriputta, one of the wisest among the Buddha's disciples and the one who the Buddha said had turned the wheel of Dhamma in his stead, said the following on the four noble truths:

> Friends, just as the footprint of any living being that walks can be placed within an elephant's footprint, and so the elephant's footprint is declared the chief of them because of its great size; so too, all wholesome states can be included in the Four Noble Truths. In what four? In the noble truth of suffering, in the noble truth of the origin of suffering, in the noble truth of the cessation of suffering, and in the noble truth of the way leading to the cessation of suffering.
>
> *The Greater Discourse on the Simile of the Elephant Footprint,*
> MN 28; trans. Bhikkhu Bodhi

The noble truth of suffering (*dukkha ariyasacca*) states that beings are fundamentally in a situation in which they inevitably experience suffering. In Buddhism it is said that there are eight kinds of suffering: birth, aging, sickness, death, separating from loved ones, uniting with enemies, not getting what we desire, and lastly the five aggregates of clinging (*pañcaupādāna-kkhandha*). The latter can be the ground or reason for the former seven sufferings because the aggregates are our existence, by which any suffering can be experienced. The *Dhammacakkappavattana Sutta* describes the relationship between the different kinds of suffering like this:

> Now this, bhikkhus, is the noble truth of suffering: birth is suffering, aging is suffering, illness is suffering, death is suffering; union with what is displeasing is suffering; separation from what is pleasing is suffering; not to get what one wants is suffering; in brief, the five aggregates subject to clinging are suffering.
> *Dhammacakkappavattana Sutta*, SN 56:11; trans. Bhikkhu Bodhi

The five aggregates are the five factors that constitute sentient beings: material form (*rūpa*), feeling (*vedanā*), perception (*saññā*), mental formations (*saṅkhāra*), and consciousness (*viññāṇa*). When clinging is involved with them, they are called "the five aggregates of clinging," and the remaining seven of the eight kinds of suffering all originate from them. In other words, we experience the remaining seven kinds of suffering because the five aggregates of clinging are present. Essentially, we are inevitably subject to suffering because we exist.

The five aggregates of clinging comprise the ultimate realities (*paramattha*) of materiality and mentality. Knowledge of materiality and mentality therefore becomes knowledge of the noble truth of suffering. The ultimate realities of materiality and mentality aren't visible to the naked eye, but rather can only be seen when the eye of wisdom is formed through the cultivation of the access or absorption (jhāna) concentrations. That is why, in the Pa-Auk tradition, we first open the eye of wisdom by cultivating access or absorption concentrations through the practice of samatha and vipassanā meditation, and afterward we know and see the noble truth of suffering by seeing materiality and mentality. I will examine these in detail in chapter 3, "Meditation on Materiality," and chapter 4, "Meditation on Mentality."

The noble truth of origin (*samudaya ariyasacca*) is knowing the origin of suffering, or in other words why suffering arises. The Buddha explains the noble truth of the origin of suffering as craving:

> What then monks, is the Noble Truth of the Origin of Suffering? It is that craving which gives rise to rebirth, bound up with pleasure and lust, finding fresh delight now here, now there: that is to say sensual craving, craving for existence, and the craving for non-existence.
>
> *Mahāsatipaṭṭhāna Sutta*, DN 22; trans. Maurice Walshe

He also explains it as the twelve links of dependent origination:

> With ignorance as condition, volitional activities [come to be]; with volitional activities as condition, consciousness; with consciousness as condition, name-and-form; with name-and-form as condition, the six sense bases; with the six sense bases as condition, contact; with contact as condition, feeling; with feeling as condition, craving; with craving as condition, clinging; with clinging as condition, existence; with existence as condition, birth; with birth as condition, old age and death, sorrow, lamentation, pain, dejection, and anguish come to be. Such is the origin of this whole mass of suffering. This is called the noble truth of the origin of suffering.
>
> *The Discourse on Sectarian Tenets*, AN 3:61; trans. Bhikkhu Bodhi

Once we discern the ultimate realities of materiality and mentality by developing the eye of wisdom through the practice of concentration, and on that basis see past and future lives and discern the twelve links of dependent origination, we will clearly know the causes and effects of the five aggregates that constitute our existence. We will know that all phenomena exist through the relationship of cause and effect. We will know how the five aggregates of clinging, which are the foundation of the noble truth of suffering, come into existence. This is knowing and seeing the noble truth of origin.

The noble truth of cessation (*nirodha ariyasacca*) is arriving at the stage in which materiality and mentality, conditioned phenomena, have ceased. The Buddha explains the noble truth of cessation as the complete destruction of craving:

> And what, bhikkhus, is the Noble Truth of the Cessation of Suffering? It is the complete fading-away and extinction of this craving, its forsaking and abandonment, liberation from it, detachment from it.
>
> *Mahāsatipaṭṭhāna Sutta*, DN 22; trans. Maurice Walshe

He also talks about it in terms of the twelve links of dependent origination:

> And what, monks, is the noble truth of the cessation of suffering? With the remainderless fading away and cessation of ignorance comes cessation of volitional activities; with the cessation of volitional activities, cessation of consciousness; with the cessation of consciousness, cessation of name-and-form; with the cessation of name-and-form, cessation of the six sense bases; with the cessation of the six sense bases, cessation of contact; with the cessation of contact, cessation of feeling; with the cessation of feeling, cessation of craving; with the cessation of craving, cessation of clinging; with the cessation of clinging, cessation of existence; with the cessation of existence, cessation of birth; with the cessation of birth, old age and death, sorrow, lamentation, pain, dejection, and anguish cease. Such is the cessation of this whole mass of suffering. This is called the noble truth of the cessation of suffering.
>
> *The Discourse on Sectarian Tenets*, AN 3:61; trans. Bhikkhu Bodhi

Once our wisdom deepens through the practice of vipassanā meditation, having laid the foundation of samatha meditation, and meditation on materiality, mentality, and dependent origination, we experience nibbāna.

In other words, the noble truth of cessation is the experience of nibbāna in which suffering disappears completely through the systematic, step-by-step practice of meditation.

The noble truth of the path (*magga ariyasacca*) is the path that leads to the destruction of suffering—that is to say, the noble eightfold path. As the eight kinds of right paths that destroy suffering, the noble eightfold path refers to right view (*sammā-diṭṭhi*), right thought (*sammā-saṅkappa*), right speech (*sammā-vācā*), right action (*sammā-kammanta*), right livelihood (*sammā-ājīva*), right effort (*sammā-vāyāma*), right mindfulness (*sammā-sati*), and right concentration (*sammā-samādhi*). The noble eightfold path can also be categorized as the three trainings of morality (*sīla*), concentration (*samādhi*), and wisdom (*paññā*). Specifically, right speech, right action, and right livelihood concern the training of morality; right effort, right mindfulness, and right concentration concern the training of concentration; and right view and right thought concern the training of wisdom. In samatha and vipassanā meditation in the Pa-Auk tradition, we observe morality, cultivate concentration, and then practice vipassanā on the basis of concentration. By practicing this way, we know and see the noble truth of the path.

The practice of samatha and vipassanā in the Pa-Auk tradition sets the goal of directly experiencing the four noble truths that are the heart of the Buddha's teachings. I will now talk about my experiences in the following order: samatha meditation; meditation on materiality, mentality, and dependent origination; and vipassanā meditation.

2. Samatha Meditation

THE MEANING OF *SAMATHA*

The mind goes to one object at a time. It can't go to two objects at once. When the mind repeatedly goes to a certain object, a tendency to go to that object naturally forms, and we are affected by that object.

Contact with objects arises in the form of meeting with someone, in the form of thinking about something, and in the form of an action. We do these things without knowing what is actually happening. As a result, things that we don't want arise inside of us. Thoughts that we don't want keep arising, and we keep doing things that we don't want to do. Since we don't know why these things happen, we blame others and ourselves, and we cause other problems by trying to escape from the things that are arising. Our problems get bigger and bigger.

Meditation is the way of knowing these characteristics of the mind and training the mind. The practice of meditation helps the mind go toward objects that truly help us rather than those that can harm us, and prevents us from being influenced by the things that can occur when the mind returns to its past habits. When practicing meditation, we bring the mind to the object of meditation. The mind, however, turns toward this thing and that thing in accordance with its past habits, which were developed before we began the practice of meditation. During the practice, we notice these kinds of movements and continue to train ourselves to turn the mind back to the object of meditation.

For example, if the mind wanders into thought while observing the in-breath and out-breath during the practice of mindfulness of breathing, we stop thinking and return to the in-breath and out-breath. If our leg aches and our consciousness goes to the feeling of the leg aching while we sit and observe the in-breath and out-breath, we let that go and return to the in-breath and out-breath. If the mind goes toward a thought, stimulus, or feeling, regardless of what it is, we turn the mind back to the object of meditation. Even if the mind goes only slightly or subtly toward objects aside from the object of meditation, we should notice this and turn the mind back to the object of meditation. If we continue this kind of training, we can "bring the mind together," or focus and unify the mind. We will always be able to turn the mind toward one object. Jhāna is the state in which the mind has been completely brought together.

Various wholesome phenomena will arise once we reach the state of jhāna. First, the unwholesome states of mind that cause suffering will disappear, and we reach a state of purity associated with happiness. Among the many unwholesome states that are sometimes described as "defilements," the five main hindrances will disappear:

1. Sensual desire (*kāmacchanda*)
2. Ill will (*vyāpāda*)
3. Sloth and torpor (*thīna-middha*)
4. Restlessness and remorse (*uddhacca-kukkucca*)
5. Doubt (*vicikicchā*)

As a result, our suffering will also temporarily disappear while we are in the state of jhāna. And when the five unwholesome things disappear, five wholesome things arise; once we enter the state of jhāna, the five factors of the first jhāna will become clear:

1. Initial application (*vitakka*): directing and placing the mind on the object of meditation.
2. Sustained application (*vicāra*): keeping the mind on the object of meditation.

3. Joy (*pīti*): delight in the object of meditation.

4. Happiness (*sukha*): peaceful enjoyment.

5. Concentration (*ekaggata*): being fixed on the object of meditation.

That is to say, jhāna is a state that is both pleasant and happy while being focused on the object of meditation.

Once we enter jhāna, we can stay happy without suffering. Jhāna is comparable to nibbāna, in which suffering is completely absent. In a conversation with Venerable Udāyī related in the scriptures, Venerable Ānanda, the Buddha's attendant, states that the Buddha says jhāna is nibbāna here and now.

Venerable Udāyī asks Venerable Ānanda, "It is said, friend, 'nibbāna in this very life, nibbāna in this very life.' In what way, friend, has the Blessed One spoken of nibbāna in this very life?"

Venerable Ānanda replied:

Here, friend, secluded from sensual pleasures ... a bhikkhu enters and dwells in the first *jhāna* ... in the second jhāna ... in the third jhāna ... in the fourth jhāna. To this extent, too, the Blessed One has spoken of nibbāna in this very life in a provisional sense ....

Again, friend, with the complete surmounting of perception of forms ... a bhikkhu enters and dwells in the base of the infinity of space ... the base of the infinity of consciousness ... the base of nothingness ... the base of neither-perception-nor-non-perception. To this extent, too, the Blessed One has spoken of nibbāna in this very life in a provisional sense ....

Again, friend, by completely surmounting the base of neither-perception-nor-non-perception, a bhikkhu enters and dwells in the cessation of perception and feeling, and having seen with wisdom, his taints are utterly destroyed. To this extent, friend, the Blessed One has spoken of nibbāna in this very life in a non-provisional sense.

AN 9:51; trans. Bhikkhu Bodhi

Secondly, when we enter jhāna, phenomena that can lead to wholesome results in the future arise; the "future" can either be this life, the next life, or the life after that. In jhāna, many wholesome *javanas* (impulsion consciousnesses) arise. Javanas are a part of the cognitive processes of the mind, and I will talk about them in detail later when I talk about mentality. The wholesome javanas that are present in jhāna bring about good results in the future. Therefore the seeds for good results in the future are planted while we are in jhāna. In order to understand this, we either have to study the Abhidhamma or practice meditation.

Another wholesome phenomenon is that the eye of wisdom is able to be developed with the attainment of jhāna.

With the eye of wisdom we will see things that we can't see with the naked eye. Once it forms, we can see the javanas of the cognitive process of jhāna. We can see the ultimate realities of mentality and materiality that are invisible to the naked eye, and we can also see previous lives.

The ultimate reality of materiality can't be divided further as it is the fundamental stuff that forms matter. It has its own intrinsic qualities. It is not permanent, and therefore arises and passes away according to its nature, but while it exists it retains its intrinsic qualities. In contrast, things like our arms and legs, which we habitually attach names to, do not actually exist. We can see this once the eye of wisdom opens.

The same is true for seeing things in relation to mentality. The ultimate reality of mentality consists of consciousness (*citta*) and mental factors (*cetasika*). Since we are usually unable to see them, however, we regard the mind as a single "lump." For example, everyone knows when anger has arisen, but not everyone sees what kinds of phenomena are actually arising when we get angry. We can't see the cognitive processes of the mind, or the consciousness and mental factors that are present inside of the mind. I will talk about this in detail in chapter 4.

I see the formation of the eye of wisdom as the most meaningful thing in jhāna. In several suttas, the Buddha said that we can see phenomena as they are if we cultivate concentration—and jhāna is one form of concentration (*samādhi*). For instance, in the *Sutta on What Purpose?* in the Anguttara

Nikāya, Venerable Ānanda asks the Buddha, "And what, Bhante, is the purpose and benefit of concentration?" The Buddha replies, "The purpose and benefit of concentration is the knowledge and vision of things as they really are" (AN 10:1; trans. Bhikkhu Bodhi).

Samatha is the meditation practice of cultivating the concentration. Through it, we see ultimate reality with the eye of wisdom and we practice vipassanā, the meditation of insight into the characteristics of ultimate reality. Therefore samatha is said to be the basis for vipassanā.

Samatha is training the mind to bring itself together. In order to bring the mind together, the mind has to return to the object of concentration when it wanders away. It has to both let go and come back. When seen from that fundamental angle, samatha is the practice of letting go. There is nothing to grasp. We will only be miserable if we grasp on to things. If our samatha training goes well, we will be able to easily let go when there are things that make us miserable. Through samatha, our minds will be unaffected by emotions or ignorance and we will be able to see things as they are.

Although there are some differences in degree among people, people generally aren't able to see things as they actually are. They live their lives affected by their emotions or in an ignorant state. Escaping temporarily from this is the goal of samatha meditation.

There are three shrouds that prevent us from seeing things as they are. The first is a personal shroud: seeing things in a distorted way because we are affected by the things we experience in our own lives. For example, those who have an academic inferiority complex will place emphasis on education when seeing others and the world. As a result, the influence of the inferiority complex, or the distortion caused by it, will arise in all kinds of forms.

The second is a cultural shroud: obstructions to our ability to see objects as they are because we are affected by the environment in which we are born and live. Culture comprises the values and lifestyles that the people of a certain region share. It can also be understood as the personality of the people of that region. None of us can be free from the effects of culture, as it formed over time through the natural environment or the influence of those who lived before us.

The third shroud consists of the limitations that we have as humans. As humans, everyone wants to live, doesn't want to die, and wants to live comfortably and well. And we are also affected by our bodies and minds. In this way, the limitations that we all have as humans prevent us from seeing things as they are.

Once we escape from these three shrouds, we will finally be able to see objects as they are. In order to do that, we have to open the eye of wisdom through the practice of concentration.

THE FORTY METHODS OF CULTIVATING SAMATHA

The cultivation of *samādhi* (concentration) is called *samatha*. Within samādhi there is momentary concentration (*khanikasamādhi*), access concentration (*upacārasamādhi*), and absorption concentration (or jhāna). Absorption concentration is therefore also called *jhānasamādhi*.

In Buddhaghosa's *Visuddhimagga* (*The Path of Purification*), there are forty subjects of samatha meditation. This means that there are forty ways of cultivating samādhi. They are listed in table 1.

All of these lead as far as the attainment of access concentration. Some also lead to the first jhāna, some to the third jhāna, some to the fourth jhāna, and some to the immaterial jhānas.

These differences are related to the characteristics of the subjects of samatha. For example, in the case of analysis of the four great elements (which is also known as the four elements meditation) we can only attain as far as access concentration, not any of the jhānas, because there are many objects in the four elements meditation and we have to be aware of each of the different properties of the four great elements. Only the Buddha truly knows which meditation subject is suitable for any given person.

Nowadays, during a time when the Buddha is not present, we have to find the subject that best suits us among the forty meditation subjects. The Pa-Auk

Forest Monastery guides us in meditation on many of the forty meditation subjects: recollection of the Buddha, mindfulness of the body, recollection of death, mindfulness of breathing, the ten kasiṇas, the four immaterial states, the four sublime abidings, the four elements meditation, and meditation on foulness.

Meditation on foulness at the Pa-Auk Monastery is the practice of contemplating the dead forms of other people we have come across in our lives. In the *Visuddhimagga*, the ten objects of foulness are the corpse and its changing forms as time passes. Nowadays it is difficult to observe a corpse that changes its form as time passes. So at the Pa-Auk Center, any corpse that the practitioner has seen any time in his or her life replaces all ten objects of foulness.

In terms of the ten recollections, recollection of the Buddha, mindfulness of the body (via discerning its thirty-two constituent parts), recollection of death, and mindfulness of breathing are taken as meditation subjects undergone formally through the Pa-Auk Center, and the rest are seen as subjects that can be practiced on our own. Although the perception of the repulsiveness of food is absent from the meditation subjects of the Pa-Auk meditation, this also isn't difficult to do by oneself. If we look at it this way, it's possible to say that all forty meditation subjects in the *Visuddhimagga* are being practiced at the Pa-Auk Center today.

Mindfulness of Breathing (*Ānāpānasati*)

At the Pa-Auk Center, the practice of samatha usually begins through *ānāpānasati*, or mindfulness of breathing. If the practice of ānāpānasati isn't going well, we sometimes switch to the four elements meditation, and then if that goes well, we sometimes return to ānāpānasati. After we attain jhāna, sometimes we practice other samatha meditations and sometimes we don't, depending on the decision of the practitioner. In my case, I practiced all twenty-four kinds of samatha meditation mentioned above, beginning with ānāpānasati. I will therefore first examine in detail how to experience jhāna through ānāpānasati.

1. Forty Ways of Cultivating Samādhi

		Level Obtained
the ten kasiṇas	the earth kasiṇa	fourth jhāna
	the water kasiṇa	fourth jhāna
	the fire kasiṇa	fourth jhāna
	the wind kasiṇa	fourth jhāna
	the black kasiṇa	fourth jhāna
	the yellow kasiṇa	fourth jhāna
	the red kasiṇa	fourth jhāna
	the white kasiṇa	fourth jhāna
	the kasiṇa of light	fourth jhāna
	the kasiṇa of enclosed space	fourth jhāna
the ten subjects of foulness	the swollen corpse	first jhāna
	the discolored corpse	first jhāna
	the festering corpse	first jhāna
	the fissured corpse	first jhāna
	the gnawed corpse	first jhāna
	the dismembered corpse	first jhāna
	the scattered corpse	first jhāna
	the bleeding corpse	first jhāna
	the worm-eaten corpse	first jhāna
	the skeleton	first jhāna
the ten recollections	recollection of the Buddha	access concentration
	recollection of the Dhamma	access concentration
	recollection of the Sangha	access concentration
	recollection of morality	access concentration
	recollection of liberality	access concentration
	recollection of the attributes of heavenly beings	access concentration

		Level Obtained
the ten recollections (*continued*)	mindfulness of the body	first jhāna
	recollection of death	access concentration
	mindfulness of breathing	fourth jhāna
	recollection of peace	access concentration
the four sublime abidings (*brahmavihāra*)	loving-kindness (*mettā*)	third jhāna
	compassion (*karuṇā*)	third jhāna
	sympathetic joy (*muditā*)	third jhāna
	equanimity (*upekkhā*)	fourth jhāna
the four immaterial jhānas (*arūpajhāna*)	boundless space (*ākāsānañcāyatana*)	immaterial jhānas
	boundless consciousness (*viññāṇañcāyatana*)	immaterial jhānas
	nothingness (*ākiñcaññāyatana*)	immaterial jhānas
	neither-perception-nor-nonperception (*nevasaññā-nāsaññāyatana*)	immaterial jhānas
one perception	the perception of the repulsiveness of food (*āhārepaṭikkūlasaññā*)	access concentration
one analysis	the analysis of the four great elements (*catudhātuvavatthāna*)	access concentration

Ānāpānasati is the practice of focusing the mind on the in-breath and out-breath. This method of practice appears in nearly identical passages in the *Mahāsatipaṭṭhāna Sutta* and in the *Ānāpānasati Sutta*. In the latter, Buddha said:

Breathing in long, he understands: "I breathe in long"; or breathing out long, he understands: "I breathe out long." Breathing in short, he understands:

"I breathe in short"; or breathing out short, he understands: "I breathe out short." He trains thus: "I shall breathe in experiencing the whole body"; he trains thus: "I shall breathe out experiencing the whole body." He trains thus: "I shall breathe in tranquillising the bodily formation"; he trains thus: 'I shall breathe out tranquillising the bodily formation."

MN 118:18; trans. Bhikkhu Ñāṇamoli and Bhikkhu Bodhi

According to the Saṃyutta Nikāya and the *Visuddhimagga*, in ānāpānasati the "body" means the "breath." So we can interpret the above passage to mean that the "whole body" is the "whole body of breath" and "tranquillising the bodily formation" means "tranquillising the breath."

Whenever, Ānanda, a bhikkhu, when breathing in long, knows: "I breathe in long"; or, when breathing out long, knows: "I breathe out long"; when breathing in short, knows: "I breathe in short"; or, when breathing out short, knows: "I breathe out short"; when he trains thus: "Experiencing the whole body, I will breathe in"; when he trains thus: "Experiencing the whole body, I will breathe out"; when he trains thus; "Tranquillizing the bodily formation, I will breathe in"; when he trains thus: "Tranquillizing the bodily formation, I will breathe out"—on that occasion the bhikkhu dwells contemplating the body in the body, ardent, clearly comprehending, mindful, having removed covetousness and displeasure in regard to the world. For what reason? I call this a certain kind of body, Ānanda, that is, breathing in and breathing out. Therefore, Ānanda, on that occasion the bhikkhu dwells contemplating the body in the body, ardent, clearly comprehending, mindful, having removed covetousness and displeasure in regard to the world.

Kimbila Sutta, SN 54:10; trans. Bhikkhu Bodhi

"'Experiencing the whole body I shall breathe out . . . shall breathe in,' thus he trains himself," means, "making clear, making plain, the beginning, middle and end of the entire exhaling body, I shall breathe out," thus he trains himself. "Making clear, making plain, the beginning, middle and end of the entire inhaling body, I shall breathe in," thus he trains himself.

Visuddhimagga; trans. Pe Maung Tin

This method is very simple, and it is called the four stages of focusing on the breath.

The Four Stages of Focusing on the Breath

The first stage is knowing that the breath is long if it is long. The second stage is knowing the breath is short if it is short. The third stage is knowing the whole body of breath, to know from the beginning to the end as much as one can. The fourth is experiencing the subtle breath.

Among these, there is no particular order for the first two stages. We simply observe the breath comfortably without agitation, regardless of what kind of breath it is. There is a reason why the breath is sometimes long and sometimes short. There is no need to react emotionally regarding which it is. Some practitioners enjoy breathing in certain ways. They think they are practicing well when they breathe that way, and when they don't, they think that they aren't practicing well and become agitated. This occurs when practice has not yet become stable. It's important to know that there is a reason for the arising of every kind of breath and to simply try our best, while remaining in a relaxed state regardless of what kind of breath we are breathing. If the mind can do this, we can say that our practice has become relatively stable.

The body and mind are always in a conditioned state. They are in their present state in accordance with various causes up to that moment. This state is not fixed; it can change in the future. The same goes for the breath. It is not always the same breath; it is the breath that has been conditioned up to that moment. If we observe the breath carefully while meditating, we will be able to know that the breath differs depending on the stage of our practice. People who are in the fourth stage of breathing mentioned above breathe subtly even when they walk. Regardless of what kind of breath is observed, it's important to know that it reflects our current state, and to make up our minds to concentrate on the breath in that state.

If we faithfully and naturally practice the first two stages in this way, we can proceed to the third stage, in which we need to progressively know, from the beginning to the end, a single breath according to improvement of mindfulness and concentration. I think this stage is very important; the fourth stage won't be stable if we enter it without sufficiently passing through the third stage.

The fourth stage is where the subtle breath appears.

The Pa-Auk method of meditation, however, doesn't just mention the subtle breath alone. During an intensive retreat that occurred in 2009 for three months at a center that opened in Taiping, Pa-Auk Sayadaw said, "The fourth stage of the subtle breath includes everything from the subtle breath, to the *nimitta* (sign of concentration), up to the jhānas." He wrote about this in his voluminous book *Nibbāna Gāminipaṭipadā*:

> Furthermore, these instructions,
> 1. the long
> 2. the short
> 3. the beginning, middle and end of the whole breath must be known;
> 4. he has to train in order to tranquilize in-breaths and out-breaths, are, indeed, instruction for attaining absorption.

If, having been stably in the third stage of knowing from the beginning to the end every single breath, we are able to keep track of every single breath while we sit or during daily activities, the subtle breath of the fourth stage will naturally arise. Then our breath will be subtle whenever we sit, and if we continue seeing the subtle breath, the nimitta will appear—though, for some meditators the nimitta may appear at earlier stages.

However, for those practitioners who have experienced the subtle breath and nimitta without having sufficiently gone through the third stage, the subtle breath and nimitta won't always be there; it'll sometimes appear and disappear. I have met many such practitioners. In any case, it's important to try not to miss a single breath. In order to do so, the mind mustn't go to other places. If the mind goes to other places, we must return it to the breath without agitation.

Nimitta

Once the state of not missing a single breath stabilizes, the subtle breath will appear naturally.

The subtle breath is a state in which the breath is so subtle that we may not be able to perceive it all the time. In the third stage, we were observing the breath clearly, as if we were seeing it with our eyes, from the beginning to the end of a single breath. However, in the fourth stage, we are now unable to observe the breath clearly. The breath is still there at this stage—it is cut off only in the fourth jhāna—but it has just become so subtle that we are unable to observe it clearly. It may disappear sometimes. Some practitioners may feel uneasy about this, but there is absolutely no need to feel this way; this is something we should welcome. It is a good phenomenon that has come naturally as a result of having observed the in-breath and out-breath well.

Thus, there is a positive side and a negative side to entering the stage of the subtle breath.

The positive side is that we arrive at the subtle breath because we have observed our breaths well, without missing any of them. The negative side is that the breath becomes so subtle we are unable to detect it. We can move on from this stage if we maintain the positive side and supplement the negative side. Maintaining the positive side means sustaining the subtle breath without agitation. Some practitioners breathe forcefully in order to find their breath; this isn't good. There is a reason why the breath becomes subtle—it's part of a process that we have to maintain. Supplementing the negative side means increasing our level of concentration so that we can observe even the subtle breath. If we understand that the subtle breath is around the nose and focus the mind in that area, our level of concentration will rise and we will be able to detect the breath again.

Once this happens, light appears together with breath. Light comes in when breathing in, and light goes out when breathing out. The breath and light become one. Pa-Auk Sayadaw calls this phenomenon "the unification of breath and light." The light we perceive when we enter the state in which the breath and light are one is called the *nimitta*, and from that point onward that light becomes the object of meditation. The nimitta is not just any kind of light; it is the light that is the object of meditation. Light may also appear when we focus even if we haven't practiced meditation for a long time. But such light is not an object of meditation; in that case the breath is still the object of meditation.

This distinction is important. The principle of light that forms when focusing is as follows.

When we say that we are focusing, we are using the mind. When we use the mind, materiality is formed by the mind. This materiality in turn produces temperature-born materiality. (I will talk about this in detail in chapter 3.) These types of materiality have color. If we continue to focus, lots of sublime materiality is created, and if it is supported by the sharp wisdom faculty, it appears as bright light. Since this light has formed as a result of us having focused on the breath, it either weakens or disappears if we focus on it too early. On the other hand, when we focus on the light that has stably unified with the breath, the light becomes continuously brighter and stronger.

Those who practice ānāpānasati may sometimes be initially suspicious of light. Since the Buddha didn't specifically speak about light, they sometimes wonder, "Will light arise solely because I focus? How can the breath turn into light? Is light emphasized too much in Pa-Auk meditation?" Once, I too asked Sayadaw U Revata about this. He replied, "There has to be light in order to enter jhāna." Now I also know this. Before I'd actually experienced nimitta, I thought that it would be easy to enter jhāna if the nimitta had simply formed, but this actually wasn't the case. Just as the nimitta forms when focusing properly on the breath, we must focus properly on the nimitta to be able to enter jhāna.

Whether we are seeing the breath or the nimitta, there are two important things to remember in samatha meditation. The first thing is to keep away from the defilements. This goes without saying while we are sitting, but we must also distance ourselves from the defilements even during our daily activities. Those who practice samatha must make an effort to train their minds to be away from the five hindrances. The second thing is concentrating on the object of meditation. So, in summary, samatha is continuously concentrating in a state that is devoid of defilements. Once we do this well, we can enter jhāna.

We must focus on the breath all day if possible. During times when it's difficult to focus on the breath, such as when we take a shower or eat, we must focus on what we are doing at the present moment. In addition, even if thoughts are present, we mustn't follow them. That way we will be able to focus easily on the breath or the nimitta when we sit down. Samatha is training the mind to bring itself together around one object. The mind has to be brought together.

Also, while we practice samatha meditation, we must try to do so in such a way that concentration is developed when we focus on an object of meditation, whether it is the breath or the nimitta. If we aren't careful, we will start comparing our previous practice to our current practice, which prevents us from being immersed in our present practice. We must do our best with the practice at this moment, and make sure that our previous sittings don't come up when we sit to practice. In order to support this, after I finished sitting, I didn't reflect upon or record anything about how the practice went. This is because if I hadn't been careful, I would have started comparing my previous practice to my present practice. I reported my practice to the teacher with my memories during interviews and then later recorded what I reported to him for future reference.

The Method of Seeing Nimitta

Although the nimitta that first forms is in fact light, it is unclear, like fog or clouds, and is called "the taken-up sign" (*uggaha-nimitta*). Meditators need to wait until it is stable and strong, which means when the unification of light and breath is stable. If we focus on this, it will become brighter and brighter, until it becomes very bright like a shining gem or the morning star. This sign is called "the counterpart sign" (*paṭibhāga-nimitta*). The types of taken-up signs and counterpart signs will differ depending on the practitioner.

Even if the nimitta is present and fully formed, it is still good to observe the breath when we first sit down to practice. We should observe the breath comfortably and as much as possible, regardless of whether it is subtle or not. Once we are completely unable to observe the breath and can only see light in the place of our breath, we should then observe the light. If we can detect the breath again, it is good to observe the breath. If we do this, we will always be focused on just one object, whether it is the breath or the light. We are bringing the mind together. Here, we must keep in mind that the light that unifies stably with the subtle breath is the object that can lead to jhāna absorption concentration.

If we observe the light this way, it'll become stronger and stronger. If the mind focuses on one object continuously without wandering away, at some point we will experience the light pulling us in. Then the light makes us focus, whereas before we focused on the light. Pa-Auk Sayadaw said, "If we observe the nimitta, the nimitta will pull us in like a magnet."

This state is very important. Once, while I was practicing in an intensive meditation retreat in Malaysia in 2009, the light became very bright and my concentration seemed to be fixed on one object. So I told Pa-Auk Sayadaw about this, with the sense that it might be enough. But he told me to continue focusing. Then one day, while I continued to practice, I experienced the light pulling me in. When I reported it, thinking that it was strange and extraordinary, he said that it was "absorption," and he gave me a new task: "From now on try sitting for three hours at a time." Once the phenomenon of absorption occurred, it wasn't difficult for me to observe the nimitta.

Regardless of what kind of phenomena may be present, the most important thing is concentration. While learning from Pa-Auk Sayadaw, this was the word that I heard the most. Rather than giving me specific instructions, he helped me focus without being drawn in by other things. For example, when I asked Sayadaw, after my breath first became subtle, "The subtle breath is important, isn't it?" he said that *concentration* was important. Through my practice, I know from experience that all of the important things that we experience in meditation come through concentration. And so I believe that concentration is indeed a master key that opens all of the treasure chests. Before having developed concentration, the meditator cannot yet begin to practice to know and see the Dhamma as it really is. Only after having developed concentration, can the meditator start to practice to know and see the Dhamma as it really is. And the whole practice ends with the attainment of Path Knowledges associated with concentration. So, it wouldn't be an exaggeration to say that meditation begins and ends with concentration.

Four Kinds of Jhāna

2. The Four Material Jhānas and Their Factors

First Jhāna	Initial Application Sustained Application Joy Happiness Concentration
Second Jhāna	Joy Happiness Concentration
Third Jhāna	Happiness Concentration
Fourth Jhāna	Equanimity Concentraion

If we continue to observe the breath or the nimitta as described above, we enter a state in which we concentrate automatically. Once we reach that state, we won't be able to go to another object even if we want to, and it'll be impossible for us to have other intentions aside from focusing on that one object. Our arms and legs will feel immobilized, our body will be fixed right where it is, and our mind will also be fixed on the nimitta. It becomes impossible to have any intention of doing something else. There is only concentration on the nimitta. Time will flow by without our noticing. This is the state of jhāna.

At this time the five factors of the first jhāna become clear: initial application, sustained application, joy, happiness, and concentration. Examination of the jhānic factors is done in the mind door (*manodvārā, bhavaṅga*) *after* exiting jhāna, because jhāna is a state in which the mind is absorbed in one object, so we cannot examine jhānic factors while in it. We can say that we have entered the first jhāna if the five factors of the first jhāna are clearly present when we examine the jhānic factors. In the scriptures, the first jhāna is expressed in the following manner: "Quite secluded from sensual pleasures, secluded from unwholesome states, I entered upon and abided in the first jhāna, which is accompanied by applied and sustained thought, with rapture and pleasure born of seclusion." (*Bhayabherava Sutta*, DN 4: trans. Bhikkhu Ñāṇamoli and Bhikkhu Bodhi)

Once we are certain of jhāna, we cultivate the five masteries of jhāna. These are the ability to (1) enter jhāna whenever we want, (2) stay in jhāna as long as we want, (3) exit jhāna whenever we want, (4) turn our mind to the factors of jhāna, and (5) examine the factors of jhāna. Once we have these kinds of abilities, we can say that we have stably entered jhāna. We can't say so if, for instance, we are able to enter jhāna once in a while but have difficulty reentering it. We train in the five masteries for all four stages of material jhāna and for the immaterial jhānas. Once we are equipped with the five masteries of a certain jhāna, we can enter into that jhāna without difficulty.

Now let's look at how we can enter each stage of jhāna and progress to the next. We can attempt to enter the second jhāna once we have cultivated the five masteries of the first jhāna successfully. Having entered the first jhāna and being trained in its five masteries means that the mind is in a malleable state and we can now easily direct the mind to do according to our intention.

The first jhāna is entered from a nonjhānic state. Although the first jhāna is a state in which the mind is brought together, it is close to the nonjhānic state, and so we may return to that nonjhānic state at any time. And so keeping this in mind, we contemplate in the following manner: "The first jhāna is close to the five hindrances. Initial application and sustained application are gross factors. I will remove initial application and sustained application, and enter and dwell in the more tranquil second jhāna." Then, once initial application and sustained application disappear, we will enter into the state of the second jhāna.

Initial application and sustained application are continuous efforts that turn toward the counterpart sign (*paṭibhāga-nimitta*), the object of samatha. Once these are absent, the first jhāna ceases. In the second jhāna, jhāna is sustained without these efforts. Once we enter the second jhāna, we are able to know how gross the initial application and sustained application of the first jhāna were. It feels like we just put down a heavy pot that we were holding.

The second jhāna is a state in which the light is brighter and we focus better, because initial and sustained applications have been removed. Now we no longer have to grasp on to the nimitta in order to sustain jhāna. The mind naturally continues to dwell with the object through the mental factor of concentration, which is always present in every consciousness.

The second jhāna is further from a nonjhānic state than the first and has fewer gross jhānic factors. The scriptures say the following concerning the second jhāna: "With the stilling of applied and sustained thought, I entered upon and abided in the second jhāna, which has self-confidence and sin-gleness of mind without applied and sustained thought, with rapture and pleasure born of concentration." (*Bhayabherava Sutta*, MN 4: trans. Bhikkhu Ñāṇamoli and Bhikkhu Bodhi)

The jhānic factors of the second jhāna are joy, happiness, and concentra-tion. Once these three factors become clear upon exiting the second jhāna and examining its jhānic factors, we train in the five masteries of the second jhāna. Once we are skilled in the second jhāna through the five masteries, we then attempt to enter the third jhāna.

Just as when we entered the second jhāna from the first jhāna, we contem-plate the properties of the second jhāna and keep the intention associated with entering the third jhāna deep in our minds: "The second jhāna is close to the first jhāna, and the joy of the second jhāna is a gross factor. I will eliminate joy, and enter and dwell in the more tranquil third jhāna." Then a change will arise in the mind, joy will disappear, and we will enter the third jhāna where only happiness and concentration remain.

Once joy disappears, we are able to know that joy was a gross factor. And we are able to know that joy disappears while happiness remains because joy and happiness are clearly different. Joy is delight toward the counterpart sign. As joy disappears, we become calmer and more stable. In other words, the mind becomes more stable and concentrated in the third jhāna as a result of the disappearance of gross joy toward the object of meditation. In jhāna, our dependence on and emotional reactions to external objects decrease more and more, and we become more and more engrossed in the mind's ability to know the object.

In the scriptures, the third jhāna is expressed as follows: "With the fading away as well of rapture, I abided in equanimity, and mindful and fully aware, still feeling pleasure with the body, I entered upon and abided in the third jhāna, on account of which noble ones announce: 'He has a pleasant abiding who has equanimity and is mindful.'" (*Bhayabherava Sutta*, MN 4: trans. Bhikkhu Ñāṇamoli and Bhikkhu Bodhi)

Once we are able to enter the third jhāna, we train in its five masteries. And once we have attained the masteries of the third jhāna, we can attempt to enter the fourth jhāna.

We enter the fourth jhāna from the third jhāna in the same manner as described previously. We contemplate as follows: "The third jhāna is close to the second jhāna and the happiness of the third jhāna is a gross factor. I will eliminate happiness, and enter and dwell in the more tranquil fourth jhāna." Then a change will occur in the mind, happiness will disappear, and equanimity will arise.

The fourth jhāna is a state in which only equanimity and concentration remain. We will look at an object as it is with equanimity, neither disliking it nor liking it. We become solely focused on the object.

I had a rather interesting experience while in the fourth jhāna. When I practiced samatha meditation at the monastery, it felt like there was a slight agitation in my mind and like my heart was moving very subtly anytime I was contacted by someone. I felt this way up through the third jhāna, but as I entered the fourth jhāna the movement stopped. I was able to experience this phenomenon about three times, whenever I entered the fourth jhāna. As I went from the first jhāna to the second and then to the third, the gross factors concerning the object of meditation fell away and I reached the fourth, where there was only concentration. I was now in a state in which I could know the object solely as it was. The first through third jhānas were good, but it felt like the fourth jhāna was a completely different level of jhāna.

The scriptures describe the fourth jhāna as follows: "With the abandoning of pleasure and pain, and with the previous disappearance of joy and grief, I entered upon and abided in the fourth jhāna, which has neither-pain-nor-pleasure and purity of mindfulness due to equanimity." (*Bhayabherava Sutta*, MN 4: trans. Bhikkhu Ñāṇamoli and Bhikkhu Bodhi)

Once the fourth jhāna becomes somewhat certain, we train in the five masteries of it, until we become skillful.

Jhāna Is a System for Dealing with Defilements

The depth of jhāna will differ depending on the past accumulated practices of the practitioner. Jhāna has no single standard.

Jhāna is very important for controlling the mind and attaining wisdom. The importance of jhāna appears often in the Nikāyas, and the Buddha always refers to samatha and vipassanā as practices that must be cultivated. But for some time there has been a tendency for jhāna to be belittled or regarded negatively. For example, there is a misperception that although entering jhāna is peaceful, the peace isn't maintained when we exit jhāna. Of course the state of jhāna is different from the state of having left jhāna; once we exit jhāna, defilements can come into the mind. But this doesn't mean that the mind after exiting jhāna is a normal state of mind.

Samatha is the practice of letting go. In order to bring the mind in unity toward one object, we must let go whenever the mind goes toward other objects and constantly return to the original object. Continuously training like this is the practice of samatha meditation, and as a result, jhāna is the building of a system of bringing the mind together. Because of this, if the mind is well trained, we can easily enter jhāna while practicing samatha meditation, and even in ordinary life we can easily let go when the mind has gone to an object that we don't want and turn the mind to the object that we do want. We will be able to control the mind while living our lives. This is thanks to an effective system for dealing with defilements being established within us via our practice of jhāna.

Up to this point we have looked into how we can cultivate jhāna through ānāpānasati and what kind of state jhāna is. Now we will look into jhāna experienced through other meditation subjects. If we want to experience jhāna through all the samatha meditation subjects that the Pa-Auk Center provides, we proceed in the following order: After ānāpānasati, we begin meditation on the thirty-two constituent parts of the body, then the kasiṇas, the four immaterial states, the four sublime abidings, and the four protective meditations (loving-kindness, recollection of the Buddha, meditation on foulness, and recollection of death).

MEDITATION ON THE THIRTY-TWO CONSTITUENT PARTS OF THE BODY

In the *Mahāsatipaṭṭhāna Sutta* of the Dīgha Nikāya, the Buddha said that our bodies are composed of thirty-one parts—omitting the brain. But in the *Paṭisambhidāmagga* (The Path of Discrimination) of the Khuddaka Nikāya, it is said that the body is composed of thirty-two parts—including the brain. Thirty-two parts are also mentioned in the *Visuddhimagga*. And according to the *Mindfulness of the Body Sutta* of the Majjhima Nikāya, mindfulness of the body consists of mindfulness of breathing, awareness of the four postures, full awareness of actions, mindfulness of the foulness of the body (with its thirty-one constituent parts), analysis of the elements, the nine charnel ground contemplations, and the four jhānas.

If we enumerate the thirty-two constituent parts one by one, they are as follows: head hairs, body hairs, nails, teeth, skin, flesh, sinews, bones, bone marrow, kidneys, heart, liver, membrane, spleen, lungs, intestines, mesentery, contents of the stomach, feces, brain, bile, phlegm, pus, blood, sweat, fat, tears, grease, spittle, snot, oil of the joints, and urine.

After attaining jhāna through ānāpānasati, moving from the first jhāna to the second, from the second to the third, from the third to the fourth, and identifying the factors of jhāna upon exiting the fourth jhāna, we discern the thirty-two constituent parts of the body one by one at the mind door with the eye of wisdom. For example, if we turn our attention toward seeing our head hair, we can see our head hair. If we turn our attention to the heart, we can see the heart. Afterward, we observe the thirty-two constituent parts of the body all at once.

When we can clearly see the thirty-two constituent parts of our own bodies, we try to observe the thirty-two constituent parts of the bodies of others: other practitioners around us and other beings that we meet in our lives. When practicing the meditation on the thirty-two constituent parts of the body, we sometimes see people as a pile of bones. When that happens, we see the body as impure rather than beautiful or handsome.

While I was a medical student, I was very shocked when I performed my first autopsy.

Before doing so, I had thought that the body would be made up of a solid lump. But as I performed the autopsy, I saw that the body was wrapped around in membranes when I peeled the skin off with a scalpel, and I had to peel off each layer of membrane in order to reach the internal organs. Seeing the exquisiteness of the body's composition made me think of the engine of a car. In this way my illusion about people's bodies was shattered, and I came to know the true form of human physical existence.

Through meditation on the thirty-two constituent parts of the body, I observed my own body in its living state, rather than merely observing other people's corpses through autopsies. I felt much disgust when I practiced. My skin looked different from what it normally looked like; it was quite wrinkled and rough, which was embarrassing to look at. My teeth also looked different from when I brush them; they looked like solid rocks and seemed to be heterogeneous. My hair, which was rooted deep in my skin, was far from being beautiful. It was the same for my fingernails and toenails. My muscles, bones, bone marrow, internal organs, blood, and other things felt very vivid. The being that I thought was "me" was actually just composed of these component parts. Through this practice, I saw vividly the true form of my body, which I had forgotten about even as a doctor, and afterward what the body really was became deeply engraved in my mind.

Meditation on the thirty-two constituent parts of the body is also helpful for people who have strong sexual desire toward the opposite sex. This is because through this practice we see forms as they are and not even as men or women.

When we focus on any one of the thirty-two constituent parts of the body (our bones, for example) as an impure object, we will enter the first jhāna.

Since the meditation on the thirty-two constituent parts of the body is a practice concerning the impurities of the body, the initial application and sustained application concerning the impurities of the body must be present. Therefore we can only enter the first jhāna through this meditation, since the factors of initial application and sustained application are absent in the second jhāna.

Meditation on the thirty-two constituent parts of the body is connected to the samatha practices of the kasiṇa meditations and the four elements meditation. For example, we use the white color from our bones, one of the thirty-two constituent parts, in the white kasiṇa meditation. And the thirty-two constituent parts of the body are also used when we observe materiality in the four elements meditation. I will talk more in detail about these practices in the appropriate chapters.

SAMATHA THROUGH THE KASIṆAS

The kasiṇa meditations are essential for attaining the immaterial jhānas and supernatural powers. The expansion of the kasiṇa is necessary in order to enter the immaterial jhāna of boundless space. In addition, in order to attain supernatural powers we need to train ourselves to freely enter and exit from various types of *kasiṇajhānas*.

There are ten kinds of kasiṇas: the earth kasiṇa, the water kasiṇa, the fire kasiṇa, the wind kasiṇa, the black kasiṇa, the yellow kasiṇa, the red kasiṇa, the white kasiṇa, the kasiṇa of light, and the kasiṇa of enclosed space. According to the Pa-Auk meditation tradition, we first practice with the color kasiṇas, starting with the white kasiṇa and then proceeding to the blue or black, the yellow, and the red kasiṇas. (We can also change the order of practicing with the blue or black, yellow, and red kasiṇas.) Afterward we practice with the earth, water, fire, and wind kasiṇas, respectively, and then we practice with the kasiṇa of light and the kasiṇa of enclosed space. We will look at each of the kasiṇas in this order.

The White Kasiṇa

We can practice the white kasiṇa meditation through two methods. We can either use a piece of white paper or white cloth, or we can use the white bones in our bodies. Among these two, I will principally look at the practice of kasiṇa meditation using a piece of white paper.

First we look continuously at the white paper. Then we close our eyes and recall the white color that we have just seen. Since we are doing this after we have attained the jhānas through ānāpānasati and meditation on the thirty-two constituent parts of the body, our level of concentration is strong and we may be able to easily recall the color, but we may also not be able to. When we look at the white color, we must engrave it in our minds to the point where we can recall it anytime, even when our eyes are closed. The white color that we see from the white paper must be engraved firmly in our minds. This differs somewhat from ānāpānasati; in the kasiṇa meditations, an effort is required to actively engrave the kasiṇa in the mind, whereas in the ānāpānasati there is just focus on the breath and letting go of any other object.

I think that our level of concentration further increases through the practice of kasiṇa meditation. The ability to grasp the kasiṇa must be strong in order to be able to recall it even when our eyes are closed. If we do not make that effort, but rather casually think that we will eventually see the kasiṇa even with our eyes closed, it may be difficult to recall the kasiṇa.

Once we are able to see the white color even when our eyes are closed, we concentrate on it. When the white color takes the form of a disc and becomes relatively stable through concentration, we then expand it in the ten directions of north, west, south, east, northwest, northeast, southwest, southeast, below, and above. The white disc will become more stable as we expand it. At first we expand it little by little in one direction until we can't expand it any further. Then we expand it in the other directions. Once we have expanded the white color in every direction, the whole world becomes white. One practitioner told me that the world filled with the white color was very pleasant, but which kasiṇas are regarded as pleasant and leave a deep impression depend on the practitioner.

Then we focus on the white color at the center of the field in which the white color has expanded in every direction. Sometimes light is also present when practicing the white kasiṇa meditation; this is all right as long as the white color is there with it. There is no need to pay attention to the light. What is important is the presence of the white color.

Once we are able to focus continuously on the white kasiṇa for one to two hours and the five factors of the first jhāna become clear, we have entered the first jhāna. We then exit the first jhāna and examine the five factors. Once the first jhāna becomes clear, with the presence of initial application and sustained application on the white kasiṇa as well as joy, happiness, and concentration, we train in the five masteries of the first jhāna.

The method of entering the second, third, and fourth jhānas in the meditation on the white kasiṇa is as follows:

First, we contemplate in the following manner in order to enter the second jhāna from the first: "Since the first jhāna is close to the five hindrances, and the initial application and sustained application on the white kasiṇa are gross factors, I will eliminate those factors, and enter and dwell in the more tranquil second jhāna." Then a change will occur in the mind and we will enter the second jhāna. Here, initial and sustained application are absent and only joy, happiness, and concentration remain. Then we train in the five masteries of the second jhāna.

Next, we contemplate in the following manner in order to enter the third jhāna from the second: "Since the second jhāna is close to the first jhāna and joy is a gross factor, I will eliminate joy, and enter and dwell in the more tranquil third jhāna." Then a change will occur in the mind and we will enter the third jhāna. Here, only happiness and concentration remain. Then we train in the five masteries of the third jhāna.

Afterward, we contemplate in the following manner in order to enter the fourth jhāna from the third: "Since the third jhāna is close to the second jhāna and happiness is a gross factor, I will eliminate happiness, and enter and dwell in the more tranquil fourth jhāna." Then happiness will turn into equanimity and only equanimity and concentration will remain. This state is the fourth jhāna. Then we train in the five masteries of the fourth jhāna until we become skillful. We enter the first through the fourth jhānas through this method for the other kasiṇa meditations as well.

The method of using the white bones in our own bodies is the same as using white paper, except for the initial material. First we take the white color from our bones. It actually doesn't matter whether they are our own bones or the bones of the practitioner sitting in front of us. We stably maintain that white color from those bones and then we expand it. The process of entering jhāna is the same as the process of entering jhāna by taking the white color of paper.

The Yellow Kasiṇa

The meditation on the yellow kasiṇa is the same as described above. Just as we could for the white kasiṇa, we can either use color from the outside or the yellow color that is in our bodies: for instance, we can use yellow paper or a piece of yellow cloth, or we can use the yellow color from our abdominal fat. What is important is being able to recall the yellow color at any time. We maintain the yellow color by recalling it stably, and then we expand it. Once we have completely expanded the yellow color, the whole world becomes yellow. The method of entering jhāna by recalling the yellow color is the same as described for the white kasiṇa.

The Blue and Red Kasiṇas

The blue and red colors can either be obtained from colored paper or a piece of cloth, or they can be obtained from the internal organs and the color of the blood in our bodies. We can also use the color black instead of blue. As before, we see the blue (or black) or red color, maintain and expand it, and make a kasiṇa of it. Once the blue (or black) or red color has expanded infinitely, the whole world becomes full of that color. Only that color is present. The method of entering the jhānas with the kasiṇas of these colors is the same as described for the white kasiṇa.

The Earth Kasiṇa

To practice with the earth kasiṇa, we draw a circle of approximately twelve inches (30 cm) in diameter on the ground—clearly, so that we can distinguish it from the surrounding earth. We remove things such as stones and tree branches from the circle, and then we even out the dirt so that the circle is level. If we do not have a place outside to do this, we can fill a box or other container with level earth and draw a circle in that. If we do it this way, we can even carry the box around with us.

Then we look continuously at that circle of earth. We try to recall it with our eyes closed. Once recollection of the circle becomes stable, we expand it. Once it has expanded in all directions, the world becomes completely full of dirt. Dirt is laid out everywhere, endlessly. After expanding the earth kasiṇa infinitely, the method of entering jhāna through it is the same as the method for the color kasiṇas.

The Water Kasiṇa

We can use either water that is in a bowl or water that is standing in a clear puddle. It's better if the water is abundant and clean, without any debris. All we have to do is to see that water and be able to recall it at any time. Once the water kasiṇa has expanded infinitely, the whole world becomes filled with water. It's like being in the middle of a large sea. The sea is everywhere. The method of entering jhāna through the water kasiṇa is the same as the method for the color kasiṇas.

The Fire Kasiṇa

It's best to use fire from wood or fire that burns vigorously in a conventional fireplace. If all else fails, we can also use a candle flame. All we have to do is be able to recall the fire at any time. By our maintaining that fire and expanding it, the world becomes covered in fire. There is only fire in the world, as though we were witnessing the spectacle of the Big Bang or the moment when the universe is destroyed. The method for entering jhāna through the fire kasiṇa is the same as for all the other kasiṇas that have been mentioned so far.

The Wind Kasiṇa

When we close our eyes, we can see movement such as heat shimmering, or we can feel the presence of the wind. Once this becomes firm, all we have to do is expand it. When the wind has expanded indefinitely, the whole world becomes filled with blowing wind. When we practice meditation on the wind kasiṇa, it feels like wind is everywhere, and there is nothing in the world except wind. The method for entering jhāna through the wind kasiṇa is the same as for the other kasiṇas.

The Kasiṇa of Light

We can either use the light that formed from our practice or we can use natural light. Since light has been formed from our practice of ānāpānasati or from other previous kasiṇa meditations, the former is not difficult; there will always be light when we practice if we enter jhāna by practicing samatha meditation. If we practice meditation on the kasiṇa of light using light formed from our practice, the light will become extremely bright. Once we expand the existing light, the world will be completely filled with light. There is only light in the world. Once the kasiṇa of light is formed, we enter jhāna through the same method as the previous kasiṇas.

The Kasiṇa of Enclosed Space

We can create enclosed space through two methods. We can imagine ourselves drawing a circle in a clear, bright, cloudless sky, or we can create a beautiful engraving of a circle that we can hold up against the clear sky in order to see the enclosed space, and use that enclosed space as our object of meditation. We look at that enclosed space continuously. Once we can recall that enclosed space even with our eyes closed, we expand the enclosed space indefinitely. Then we can experience a world that has become an enclosed space, devoid of anything. We generally live our lives by filling up our surroundings with various things. The kasiṇa of enclosed space can be seen as a state in which we have cleared out everything, starting with the things closest to us and going outward toward everything in the world, until there is nothing. A kasiṇa is a world that is completely filled up with any one given object, and in this case it is empty, enclosed space. Once the kasiṇa of enclosed space is formed, we enter jhāna through the same method as the other kasiṇa meditations.

There are countless objects in the world, but not all of them receive our attention, because our attention is limited. Meditation on the kasiṇas is taking each of a specific object and creating a world in which only that one object is present. Up to this point we have looked into how to obtain the object of meditation for each of the ten kasiṇas, and how to create the kasiṇa and enter jhāna by expanding that object of meditation. The method of entering the first through the fourth jhānas and training in the five masteries of each jhāna is the same as for ānāpānasati. But unlike ānāpānasati, we can enter the immaterial jhānas through meditation on the kasiṇas.

MEDITATION ON THE IMMATERIAL JHĀNAS

There are four immaterial jhānas: boundless space, boundless consciousness, nothingness, and neither-perception-nor-nonperception. The practice of the jhāna of boundless space, the first of the immaterial jhānas, begins with contemplation on materiality after exiting the fourth jhāna of the kasiṇas.

In terms of their characteristics, the immaterial jhānas correspond to the fourth jhāna. Just as the fourth jhāna is composed of the jhānic factors of equanimity and concentration, the four immaterial jhānas are also all composed of equanimity and concentration. Therefore, in the *Visuddhimagga*, the four immaterial realms are said to carry the fourth jhāna with them in the division of meditation subjects according to the type of jhāna.

Boundless Space

In order to enter boundless space, we must first experience the first, second, third, and fourth jhānas through the practice of ānāpānasati and one of the kasinas other than the kasina of enclosed space. By practicing meditation on the immaterial jhānas, we enter the immaterial realm by transcending materiality. Since the kasina of enclosed space is not materiality, we can't use it to transcend materiality.

In the following example, I will use the earth kasina, but it's best to rotate between each of the nine kasinas, excluding enclosed space. For example, if we have practiced ānāpānasati, the white kasina, and the immaterial jhānas this time, we should practice ānāpānasati, the yellow kasina, and the immaterial jhānas next time.

We enter the first through fourth jhānas through the kasinas. After exiting the fourth jhāna and examining its jhānic factors, we contemplate as follows, in the case of the earth kasina: "Materiality brings us suffering. If materiality is present we must be born, grow old, become sick, and die, and we cannot avoid all of the sufferings that the body undergoes. Earth is materiality, and light is also materiality. I will enter and dwell in boundless space that has no materiality." Afterward, if we concentrate on space, noting, "space, space," or "boundless space, boundless space" space will slowly form within the boundless earth kasina and it will grow larger and larger. Light will also begin fading away. Eventually the earth will disappear completely and everything will be filled up with boundless space.

When I entered boundless space, I felt much more calm and tranquil than I did when I was in the four material jhānas. It felt like I was in an empty sky that was completely devoid of materiality. I hadn't had many chances to hear about the immaterial jhānas from those around me. Even in Buddhist scriptures the immaterial jhānas tend to be described less frequently than the material jhānas. So I practiced meditation on the immaterial jhānas without having many expectations. Boundless space was a new state that I hadn't previously experienced before. A pure and vast world laid itself out in front of my eyes.

When we exit boundless space, we examine its jhānic factors: equanimity and concentration. Then we train in the five masteries of boundless space. Once we have become skilled in boundless space, we exit boundless space and attempt to enter boundless consciousness.

Boundless Consciousness

We contemplate in the following manner in order to enter boundless consciousness after exiting boundless space: "Boundless space is close to the four material jhānas. I will enter and dwell in the more tranquil boundless consciousness." Then we concentrate on the consciousness (mind) that knows boundless space by noting, "consciousness, consciousness," or "boundless consciousness, boundless consciousness." Even though we pay attention to it as "boundless consciousness, boundless consciousness," we do not need to expand the consciousness to the ten directions as it cannot be done. We make consciousness the object of meditation. We enter immaterial jhāna by focusing on consciousness as object.

Equanimity and concentration, the two jhānic factors of boundless space, are mental factors. Mental factors are always present together with consciousness; the boundless consciousness of immaterial jhāna is also accompanied by the mental factors of equanimity and concentration. In order to practice meditation on boundless consciousness, we need to pay attention to the consciousness that is ultimate reality. When examining the jhānic factors of boundless space, we see and concentrate on the consciousness that is present with equanimity and concentration.

As we contemplated before entering boundless consciousness, boundless consciousness is more tranquil and extraordinary than boundless space. Once we enter boundless consciousness, it will feel as if only the consciousness that knows boundless space exists. I feel as if I become a being of boundless consciousness. Boundless consciousness isn't a state that is completely filled with consciousness, but rather a state in which we are solely focused on the consciousness that knows boundless space.

We can return to the fourth jhāna upon exiting boundless space because boundless space is formed with the four material jhānas as its point of departure and is close to the fourth jhāna, but boundless consciousness is far from the fourth jhāna because it is formed with boundless space as its point of departure. It is more tranquil and stable. Although the objects of many other jhānas are concepts that don't exist in reality, the object of boundless consciousness—the ultimate reality of consciousness—does.

After training in the five masteries of boundless consciousness until we become skillful, we make an effort to enter nothingness.

Nothingness

In order to enter nothingness after exiting boundless consciousness, we have to see the flaws of boundless consciousness and the extraordinary aspects of nothingness. We contemplate as follows: "Boundless consciousness is close to boundless space. I will enter and dwell in the more tranquil nothingness." Nothingness is more tranquil and extraordinary because of the absence of boundless space and its consciousness. The object of nothingness is the absence of consciousness taking boundless space as an object. We focus on the absence of it by noting "nothingness, nothingness." We generally think that something is always present. In nothingness we focus the mind on the fact that there is truly nothing present. We can say that we are training to bring the mind toward absence; the object of our concentration has turned from presence to absence. However, the consciousness that clearly knows nothingness will still be present. After training in the five masteries of nothingness, we make an effort to attain neither-perception-nor-nonperception, the last immaterial jhāna.

Neither-Perception-Nor-Nonperception

After exiting nothingness, we contemplate as follows: "Nothingness is close to boundless consciousness. I will enter and dwell in the more tranquil and extraordinary neither-perception-nor-nonperception." After we engrave the contents of this contemplation in our minds, we focus on the consciousness of the third immaterial jhāna by noting, "this is peaceful, this is sublime." We will then experience reaching neither-perception-nor-nonperception. This is also a new experience that differs from everything else up to this point. Unlike nothingness, which clearly knows absence, neither-perception-nor-nonperception is a state in which mental processes are very subtle.

Although the term refers only to perception (saññā), it is a state in which not only perception but all the consciousness and mental factors are neither present nor absent. That is, consciousness and mental factors are present, but they are very weak. That is why it is a state in which mental processes have become very subtle. For that reason, it is very tranquil and extraordinary. As with the other immaterial jhānas, we cultivate the five masteries for neither-perception-nor-nonperception.

Like the object of boundless consciousness, the object of neither-perception-nor-nonperception isn't a concept but actually exists in reality. The consciousness and mental factors of neither-perception-nor-nonperception can't individually become the objects of vipassanā meditation, except in special cases, but we can practice vipassanā by taking all of them together as objects.

Opening Our Eyes to the Various Worlds of Buddhism through the Immaterial Jhānas

In the Buddhist scriptures, it is said that beings who possess life can dwell in three realms, the desire realm (kāmāvacara), the material realm (rūpāvacara), and the immaterial realm (arūpāvacara). By experiencing a realm devoid of materiality through meditation on the immaterial jhānas, I was able to feel at least a little bit of the influence that materiality has on us, which I had previously taken for granted. I was able to know what it was like to be free from the suffering caused by materiality. I came to acknowledge the possibility of existing in a realm beyond materiality. I wonder indeed if I would have been able to think in this way without having experienced the immaterial jhānas. I came to know that experiencing the immaterial jhānas is essential for understanding the worldview put forth in Buddhism.

There are two types of immateriality. One is the state experienced by reaching immaterial jhānas through meditation, and the other is the world experienced by a being of the immaterial realm. There are actually beings that dwell in the state of the immaterial jhānas. Experiencing the immaterial jhānas is helpful in understanding the various forms of beings that exist.

The experience of the immaterial jhānas is also helpful in understanding and familiarizing ourselves with heavenly realms and beings in those heavenly realms. Because the heavenly realms aren't visible to our senses, it's easy to be careless and think that they don't exist. The Buddhist outlook of the world isn't limited to the world that has been proven by science or through our six senses. The world that the Buddha and his disciples have seen through the practice of advanced meditation and observation includes the heavenly realms. We will be able to experience the various kinds of worlds that are mentioned in Buddhism when we practice meditation on the four sublime abidings.

MEDITATION ON THE FOUR SUBLIME ABIDINGS

After experiencing the immaterial jhānas, we experience jhāna through meditation on the four sublime abidings (the four brahmavihāras). The four brahmavihāras are also known as the four immeasurables. They are called *brahmavihāras* because they refer to the consciousness that *brahmas* (the highest of the heavenly beings) possess as well as to the mental states that lead to rebirth in the brahma realm. The four brahmavihāras are loving-kindness, compassion, sympathetic joy, and equanimity.

Though the experiences of jhāna attained through the various meditation subjects are all meaningful and good, the jhāna I experienced through the four brahmavihāras was especially meaningful. Since meditation on the four brahmavihāras consists of spreading loving-kindness, compassion, sympathetic joy, and equanimity toward every being everywhere, we meet all beings everywhere through this practice. Through the eye of wisdom developed by cultivating the jhānas, we can see beings that we can't perceive with the naked eye. We have to be able to see, for example, heavenly beings, demons, hungry ghosts, and hell beings in order to send loving-kindness to them. By practicing meditation on the four brahmavihāras we will have the special experience of seeing beings that appear in Buddhist scriptures.

Samatha meditation up to this point consisted of entering jhāna by focusing the mind and dealing with our own defilements. What is special about practicing meditation on the four brahmavihāras is that we experience jhāna through the mind's treatment of other beings. In the context of living together with other beings in this world, we are able to practice not only for our own sake but also for the sake of those other beings. Perhaps this is why, among the four brahmavihāras, the most people practice loving-kindness meditation—it transcends religion. It is also used frequently in psychotherapy. I have used loving-kindness meditation with a patient who had lots of anger, for instance, and I have seen a significant impact.

My mind became very pure while practicing meditation on the four brahmavihāras. Many thoughts of loving-kindness arose, and as my concentration deepened the light became very bright. While practicing meditation on the four brahmavihāras, I was able to feel happy, as my mind became filled with thoughts of loving-kindness. The thought of loving others and making them happy makes us happy. When we think about sending loving-kindness toward others, for instance, loving-kindness will first arise in ourselves. Chade-Meng Tan, the developer of meditation at Google, said in a lecture that we become happy when we are kind to others. This is the law of the world. We receive benefits when we try to benefit others, and harm will come to us if we try to harm others.

To practice meditation on the four brahmavihāras, we first take four types of people as objects: ourselves, people that we respect or like, neutral people that we neither like nor dislike, and people that we dislike or hate. Once the mind no longer distinguishes between these four types of people, we then send thoughts of loving-kindness, compassion, sympathetic joy, and equanimity to all beings without any limits. We can cultivate the first, second, and third jhānas through meditation on loving-kindness, compassion, and sympathetic joy, and we can cultivate the fourth jhāna through meditation on equanimity.

Now let's look at how to practice meditation on the four brahmavihāras in order.

Loving-Kindness Meditation

Before beginning loving-kindness meditation, we first enter jhāna through the practices that we have done up to this point: ānāpānasati, meditation on the kasiṇas (excluding meditation on enclosed space), and meditation on the immaterial jhānas. We begin practicing loving-kindness meditation after experiencing the first through fourth jhānas through ānāpānasati, the first through fourth jhānas through meditation on the kasiṇas, and the four immaterial jhānas one by one. We always do this before beginning meditation on any of the four brahmavihāras.

One thing that is unique about the Pa-Auk meditation tradition is that we always repeat the previous practices when going on to the next. When we practice kasiṇa meditation, for instance, we always do so after attaining jhāna through ānāpānasati. And when cultivating the immaterial jhānas, we do so after attaining jhāna through ānāpānasati and jhāna through the kasiṇas. When we practice meditation on the ultimate realities of materiality and mentality after cultivating the jhānas, we always do so after first practicing meditation on the previously cultivated jhānas. When we practice meditation on dependent origination, we do so after practicing samatha, meditation on materiality, and meditation on mentality. The same goes for vipassanā. As a result, our jhāna becomes deeper and deeper as time passes. Thus as we progress, each time we begin our practice we are always able to enter jhāna, see materiality, mentality, and dependent origination, and practice vipassanā. The system of meditation is always at work.

After entering the first through fourth jhānas through ānāpānasati and the kasiṇas, and after entering the immaterial jhānas, from boundless space through neither-perception-nor-nonperception, we exit neither-perception-nor-nonperception and examine its jhānic factors. Then we begin practicing loving-kindness meditation.

The phrases used in loving-kindness meditation differ a bit depending on the tradition of practice, but in the Pa-Auk tradition the following four phrases taught by the Buddha are used: "May beings be free from danger, may beings be free from mental suffering, may beings be free from physical suffering, and may beings be well and happy" ("*Averā hontu, abyāpajjā hontu, anīghā hontu, sukhī attānaṃ pariharantu*"). We can change the order in which we practice these four phrases. For instance, I start with "May beings be well and happy," because I can enter jhāna quickly when I do so.

Loving-Kindness Meditation toward Ourselves

First we send loving-kindness to ourselves: "May I be well and happy." Since we have already cultivated the jhānas, our mind will be at ease and our face becomes happy and smiling when we have these kinds of thoughts. We continue to send loving-kindness to ourselves using the following phrases: "May I be free from danger, may I be free from mental suffering, and may I be free from physical suffering."

We can't enter jhāna by practicing loving-kindness meditation toward ourselves. The *Visuddhimagga* says this:

> For even if he developed loving-kindness for a hundred or a thousand years in this way, "May I be well and happy" and so on, absorption would never arise. But if he develops it in this way, "May I be well and happy. Just as I want to be well and happy and free from pain, as I want to live and not to die, so do other beings, too," making himself the example, then desire for other beings' welfare and happiness arises in him.

Once the mind has become somewhat calm, we move on to the next stage.

Loving-Kindness Meditation toward Those We Respect

Now we take a person that we respect as object: the monk who is teaching us, for instance. It can be anyone, as long as it is a person for whom we have respect, but they must be living. A dead person can't receive loving-kindness, so dead people are omitted from loving-kindness meditation. We also exclude all people of the opposite sex (or, if applicable, of the same sex) until our practice of loving-kindness has stabilized and our mind has reached a state of balance when sending loving-kindness toward various objects, to prevent the arising of sensual desire and defilements. Even family members aren't exempt here.

We recall the image of the person that we respect and send loving-kindness using the four phrases. It will be easy to focus on the person to whom we are sending loving-kindness, since we are practicing loving-kindness in a focused state after experiencing the first through fourth jhānas through ānāpānasati, the first through fourth jhānas through the kasiṇas, and the four immaterial jhānas in order. If we recite "May this person be well and happy" and keep that thought deep in our mind, the face or image of the person we respect will appear vividly. The person's peaceful and happy face and image will be fixed in front of us without disappearing. When we see that peaceful and happy face, our mind also becomes happy, and it becomes fixed in that state. When this state continues, the mind will be equipped with all five factors of jhāna—including the initial application and sustained application toward the person we are sending loving-kindness to, the feelings of joy and happiness from seeing that object, and the concentration that has gone solely to that object—and we will then enter the first jhāna. After remaining in the first jhāna for one or two hours, we exit it and examine the five factors of the first jhāna at the mind door. Once the first jhāna becomes clear, we train in the five masteries of the first jhāna.

Joy and happiness are strong in loving-kindness meditation. In loving-kindness, the jhānas are being in a state of happiness while solely seeing the happy image of the person we respect.

Once we become skilled in the first jhāna by training in the five masteries of the first jhāna, we enter the second jhāna. We enter the second jhāna by contemplating in the same way as we have done for attaining jhāna through other meditation subjects. Once we enter the second jhāna, the initial and sustained application toward the object of loving-kindness will disappear and only joy, happiness, and concentration remain. Then, after training in the five masteries of the second jhāna, we enter the third jhāna. In the third jhāna, only happiness and concentration toward the object of loving-kindness are present. Once we enter the third jhāna, we train in the five masteries of the third jhāna.

We can only enter up to the third jhāna through the practice of loving-kindness meditation. We can't enter the fourth jhāna because in it loving-kindness disappears and only tranquility remains.

Once we experience the first through third jhānas using the first phrase of loving-kindness, we practice loving-kindness meditation using the second phrase: "May the person I respect be free from danger." If we truly wish this, an image of that person safe and free from danger will present itself in front of us, and it will feel like this person is in a state of safety.

I've had an interesting experience while practicing using the second phrase. When I sent loving-kindness to a person who was already living safely, that person was safe as usual. However, when I sent loving-kindness to a person who had much anger and carried factors of danger with him, I saw an image of him safe by being deep in the ground. The depth in the ground appeared precisely in accordance to the degree of danger he was in.

Once the image of the person safe from danger becomes fixed, and the five factors of jhāna become clear by focusing on that image, we enter the first jhāna. After training in the five masteries of the first jhāna, we move to the second and third jhānas and train in the five masteries of each of those jhānas.

Once we experience the first through third jhānas using the second phrase, we practice loving-kindness meditation using the third phrase: "May the person I respect be free from mental suffering." Then we will very quickly be able to picture that person in such a state. When I practiced using the third phrase, an image of the person smiling broadly always appeared. When I saw that image, I would also become happy and smile, and sometimes I would laugh uncontrollably. Once the broadly smiling image becomes fixed, we enter the first jhāna. We also enter the second and third jhānas and train in each of their five masteries in the same way as we did for the first phrase.

After experiencing the three jhānas with the third phrase, we practice loving-kindness meditation using the fourth phrase: "May the person I respect be free from physical suffering." Then we will see an image of that person free from physical suffering and in a physically comfortable state. For example, if it's a person that was bent with back pain, we will see an image of that person with a straight back, without pain, and feeling well. When we look at that image we will follow suit and also feel well, and once that image becomes fixed we enter the first jhāna. We enter the second and third jhānas in the same way as previously, and we definitely make the jhānas our own by training in the five masteries of each of them.

After practicing with one person that we respect, we practice loving-kindness meditation in the same way ten times in total by bringing to mind about ten people that we respect or like.

Loving-Kindness Meditation toward Neutral People

Next, we practice loving-kindness meditation using the four phrases with a neutral person, one that we neither like nor dislike. Neutral people are usually people that we only know superficially or people that we know well but neither like nor dislike. These may include people like an apartment security guard, a grocery store clerk, or the manager of a restaurant.

We practice loving-kindness meditation using the first phrase on a neutral person. If we intend "May this person be well and happy," a well and happy image of that neutral person will appear. Although this person was neutral before practicing loving-kindness meditation, he or she is no longer neutral once we begin our practice. As someone we lend out our happiness to, this person becomes dear to us.

Actually, as we really practice meditation on the four brahmavihāras, not only will neutral people become dear but we will no longer have people that we dislike and hate. There will be only the sense of intentionally recalling, for the sake of our practice, people we have memories of feeling indifferent toward or disliking. If we practice loving-kindness meditation, all people completely become dear to us, whether they are neutral people or people we dislike. This is the reason why loving-kindness meditation is necessary.

Once the peaceful and happy image of a neutral person becomes fixed by practicing using the first phrase, and the five factors of jhāna are clear by completely focusing the mind on that image, we enter the first jhāna. We enter up to the third jhāna and cultivate the five masteries of each jhāna in the same way as we have done for the person that we respect or like.

Once we experience up through the third jhāna using the first phrase, we experience the first through third jhānas using the second phrase: "May this person be free from danger." In my case, whether it was a person I respect or a neutral person, when I wished "May they be free from danger," the image of that person free from danger appeared in different ways according to the degree of that person's danger.

Once we have completed practicing using the second phrase, we experience the first through third jhānas using the third phrase: "May this person be free from mental suffering." Here too a broadly smiling image of the neutral person appeared to me in the same way as it had with the person I respect or like. Once that image becomes fixed like a photograph and once the jhānic factors are clear, we enter each of the first three jhānas. We likewise train in the five masteries of each jhāna.

Once we have completed the third phrase, we sincerely wish the fourth phrase: "May this person be free from physical suffering." Once we recall the image of that person at ease with a healthy body, the mind that sees that also becomes peaceful and happy. This image becomes the object of meditation. We enter jhāna by taking that object. We also practice the five masteries of each jhāna. In this way we should practice loving-kindness meditation ten times in total by taking ten neutral people as objects.

Loving-Kindness Meditation toward Those We Dislike

Once we have finished practicing loving-kindness meditation toward neutral people, we finally practice loving-kindness meditation by taking people we dislike or hate as objects. We practice by recalling in turn about five people we dislike or hate. They can be people we have hated in the past or people that we don't hate yet but against whom we have a bit of a grudge.

Taking someone we hate as an object, we wish using the first phrase: "May this person be well and happy." Then a happy, well and peaceful image of that person will appear in front of us without much difficulty. When we look at that image we will also feel good and become happy. Once that image becomes fixed and the mind is solely focused on that object, we enter jhāna. We enter the first through third jhānas and train in the five masteries of each jhāna.

Once we have completed the first phrase, we cultivate up through the third jhāna using the second phrase: "May this person be free from danger." We also cultivate the five masteries of each jhāna. Following the second phrase, we again cultivate up through the third jhāna using the third phrase, "May this person be free from mental suffering," and also cultivate the five masteries of each jhāna. Finally, we cultivate through the third jhāna using the fourth phrase, "May this person be free from physical suffering," and also cultivate the five masteries of each jhāna. Once we have finished practicing loving-kindness meditation toward one person, we practice loving-kindness meditation toward other people that we dislike or hate using the same method.

The State of Balance

Once we cultivate loving-kindness toward the four types of people using the four phrases in this way, our thoughts of loving-kindness will be balanced. Sayadaw U Sīla has expressed this state—where loving-kindness toward the four types of people has become equal and where loving-kindness doesn't go toward any one kind of person more than another—as "the state of balance." In the *Visuddhimagga*, Buddhaghosa expresses this state of balance as follows:

> He should break down the barriers by practicing loving-kindness over and over again, accomplishing mental impartiality towards the four persons, that is to say, himself, the dear person, the neutral person and the hostile person.
>
> The characteristic of it is this. Suppose this person is sitting in a place with a dear, a neutral, and a hostile person, himself being the fourth; then bandits come to him and say, "Venerable sir, give us a bhikkhu," and on being asked why, they answer, "So that we may kill him and use the blood of his throat as an offering"; then if that bhikkhu thinks, "Let them take this one, or this one," he has not broken down the barriers. And also if he thinks, "Let them take me but not these three," he has not broken down the barriers either. Why? Because he seeks the harm of him whom he wishes to be taken and seeks the welfare of the other only. But it is when he does not see a single

one among the four people to be given to the bandits and he directs his
mind impartially towards himself and towards those three people that he
has broken down the barriers.

trans. Bhikkhu Ñāṇamoli

Loving-Kindness Meditation toward All Beings

In the Pa-Auk tradition, once we have entered this state of balance through
loving-kindness meditation, we send loving-kindness toward all beings. In
order to reach this balanced state, we first enter the first through third jhānas
using the four phrases toward ourselves, the people we like, neutral people,
and the people we dislike. Once we have determined that we have reached
the state of balance, we recall, one by one, the twelve types of beings in our
area and send loving-kindness to those beings.

If we enumerate the twelve types of beings, they are as follows: beings
(*sattā*), breathing things (*pāṇā*), creatures (*bhūtā*), people (*puggalā*), individuals (*attabhāvapariyāpannā*), women (*itthiyo*), men (*purisā*), enlightened
beings (*ariyā*), unenlightened beings (*anariyā*), heavenly beings (*devā*),
human beings (*manussā*), and beings in the lower realms (*vinipātikā*). *Beings*
refers to all living beings, *breathing things* refers to beings that breathe, *creatures* refers to beings that are born, *individuals* refers to beings that have
bodies and are easy to see, and *beings in the lower realms* refers to beings in
the four woeful states of existence; first we send metta to all living beings
generally, and then in more specific and focused ways. It may be difficult
to distinguish between beings, breathing things, and creatures. But in any
case, when practicing loving-kindness meditation, we recall all these kinds
of beings in the mind and send loving-kindness toward them.

We begin by turning our attention toward the twelve types of beings in the
town that we are in. We send loving-kindness using the four phrases to those
beings, and enter the first through third jhānas using each phrase. As we do
so, the appropriate beings will automatically appear under the light of concentration. For example, if we think "all the humans in this town," the people
living in that town will appear. If we think "the beings in the lower realms,"
hungry ghosts will appear. If we think "devas," we will see heavenly beings in

that town or above it. Just like in the game whack-a-mole—where one mole appears and disappears, and another mole appears, and then another—the appropriate beings continue to appear under the light of concentration.

We send loving-kindness to each of the beings that appear in this way.

Once we practice sending loving-kindness to all twelve types of beings in our town, we go through areas that are bigger than the town (such as the city or district), practicing loving-kindness meditation through the same method. Then we should expand the area up to the level of the country. For example, when I was practicing the four brahmavihāras at a certain temple in Kangwon province in Korea, I first took the twelve types of beings in that town as objects, and afterward I expanded my area to the district, the Kangwon province, Korea, the world, and the universe, in order, taking the twelve types of beings in those areas as objects. Aside from this method of progressive expansion, loving-kindness meditation can also be practiced by expanding in the ten directions (north, west, south, east, northwest, northeast, southwest, southeast, below, and above).

I definitely saw the twelve types of beings in my area when I sent loving-kindness toward them. For example, while I was practicing with my eyes closed, I clearly saw a tree god that was on top of a tree. In fact, there were tree gods on top of every tree. If human beings had been in their place they definitely would have fallen off, but the tree gods were well and comfortable, as if they were stuck to the trees. The tree god was larger than a person, had long arms and legs, and was wearing clothes and a hat. After seeing a tree god in this way, if I looked at a tree after finishing my sitting, I would feel the tree god's living presence as if I were seeing it. It was unclear whether I was seeing it with my eyes or with my mind.

And I didn't just see tree gods. I saw the other twelve types of beings when I turned my attention toward them as well. I also saw a hungry ghost (*peta*) that looked like Shrek (from the animated film) but was about the size of a child. There were also beings that sat in the sky not far from town that were extremely large. There were many heavenly beings (*devas*) in the sky. The heavenly beings all wore different clothes and had different appearances. Some heavenly beings were practicing meditation; others weren't. The heavenly beings also seemed to have different backgrounds: There were heavenly beings that looked wise, and others that looked less wise. There was a heavenly being that seemed to be the ruler of heaven. I also saw female heavenly beings (*devis*). Unlike women on earth, the devis had no shortcomings, incongruities, or flaws.

And although I only saw hell beings once in a while, their existence felt clear to me.

When I expanded my area to Korea, I saw families in Seoul, my mother living in my hometown, and my dog in my house. I saw these many beings even though I simply turned my attention without trying to see them. When I then expanded the area to the universe, Earth went farther and farther away and looked smaller and smaller, as if I were seeing it from space. Eventually it looked as small as a dot. The sky is much wider than Earth, and many heavenly beings live there. Among the twelve types of beings there are enlightened beings, and when I turned my attention toward them, I saw that most of them were in the sky. There weren't many on Earth. The enlightened devas in the sky had an appearance that gave the impression they were wise. I went back and forth between the sky and Earth when sending loving-kindness toward enlightened beings. Likewise, whenever I sent loving-kindness to a certain being, I moved to the place where that being was.

After having these experiences, I stopped denying the existence of these beings. And I wasn't the only one who had these kinds of experiences. Fellow practitioners who practiced meditation in the Pa-Auk meditation tradition have told me that they also had the experience of seeing all beings when they practiced loving-kindness meditation.

The existence of heavenly beings is referenced in the Nikāyas. In the *Discourse on Advice to Anāthapiṇḍika* in the Majjhima Nikāya (MN 143), there is a scene in which Anāthapiṇḍika, a famous lay disciple who donated the Jetavana Monastery where the Buddha spent much of his time, passes away and visits the Buddha as a deva. The next day the Buddha told the monks that a certain deva had visited him and talked with him. When Ānanda replied, "That deva must have been Anāthapiṇḍika," the Buddha said that it was so.

Also, if we look at the *Gayā Sutta* in the Aṅguttara Nikāya (AN 8:64), there is a scene in which the Buddha refers to knowing the devas through eight processes and says that he declared to have finally awakened to the unsurpassed perfect enlightenment only after completely knowing them through these eight facets.

In the same way as I understood after experiencing the immaterial jhānas that the realms of beings are much more diverse than what we generally experience, I began to understand the possibility of existence in the six realms of saṃsāra mentioned in Buddhism through my experience of loving-kindness meditation and the four brahmavihāras. These worlds aren't to be blindly rejected.

Ceasing Our Psychological Projections

As I sent loving-kindness to all of the beings that I could see, I felt that I was completely filled with loving-kindness. It seemed like I could send only loving-kindness even to a person who harmed me.

Someone asked me whether I was afraid when I saw various beings while practicing loving-kindness meditation. I replied that fear disappears when we practice because we see reality as it is. Regardless of what kinds of beings they are, they became those beings in accordance with the laws of cause and effect, they are beings that experience suffering, and they are objects to whom we must send loving-kindness. Our fear disappears if we look at it this way.

Fear actually arises out of ignorance. And fear that has arisen this way is projected onto the external objects. Projection is a psychological defense mechanism whereby we send what is inside of us to an outside object and see the outside object as having those qualities. For example, let's say that there is a man with much sexual desire who says that he is tempted by women who wear miniskirts. Even if the woman who is wearing a miniskirt doesn't have the thoughts or intention to tempt that man, the man feels like she does because he is projecting his own sexual desire onto that woman. The thoughts and emotions that arise in us are, in many cases, projections. So when a certain reaction arises in us, we must always first look at our own mind. Once we see the mind and change it, external objects will look different to us in some cases. This is because we are looking at the object as it is, having stopped projecting onto it. The core of Buddhism is not just taking in external objects but rather looking back at our own mind, stopping the projection of our own desire or thoughts onto those external objects, and afterward looking at things as they are. This is a very important point.

There are a total of 528 kinds of jhāna associated with loving-kindness toward all beings, if we combine those from our starting point of attaining jhāna through loving-kindness using the four phrases toward the twelve types of beings (4 × 12) and those we attain by subsequently sending loving-kindness using the four phrases toward the twelve types of beings in the ten directions (4 × 12 × 10). If we multiply this number by the first, second, and third jhānas, the number increases substantially. Thus, when we practice loving-kindness meditation in this way our minds become completely filled with jhāna and loving-kindness.

After practicing loving-kindness meditation sufficiently, we move on to meditation on compassion.

Compassion

Although we also practice meditation on compassion by taking the four types of people as objects, there is only one phrase: "May beings be free from all suffering." First we wish "May I be free from all suffering." Once the mind becomes compassionate toward ourselves to a certain extent, we move on to a person that we respect or like. As with loving-kindness, we can't enter jhāna through compassion toward ourselves because we have much craving and attachment toward ourselves. We take about ten people, in turn, of each of the other three types of people as objects.

In order to practice meditation on compassion, we need to know the suffering of the person we are sending compassion toward. No one is free from suffering. Even people who we think don't suffer will relate suffering once we start talking to them. No matter how good a person's surrounding circumstances are, there will be some discomfort in the body and the mind. Even if there isn't any of this kind of discomfort for that person, there is bound to be something that gives his or her family members or friends a hard time, and as a result, that person may also have a hard time. Therefore, if we examine things carefully, we can find the suffering of any person we are sending compassion toward.

If we find the suffering of a person that we respect or like and wish that this person's suffering disappear by thinking "May this person be free from all suffering," we can see an image of that person at ease and free from suffering. Once we see the image of that person at ease and free from suffering, our mind also becomes at ease. And once the person we like is at ease and we also continuously see that image in a state of ease, we enter jhāna. Once the five factors of initial application, sustained application, joy, happiness, and concentration are clear, as we become fixed on the image of the person at ease and free from suffering and take it as the object of meditation, we enter the first jhāna. We examine the five jhānic factors at the mind door after exiting jhāna. Afterward we cultivate the five masteries of the first jhāna. Then we enter the second and third jhānas through the same method we've discussed thus far, and we cultivate the five masteries of those jhānas.

Once we finish practicing meditation on compassion toward a person we respect or like, we practice meditation on compassion with a neutral person as object. The method is the same. Then, once we finish practicing with a neutral person as object, we practice meditation on compassion with a person that we dislike or hate as object. Once thoughts of compassion toward the four kinds of people reach a state of balance without leaning toward any one person—in other words, upon sufficiently practicing meditation on compassion toward the four types of people—we practice meditation on compassion toward all beings.

First we wish that all twelve types of beings in our town be free from suffering. We send thoughts of compassion to all of the living beings that appear at that time. Once this practice is sufficient, we expand our range more and more to the entire earth, and then to the entire universe. We send compassion to all of the beings that we come across in the process. There is no limit to the number of objects of compassion; all beings are objects of compassion, and we meet all beings in this process. We go beyond taking only people and animals as objects and turn our life into one that takes all beings as objects. Once our practice of compassion has ripened, our minds become filled with jhāna and compassion.

There are a total of 132 jhānas related to meditation on compassion for all beings, if we combine those from our starting point of attaining jhāna through compassion using the one phrase toward the twelve types of beings with those we attain by subsequently sending compassion using the one phrase toward the twelve types of beings in the ten directions. If we multiply by the first, second, and third jhānas, the number increases substantially. Once we have finished practicing meditation on compassion, we practice meditation on sympathetic joy.

Sympathetic Joy

Like meditation on compassion, there is also one phrase for meditation on sympathetic joy:

"May this being not lose what he or she has gained." We first practice meditation on sympathetic joy by taking the four types of people as objects using this phrase. In order to practice meditation on sympathetic joy, we have to see the good things that each person possesses. That way we can wish that the person does not lose them. We have to know what that person cherishes, what that person thinks he or she has gained, what makes that person feel good, and what makes that person happy. In order to do that, we have to look closely at that person. Sometimes we have to make an effort to know what's in that person's mind. Those kinds of things are present in every person. We practice meditation on sympathetic joy by observing those things. However, there are certain cases, like beings in hell, where these things are truly difficult to find. After my practice I asked Sayadaw U Revata about this.

He said we can develop sympathetic joy toward beings in the four woeful realms by paying attention to their bright potentiality, which lies hidden in their mental continuum.

Practicing meditation on sympathetic joy helps us deal with the mind. In many cases a normal person's mind suffers when others do well. By comparing ourselves to those who do well, we feel hatred toward them and berate ourselves. Somewhere there are bound to be people who are better than us, people who are better off than us, and people who are in a better state than we are. If we can't deal with these thoughts, it'll be difficult to live our lives. Even in meditation centers, it is easy to be envious when a practitioner makes progress in practice and to compare ourselves to that person rather than congratulating him or her. This is a defilement that becomes a great hindrance to our practice. We can deal with these thoughts by practicing meditation on sympathetic joy.

Actually, being sympathetically joyful is the most beneficial path for us. And it's the most rational. Although having people who are doing well beside us is actually quite good for us, we arouse emotional reactions simply because we don't know this. Through meditation on sympathetic joy, we can stop living this way. Meditation is cultivating a way of living rationally. It is the work of stopping the wrong way we have been living and continuously training ourselves to live rationally. The same goes for all the practices of samatha meditation, meditation on loving-kindness, and meditation on compassion that I have mentioned thus far. Meditation is resetting the established, false system in us, and samatha meditation is a powerful reset.

In meditation on sympathetic joy, we first take ourselves as object and wish "May I not lose what I have gained." Once we can practice meditation on sympathetic joy toward ourselves to a certain extent, we practice by recalling around ten each of the people that we respect or like, neutral people, and people that we dislike or hate, as we've done before. Once the images of those people being satisfied with what they've already gained becomes fixed and doesn't disappear, and once the five jhānic factors clearly form with those images as objects, we enter the first jhāna. Then we go on to experience the second and third jhānas, and we train in the five masteries for each jhāna.

Once our thoughts of sympathetic joy reach a state of balance—without any distinguishing or discriminating toward the four types of people—we practice by taking all beings as objects. Just as in meditation on loving-kindness or compassion, we start with our town and expand out to the universe, sending thoughts of sympathetic joy toward all of the twelve types of beings. During this time we meet all beings. Then we are completely filled with thoughts of sympathetic joy, and we can have those thoughts toward all beings. We can also enter jhāna through this meditation easily.

There are a total of 132 jhānas related to meditation on sympathetic joy for all beings, if we combine those from our starting point of using the one phrase toward the twelve types of beings and those we attain by subsequently sending sympathetic joy using the one phrase toward the twelve types of beings in the ten directions.

By practicing meditation on loving-kindness, compassion, and sympathetic joy, our minds will be completely filled with the thoughts of loving all beings. Selfish thoughts, thoughts of getting ahead of others, jealous thoughts, and thoughts of taking pleasure in the suffering of others will all disappear. Our minds transform from those that narrowly think only of ourselves to open minds that include others.

When I first saw the Dalai Lama in 2006 at a concert hall in Kanazawa, Japan, the Dalai Lama folded both of his hands together and looked one by one at all of the people in the concert hall. At that time I felt, "This person is someone who truly wishes well on others!" A narrow mind brings about suffering. When we live in the world with a narrow mind we clash with many things. On the other hand, if we live like the Dalai Lama with an open mind, we won't clash with anything. An open mind is beneficial for both ourselves and others. An open mind is something that we need. Meditation on the four brahmavihāras is the practice of cultivating an open mind. If we can practice meditation on the four brahmavihāras, things that we usually get caught up in will disappear.

In the Aṅguttara Nikāya, a brahmin householder enumerated categories of very expensive and ornate beds and then said that surely someone as famous as the Buddha could easily obtain such beds. The Buddha replied:

> Brahmin, those high and luxurious kinds of bedding are rarely obtained by those who have gone forth, and if they are obtained, they are not allowed.
>
> But, brahmin, there are three kinds of high and luxurious beds that at present I gain at will, without trouble or difficulty. What three? The celestial high and luxurious bed, the divine high and luxurious bed, and the noble high and luxurious bed.
>
> *The Venāga Sutta*, AN 3:63; trans. Bhikkhu Bodhi

One of these three beds is the bed of the brahmas; wherever he lays with the mind of the four brahmavihāras, he lays on a bed that brahmas, the highest of the heavenly beings, use. Conversely, no matter how good the bed we lay on is, it'll be like a bed of needles if the mind isn't at ease. Practicing meditation on loving-kindness, compassion, and sympathetic joy makes us into people who aren't caught up in anything. Once we have finished practicing meditation on sympathetic joy, we practice meditation on equanimity.

Equanimity

There is a something special about meditation on equanimity, the last of the four brahmavihāras. Unlike wishing for the well being of others, as in the meditations on loving-kindness, compassion, and sympathetic joy, meditation on equanimity is seeing beings with an equanimous mind on the basis of loving-kindness, compassion, and sympathetic joy. Therefore we immediately enter the fourth jhāna when we practice meditation on equanimity.

The jhānic factors of the fourth jhāna attained through meditation on the brahmavihāra of equanimity are equanimity and concentration, just like the jhānic factors of the fourth jhāna attained through other meditation subjects. The equanimity of the fourth jhāna attained through other meditation subjects is a state in which the happiness of the third jhāna has disappeared. Therefore, before attaining the fourth jhāna by practicing meditation on the brahmavihāra of equanimity, I asked Sayadaw U Sīla whether it is enough for happiness to have simply disappeared, or whether a separate factor of equanimity needs to have arisen through other meditation subjects first. He said that true equanimity can be experienced in the fourth brahmavihāra. Once I actually experienced the fourth jhāna through meditation on equanimity, I understood why Sayadaw U Sīla said that. I was able to feel, "Ah, *this* is equanimity!" The fourth brahmavihāra of equanimity is special because, unlike the equanimity of the fourth jhāna attained through other meditation subjects, not only suffering but also loving-kindness, compassion, and sympathetic joy all disappear and only the balanced mind that doesn't lean toward any being remains.

Meditation on the fourth brahmavihāra of equanimity must be practiced on the basis of meditation on loving-kindness, compassion, and sympathetic joy. Although thoughts of loving-kindness, compassion, and sympathetic joy are present in this state, it transcends them and acquires equanimity. Therefore, in any occasion where we intend to practice meditation on equanimity, we first need to experience the first, second, and third jhānas by sending loving-kindness using the four phrases with a neutral person as object; the first, second, and third jhānas by sending compassion using the one phrase toward that person; and finally the first, second, and third jhānas by sending sympathetic joy using the one phrase to that person. After completing all of these, we take that person as object for the meditation on equanimity by contemplating as follows: "Kamma is the owner of this person. This person must live according to his/her kamma." Then we immediately enter the fourth jhāna of equanimity. This equanimity is a tremendous feeling that is hard to express with words.

Afterward, we practice meditation on equanimity in the same manner by recalling around ten neutral people, one at a time. Then we practice meditation on equanimity toward ourselves, people we respect or like, and people we dislike. The order is different from previous meditations because experiencing equanimity with a neutral person is easiest. When our thoughts of equanimity do not lean toward any one of the four types of people and no longer distinguish them, we practice meditation on equanimity taking all beings as objects. In other words, we practice meditation on equanimity by taking all twelve types of beings as objects, starting with the area where we are and expanding outward to the entire universe.

There are a total of 132 jhānas related to meditation on equanimity, if we combine those from our starting point of attaining jhāna through equanimity using the one phrase toward the twelve types of beings and those we attain by subsequently sending equanimity using the one phrase toward the twelve types of beings in the ten directions.

This completes the discussion of meditation on the four brahmavihāras: loving-kindness, compassion, sympathetic joy, and equanimity. By practicing meditation on the four brahmavihāras, our minds become very pure and our concentration greatly increases. Now it's time to practice the four protective meditations.

The Four Protective Meditations

We will be protected from various kinds of dangers if we practice the four protective meditations. That's why we do this practice before entering vipassanā meditation. The four protective meditations are loving-kindness meditation from the four brahmavihāras, recollection of the Buddha, meditation on foulness, and recollection of death. I will omit loving-kindness meditation from the following discussion, since I explained it above in the section on the four brahmavihāras. So I will begin by looking into recollection of the Buddha.

Recollection of the Buddha

As with other practices, we also embark on recollection of the Buddha after practicing ānāpānasati, the kasiṇas, and the immaterial jhānas. After exiting neither-perception-nor-nonperception and examining its jhānic factors, we continuously recall the virtues of the Buddha. The ten qualities of the Buddha are also known as the ten epithets of the Buddha and are as follows:

worthy one (*arahaṃ*), perfectly enlightened (*sammāsambuddho*), perfected in knowledge and conduct (*vijjā-caraṇasampanno*), well-gone (*sugato*), knower of the worlds (*lokavidū*), the unsurpassed (*anuttaro*), the tamer of men fit to be tamed (*purisadammasārathī*), the teacher of devas and human beings (*satthādevamanussānaṃ*), the enlightened one (*buddho*), the blessed one (*bhagavā*). In Myanmar there are nine epithets of the Buddha, as "unsurpassed" and the "tamer of men fit to be tamed" are combined. All we have to do is recall one of these ten.

Arahant also signifies one who is devoid of defilements. So we can think of the Buddha as having no defilements and recall the image of the Buddha who is devoid of defilements. Another way to think of the Buddha as having no defilements is to recall an image of the Buddha that we like. Also, we can recall other virtues of the Buddha aside from the ten already mentioned. For example, we can recall "the Buddha is one who is very equanimous," or we can think of the Buddha as being deeply absorbed in jhāna and recall an image of the Buddha deeply absorbed in jhāna. Or we can recall him as having much compassion. We can either recall the Buddha or a statue of the Buddha.

When we recall any virtue of the Buddha, we will be able to focus on the image of the Buddha with that virtue and much joy will arise in us. The Buddha will be inside of us. We will be meeting with a being who is wiser and more compassionate than anyone else in this world. The Buddha is nobler and purer than any other object of meditation.

We can't enter jhāna through this practice, but we can enter access concentration. As explained in Bhikkhu Ñāṇamoli's translation of the *Visuddhimagga*: "Owing to the profundity of the Enlightened One's special qualities, or else owing to his being occupied in recollecting special qualities of many sorts, the jhāna is only access and does not reach absorption."

Meditation on Foulness

Just like when we practice the recollection of the Buddha, we practice meditation on foulness after first practicing ānāpānasati, the kasiṇas, and the immaterial jhānas, and after exiting neither-perception-nor-nonperception and examining its jhānic factors. The object of meditation on foulness is a dead person that we have seen directly sometime during our lives. However, we don't practice with the image of a dead person of someone we might be attracted to. For instance, in the Pa-Auk Sayadaw tradition, we are told we shouldn't practice with the image of any person of the opposite sex, even if that person is one of our family members.

A corpse is generally a repulsive object. This is why we take it as the object of meditation on foulness. When we focus on a dead person as object, at first it's frightening and we may also think that it's unclean. However, after a short time light will be present and we will see the object with ease as it becomes fixed. The object won't be repulsive at all but rather it'll become a pleasant object, and it will look as if it is peacefully in eternal sleep. We can enter jhāna through this object. Once the five jhānic factors become clear, we enter the first jhāna. We can only enter the first jhāna through this practice.

> Just as it is only by virtue of its rudder that a boat keeps steady in a river with turbulent waters and a rapid current, and it cannot be steadied without a rudder, so too [here], owing to the weak hold on the object, consciousness when unified only keeps steady by virtue of applied thought, and it cannot be steadied without applied thought, which is why there is only the first jhāna here, not the second and the rest.
>
> *Visuddhimagga*, trans. Bhikkhu Ñāṇamoli

Once we practice meditation on foulness with a dead person that we have encountered at some point, our perception of death will change. This happened to me. Once, while I was majoring in psychiatry, I was on night duty and I saw the body of a person who had died a terrible death from a car accident in the emergency room. I returned to the night-duty room to sleep but I couldn't, because I kept recalling that image. But later, as I practiced meditation on foulness by taking all the dead people that I had encountered in my life as objects, my own perception of dead people changed substantially.

I was unable to feel any foulness from the objects of meditation, and I saw them as not being unclean at all, despite the fact that they were objects of meditation on foulness. This happened to the point where I wondered whether this was okay. When I asked Sayadaw U Sīla about this, he said that it was fine.

Once we practice meditation on foulness, our perception of death and dead people, things which all beings instinctually avoid, will change and we will accept these things. In truth, we will all die some day, and we will leave behind our dead bodies. There is no reason to see that as unclean. Meditation helps us get rid of the biases inside of us and accept things as they are.

Recollection of Death

As with the other protective meditations, we practice the recollection of death after practicing ānāpānasati, the kasiṇas, and the immaterial jhānas. After exiting neither-perception-nor-nonperception and examining its jhānic factors, we contemplate in the following manner: "I too will die." Then we move from the present moment closer and closer to the moment of death through the eye of wisdom. We see the image of our body aging as time passes, and eventually we see the image of our death. We can see our situation of the time of our death and we can also know our age at that time.

Death unfolds itself in various forms. Sometimes it appears in an ordinary form of death; sometimes it appears as darkening, with light disappearing in the mind door; and sometimes it appears in the form of the disappearance of materiality formed by kamma, consciousness, and nutriment. We can attain up to access concentration through this practice.

Seeing my own dead body helped me accept, not just in my mind but ontologically, that I too would die someday. It was a different experience than just thinking about it as a fact. What we have seen through samādhi always appears vividly and takes effect on our minds, and this goes for the recollection of death as well. Speaking from a psychoanalytical point of view, I felt that it had a very big impact on my unconscious. Living beings are all approaching death. What's important is the state in which we face death.

Death is not just an ending, it is also another beginning. How we proceed with this beginning is important.

When We Bring the Mind Together, We Will Obtain Power

Samatha meditation is the path of training the mind in two ways.

The first way is training to let go. Since we are bringing the mind toward one object in samatha meditation, we have to bring the mind back to the object of meditation when it has gone somewhere other than toward the object of meditation. In order to do that, the mind that has gone toward another object has to let that object go. In samatha meditation, the practice of letting go occurs naturally, as we repeat this process continuously.

Once we are well-trained in this, if the mind has gone to an object that is harmful to us or an object that we don't want, we will easily be able to let it go and return to the object of meditation. We can easily escape from any object's influence. Thus, nothing in the world will be able to make us suffer. Suffering arises when the mind has gone to a certain object and has been affected by it. But since we can always gather the mind from that object, suffering won't be able to take hold in us. Therefore if we practice samatha meditation we can live our lives without suffering.

The second way is training to focus. When the mind is focused on one object, we will obtain great power. Although we can't burn a piece of paper with the sunlight that comes in through our window, we can burn it if we focus the sunlight by using a magnifying lens. Likewise, a mind that is unified has great power. Things we have experienced through samatha or a powerful state of focus will always remain in our memory and will affect our minds greatly. Principles like this also operate in hypnosis.

Just as a laser cuts through steel, a mind that has been brought together can cut through to the fundamental nature of whatever it sees. When people see something, they usually can't see it as it is, since they are affected by past experiences and emotions when seeing it. So not only are they unable to see its fundamental nature, but they forget about it soon afterward. If we live this way, we won't be able to possess great power. There has to be lightning-like insight in order to move people and to carry out the changes that guide a generation. Steve Jobs, who turned Apple into one of the best companies in the world, knew this very well. And so he said that we can move mountains when the mind is focused.

We will be able to move the mind at will once, through the practice of samatha meditation, it is no longer affected by our past experiences, emotions, and preconceptions. In other words, there will be fewer defilements, which are the forces that disrupt the mind's movement. There is great power in a mind that has been cultivated through samatha. With that power, we will be able to turn the mind in the direction that we want.

In this way, samatha meditation isn't just necessary for our practice. It is also necessary so that we can live our lives with less difficulty. Just as the body needs exercise, the mind also needs the training of samatha.

Up to this point we have looked into samatha meditation. We cultivate samatha in order to purify the mind and eliminate our defilements temporarily so that we can meditate on materiality, mentality, dependent origination, and vipassanā. We can only practice meditation on materiality, mentality, dependent origination, and vipassanā with the eye of wisdom that forms from cultivating samatha.

3. Meditation on Materiality

The Four Elements Meditation

In order to practice meditation on materiality, we first have to practice the four elements meditation, one of the samatha practices. The four elements meditation is a samatha practice in which we can attain access concentration while at the same time seeing the ultimate reality of materiality. Therefore the four elements meditation is included in the forty meditation subjects mentioned in the *Visuddhimagga*. Let's look closely at the process of attaining access concentration through the four elements meditation and seeing materiality with that samādhi.

There are two ways of beginning the practice of the four elements meditation: after first cultivating the jhānas, and without first cultivating the jhānas. The four elements meditation isn't very difficult if we practice it after experiencing jhāna through ānāpānasati. To me, cultivating samādhi for the first time through the four elements meditation seems like it would take a lot of time and wouldn't be easy, although there are probably differences from person to person. In any case, the method of practicing the four elements meditation is the same for those practicing after attaining jhāna as for those who haven't yet experienced jhāna.

Since I first practiced the four elements meditation after practicing ānāpānasati, the meditation on the thirty-two constituent parts, and meditation on the kasiṇas, I always cultivated the first, second, third, and fourth jhānas one by one through ānāpānasati and meditation on the kasiṇas before beginning my practice of the four elements meditation. After exiting the fourth jhāna attained through meditation on the kasiṇas and examining its jhānic factors, I began practicing the four elements meditation. I practiced the four elements meditation by discerning the four great elements from the thirty-two constituent parts of the body.

First we train in discerning the four great elements. The four great elements are the earth element (*paṭhavīdhātu*), the water element (*āpodhātu*), the fire element (*tejodhātu*), and the wind element (*vāyodhātu*). Although earth, water, fire, and wind are considered to be materiality, strictly speaking they refer to their material qualities or properties, or in other words to the state of energy that they possess. Of course these qualities can take physical form when they are combined; in modern physics, it is said that energy has mass. But the earth of the four great elements refers to things that have the fundamental *properties* of earth, not necessarily something that has a solid form. Regardless of where they are or how big or small they are, everything that has the property of earth is "earth." The same goes for water, fire, and wind. In order to discern the ultimate reality of the four great elements, we have to know the properties of the four great elements. Therefore the four elements meditation begins with knowing the properties of the four great elements.

The Twelve Properties of the Four Great Elements

There are six properties of the earth element, and they are divided into two groups. One group is hardness, roughness, and heaviness, and the other group is softness, smoothness, and lightness. Hardness and softness can't exist together; this also applies to roughness and smoothness, and to heaviness and lightness. Other properties can exist together.

The water element has the two properties of flowing and cohesion. The fire element has the two properties of heat and coldness. The wind element has the two properties of supporting and pushing.

Thus there are altogether twelve properties of earth, water, fire, and wind. This method of division is quite different from the classification of matter in the field of natural science, in which there are over one hundred of just the chemical elements. Although the chemical elements in the field of natural science are very small, they all have form. If the Buddha were to see the chemical elements, he would say they are not fundamental materiality that can't be divided any further, but rather composite materials that have the four great elements within them.

We can discern the four great elements with the twelve properties of earth, water, fire, and wind. There is materiality when these twelve are present. Although I didn't have many difficulties concerning earth properties, I couldn't understand why water has the property of cohesion, why everything that was in a state of cohesion is seen as water. For example, if our eyeglasses are in a fixed state, it means that the water element of cohesion is there. The property of cohesion is a property of water, and if there is cohesion it means that, among the four elements, the water element is present. In order for there to be cohesion, there needs to be something that creates cohesion. If there isn't anything that creates cohesion, materiality can only exist separately. Just as flour can't stick together without water, materiality can't stick together without the water element. Therefore the Buddha saw the force that creates cohesion as water. And so if there is something that is lumped together, he viewed that as the presence of the water element. He also saw flowing as water. As long as there is materiality, there is always either flowing or cohesion. This is because of the properties of the water element within materiality.

Though I understood heat as a property of fire, another thing I couldn't understand was why cold is also seen as a property of fire, since there is no warmth. Eventually I also came to understand that in my own way. Heat and cold are always present for things that exist in this world. When the element of fire is present there is warmth, and when that warmth goes to another place, it becomes cold. Therefore heat and cold are phenomena caused by fire. Heat and cold are present as long as there is materiality.

Finally, in the case of wind, although I understood pushing, I couldn't understand why support was included as one of the properties of wind. Support occurs when materiality maintains a certain state. Support is being in a certain position continuously. Why did the Buddha include this as being wind? I came to understand that support requires force. If only one force is at work, the situation will unfold according to the influence of that force. When something is supported, various forces are at work. For example, a weak patient can't remain sitting. We can maintain a certain posture only when there is a force working in one direction and a force working in the opposite direction as well. We can see this as pushing arising in several directions. Support can therefore be seen as the result of various kinds of pushing. Thus, just as pushing is a property of wind, support is also a property of wind. When we look at it this way, the four great elements explain material phenomena well. There are no material phenomena that can't be explained through the four great elements.

Discerning the Four Great Elements from the Thirty-Two Constituent Parts of the Body

Now let's look into practicing the four elements meditation through examining the thirty-two constituent parts of the body. We discern the twelve properties of the four great elements one by one in the thirty-two constituent parts of the body.

First we discern the six properties of the earth element. We clearly discern hardness, roughness, heaviness, softness, smoothness, and lightness, one by one in order. As the eye of wisdom opens when we cultivate jhāna, we will discern these naturally if we turn the mind toward what we are trying to see. For example, when we try to find hardness, our consciousness goes toward the direction where there is hardness, such as our bones or our teeth. At first this was quite marvelous for me. There was no doubt about it when I checked to see if the eye of wisdom was pointing things out correctly. Therefore I later began to have faith in the eye of wisdom. When I turned my attention toward hardness, I discerned hardness wherever it was present. When I turned my attention toward heaviness, my consciousness went toward a place with heaviness, such as the places where my organs faced downward; and when I looked for lightness, my consciousness went toward things that faced upward, such as my head hairs or my body hairs. When I turned my attention toward softness, I perceived soft surfaces; and when I looked for smoothness, I perceived things such as my internal organs or globules of fat.

After discerning the six properties of the earth element, we discern the two properties of the water element: flowing and cohesion. If we turn the mind toward flowing, we perceive places where there is flowing, such as our blood vessels or lymph glands. If we look for cohesion, we discern cohesion from our entire body.

After discerning the properties of the water element, we discern the two properties of the fire element: heat and cold. If we try to discern heat, our consciousness will go toward places such as the inside of our body or our armpits, and we will actually feel warmth there. On the other hand, if we try to feel coldness our consciousness will go toward places that are exposed to the outside, such as our fingertips and toes, and we feel coldness there.

Then we discern the two properties of the wind element: pushing and support. If we try to discern pushing, our consciousness will go toward several places inside our body where wind moves. If we try to discern support, our consciousness will go toward the posture we are holding now and support will be perceived.

As we discern the twelve properties of the four great elements in the thirty-two constituent parts of the body, the thirty-two constituent parts will disappear and turn into a mass of light. Even when the body turns into a mass of light, there is still no problem in discerning the twelve properties of the four great elements. For me, this happened after practicing for about two days.

If I had tried to find the four great elements while observing the thirty-two constituent parts of the body merely by thinking "this must be hardness because it is the bone," I wouldn't have been able to find hardness once only light remained. But I was able to discern hardness within light even when only light was present because I had looked for hardness with the eye of wisdom. There was no doubt in me due to my faith in the eye of wisdom.

In order to discern the twelve properties clearly and quickly, it's better to take only a part of the word. For example, hardness, roughness, and heaviness become "hard-rough-heavy." The same goes for the other properties. By doing this, I discerned the twelve properties about two and a half times in one minute.

Through this we will see the body not as bones, skin, and blood but as the four great elements. We will observe the phenomena that arise as the four great elements not only while we are sitting but also while we are eating, walking, or lying down. For example, the phenomenon of pushing is present when we walk. Therefore we will know "the pushing phenomenon of the wind element is present" rather than just knowing that we are walking. In this way our view of ourselves and others as well as the things in this world will change. We will see the lumps that we had seen up to this point as hands, arms, trees, etc., as the fundamental materiality of the four great elements.

As my practice of the four elements meditation deepened, I felt the twelve properties vividly in my body when I looked for them. For example, when I thought "smoothness," I vividly felt the smoothness of my entire body and felt very good. When I thought "hardness," I vividly felt the hardness of my entire body.

In the four elements meditation, there is a stage where we see *kalāpas*. Kalāpas are the smallest unit of mass in which materiality can exist. The four great elements can't exist individually on their own; they always exist as a group of materiality in the form of kalāpas. In the stage of seeing kalāpas, the kalāpas that have clumped together must fall apart.

When he thought I would see kalapas after hearing I could discern the properties of the four great elements vividly within light, Sayadaw U Sīla told me to look for space within the mass of light by saying "space, space." At first nothing really changed when I did that, but as I looked for space by saying "space, space" during the following sitting, I saw space, and kalāpas casting a bright light began revealing themselves. It was a mysterious experience in which the mass of light transformed into individual kalāpas. For about a day the mass of light would turn into kalāpas only when I looked for space, but afterward the kalāpas were always present. Once this happens we can discern materiality from the kalāpas. If we can see the materiality of the kalāpas, we have entered the state of momentary concentration (*khaṇikasamādhi*).

Access concentration can be achieved through the four elements meditation. And it is from this point that the practice of seeing materiality through meditation on materiality actually begins.

MEDITATION ON MATERIALITY

All existing things have two aspects; in other words, things exist both in conventional reality (*sammuti*) and in ultimate reality (*paramattha*). Conventional reality refers to putting certain labels through mutual agreement on forms that we perceive through our sense organs. For example, a Korean person will look at a hand and say "*son*," look at a foot and say "*bal*," and look at a rock and say "*dol*." This is conventional reality. Concepts created by humans are also included in conventional reality.

On the other hand, ultimate reality has its own inherent characteristics, which can't be broken down any further, and therefore doesn't change— unlike the "hand" of conventional reality, for instance, which changes its color and size when the weather is cold. Therefore ultimate reality becomes the smallest unit of measurement. Of course this doesn't mean that ultimate reality is permanent, just that it doesn't change its characteristics while it exists. Ultimate reality also arises and passes away in accordance with its conditions. There are four ultimate realities: materiality (*rūpa*), consciousness (*citta*), mental factors (*cetasika*), and nibbāna.

Meditation on materiality is the practice of seeing the ultimate reality of materiality. We will see consciousness and mental factors in meditation on mentality. And nibbāna can be experienced when the wisdom of vipassanā has ripened.

Meditation on materiality is discerning, one by one, materiality composed of kalāpas, the smallest unit in which materiality can exist. It is knowing what materiality is through this process. There are twenty-eight kinds of materiality, and they are divided into two categories: concrete materiality and nonconcrete materiality. There are eighteen kinds of concrete materiality, which exist in reality, and ten kinds of nonconcrete material phenomena, which are produced by concrete materiality. In meditation on materiality, we actually see both concrete materiality and nonconcrete materiality, but we first discern the eighteen kinds of concrete materiality in the kalāpas.

There are three types of kalāpas. They are kalāpas (1) from eight kinds of materiality gathered together, (2) from nine kinds of materiality gathered together, and (3) from ten kinds of materiality gathered together. Therefore at the very least there are always eight kinds of materiality gathered together. These eight kinds of materiality are the earth element, the water element, the fire element, the wind element, color, smell, taste, and nutriment. These eight kinds of materiality are always present regardless of what kind of kalāpa it is. For kalāpas composed of nine kinds of materiality, life faculty is added to the eight basic kinds of materiality. For kalāpas composed of ten kinds of materiality, one of either the eye sensitivity, ear sensitivity, nose sensitivity, tongue sensitivity, body sensitivity, heart base, femininity, or masculinity is present with the nine others.

Eight Kinds of Basic Materiality

We discern materiality in the kalāpas one by one. Since there are always the eight basic kinds of materiality, we can discern the earth element, the water element, the fire element, the wind element, color, smell, taste, and nutriment in every kalāpa. When we discern the materiality of the earth element for one particular kalāpa, we perceive whether the six properties of the earth element are present in that kalāpa. At first the kalāpa isn't easy to discern, since it appears and disappears very quickly, but if we train a little bit we can discern hardness, roughness, heaviness, softness, smoothness, and lightness within the kalāpa. Then we can see that the earth element is present in that kalāpa.

Once we have become skilled at discerning the materiality of the earth element, we discern the flowing and cohesion of the materiality of the water element. This isn't difficult since we have been trained in quickly discerning the twelve properties of the four great elements through the four elements meditation. Then we discern the heat and cold of the materiality of the fire element and the pushing and supporting of the materiality of the wind element. Although there are eighteen kinds of concrete materiality, they actually are just the four great elements plus materiality derived from the four great elements. In other words, the fourteen other concrete materialities are all derived from the four great elements.

After discerning the four great elements, we discern color from the kalāpas. We start with the kalāpas in the eye and then discern color from the kalāpas in the ear, nose, tongue, body, and heart. The colors will differ based on their

3. Types of Materiality

concrete materiality	earth element
	water element
	fire element
	air element
	color (visible form)
	smell
	taste
	nutriment
	sound
	eye sensitivity
	ear sensitivity
	nose sensitivity
	tongue sensitivity
	body sensitivity
	heart base
	femininity
	masculinity
	life faculty
nonconcrete materiality	element of space
	bodily intimation
	vocal intimation
	lightness
	malleability
	wieldiness
	production
	continuity
	decay
	impermanence

location. In my case, when I first discerned color from the kalāpas, I perceived white from the eye, black from the ear, green and red from the nose, green from the tongue, yellow from the body, and white and red from the heart. Later on I perceived a variety of colors based on their location. When we look to discern color from the kalāpas, we will be able to intuitively know what the color will be. It becomes immediately visible through the eye of wisdom.

We discern smell starting from the nose and then going to the eyes, ears, tongue, body, and heart. The reason we start with the nose is because smell is discerned clearly from the nose. When I first discerned smell, the kalāpas in my nose smelled like cosmetics (skin lotion). I wasn't able to sense this smell at all before practicing meditation, but the smell of cosmetics was definitely there. My eyes smelled like eye wax or water, my ears smelled stinky, my tongue smelled yucky, my body smelled slightly sweaty, and my heart smelled like blood.

I also discerned taste from my eyes, ears, nose, tongue, body, and heart. My eyes tasted slightly salty or like plain water. My ears and nose tasted slightly salty. My tongue tasted like spit, and my body tasted salty. My heart tasted like blood. There was a taste for each kalāpa.

I saw nutriment as forms, like round objects being piled up. When I drew what I saw and showed it to Sayadaw U Sīla, he said that nutriment has the form of an egg yolk being cut in half.

The Materiality of Life Faculty

After seeing the eight basic materialities in this way, we discern the materiality of life faculty. There are kalāpas that have life faculty and kalāpas that don't. In order to be able to see this, we first must understand that there are kalāpas that are translucent and kalāpas that are opaque.

The translucent kalāpas reflect and shine brightly, while the opaque kalāpas don't reflect or shine. The materialities of eye, ear, nose, tongue, and body sensitivity are all translucent kalāpas. Only the kalāpas that have sensitivity are translucent kalāpas; the kalāpas that lack sensitivity are opaque kalāpas. The materiality of life faculty is present in all translucent kalāpas and some (but not all) opaque kalāpas. So we first discern the materiality of life faculty in translucent kalāpas.

The materiality of life faculty is materiality that has the function of sustaining other materiality, and it is present if we feel that materiality is sustaining other materiality in the same kalāpa. If we don't feel that way, then the materiality of life faculty is absent. Since all translucent kalāpas have the materiality of life faculty, we can clearly perceive that it is present.

When we look for the materiality of life faculty in opaque kalāpas, there are some kalāpas where we can discern the materiality of life faculty and some kalāpas where we can't.

After discerning the materiality of life faculty in this way, we discern the materialities of masculinity and femininity.

The Materiality of Sex

The kalāpas that have the materialities of masculinity and femininity (together called "the materiality of sex") are opaque kalāpas that have the eight basic materialities as well as the materiality of life faculty. Therefore, in order to discern the materiality of sex, all we have to do is find it in the opaque kalāpas with the materiality of life faculty. As a man, I discerned the materiality of masculinity in myself. The materiality of masculinity feels like the masculine attributes of manliness, intrepidness, gallantry, and coarseness that we talk about in the dichotomy of gender archetypes. If we feel these things, it means the materiality of masculinity is present. We can also find the materiality of femininity by discerning its archetypal qualities in this way.

The Five Sensitive Materialities and the Heart Base

Next we discern the five sensitive materialities: eye, ear, nose, tongue, and body. We begin with eye sensitivity. Once we make up our minds to discern eye sensitivity, the eye of wisdom will move to a place where it is present. Then all we have to do is look for eye sensitivity.

Eye sensitivity can be discerned if the reflection of color is present. In eye sensitivity, colors that are reflected a little distance away are perceived clearer than colors that are very close. But although eye sensitivity is present in an eye, body sensitivities are also present. The same goes for the ear, nose, tongue, and the heart base: each has its own sensitivity as well as its body sensitivity. So we must keep in mind that among the translucent kalāpas, only the ones that reflect light are materialities of eye sensitivity.

After discerning the materiality of eye sensitivity, we discern ear sensitivity. If we turn the mind toward perceiving ear sensitivity, our attention will again move to the place where it is present. All we have to do is notice the sounds that come in contact with the materiality of ear sensitivity. Two types of sounds are discerned: sounds that are heard when kalāpas run into each other or hit each other or crash each other, and sounds that are heard from the inside or outside. It doesn't matter what sound it is; when sounds come in contact with materialities in translucent kalāpas, those are materialities of ear sensitivity.

When discerning the materiality of nose sensitivity, all we have to do is discern smells present in all the kalāpas or external smells coming into contact with nose sensitivity in our nose. When we discern tongue sensitivity, all we have to do is discern the tastes in all the kalāpas or the external tastes coming into contact with tongue sensitivity. For the materiality of body sensitivity, we discern the hardness that is the property of the earth element coming into contact with body sensitivity.

Finally, after we have discerned the five sensitive materialities, we discern the heart base in the opaque kalāpas right below the mind door. The heart base is the materiality that is the support for all mental processes and has the feeling of a dependable place.

Thus we have discerned the eighteen kinds of concrete materiality.

The Ten Kinds of Nonconcrete Materiality

Since the ten kinds of nonconcrete materiality are phenomena that are produced by concrete materiality, we have to discern them when we are prepared to do so.

Before discerning nonconcrete materiality, we first observe mind-born materiality. Sayadaw U Sīla told me, "Look at what kinds of phenomena are present when you come out of the fourth jhāna and have the intention to see the mind door." When I tried doing that, something surprising occurred. Materiality was formed by the mind that had the desire to look toward the mind door. Kalāpas formed like white smoke and spread out everywhere. I then thought, "This must be the mind-born materiality!"

Next Sayadaw U Sīla told me to see what phenomena were present when I tried moving my finger. So as I watched, mind-born materiality spread from the mind door to my finger, and my finger moved as they touched it. The pushing of the predominant wind element of the kalāpas formed by the mind intending to move makes the finger move.

The movement of the body is bodily intimation, which is one of the non-concrete materialities. I came to know that bodily intimation was a material phenomenon by seeing *how* the body moves when it moves. When I had previously studied the Abhidhamma, I didn't understand why bodily intimation was deemed materiality, but I understood what I learned in the Abhidhamma once I saw it directly through actual practice. The things that appear in the Abhidhamma are things that are experienced by practicing meditation, so it was hard to understand them without practicing.

The same goes for the nonconcrete materiality of verbal intimation. When we think of speaking, the desire to speak produces mind-born materiality, which spreads thoughout the body including in the area of the vocal cords. In this way, sounds are made when the materiality of the earth element in the kalāpa produced by the mind and the materiality of the earth element produced by kamma in the vocal cord come in contact. Therefore the sound of our speech is also a material phenomenon. This is something we can experience by practicing, and we can know this well if we practice systematically with the help of the light of concentration.

Materiality was produced when I made up my mind to move my body, and I saw materiality being produced by the mind, and it caused the actions according to my intention. I naturally became focused on the present. I saw materiality being created in every mental activity.

Some years before having this experience of seeing the body move when making up my mind to do so, I had a similar experience when I practiced observing the mind and body in Myanmar in 2003. My teacher Sayadaw U Janaka said, "Think about trying to move your hand," and I found it extremely amazing that my hand would move automatically in response to just that thought. Through that experience I came to know that my will moves my body. Afterward I was able to prostrate whenever I made up my mind to prostrate and I was able to walk whenever I made up my mind to walk—my body moved automatically in response to the intention. I came to understand that in hypnosis, when someone says, "Your hand is becoming lighter and will now float like a balloon," the fact that the hand moves upward also follows this principle. But in this later time of practice, I came to know that when will is present, it is carried out when mind-born materialities are produced. The relationship between the body and mind became clearer to me than it had been before.

The Regeneration of Materiality

Among the various materialities there are those that regenerate and those that don't. Those that regenerate are the temperature and nutriment inside the kalāpas. Now let's look a little more into the regeneration of materiality.

Materiality is produced in four ways: by kamma, mind, temperature, and nutriment.

Materiality produced by kamma includes the eye, ear, nose, tongue, and body sensitivities, the heart base, masculinity, femininity, and life faculty. I have explained materiality produced by the mind above. Temperature-born materiality is produced by the temperature (the fire element) of different kalāpas, and nutriment-born materiality is produced from food. The regeneration of nutriment-born materiality is a bit complex. It is regenerated with the help of the digestive heat from a life-faculty materiality produced by kamma. Once regenerated, nutriment-born materiality arises. Then, this materiality spreads throughout the entire body. On the other hand, with the help of the nutriment of the nutriment-born materiality and the digestive heat, new kalāpas are regenerated from the nutriments of the kalāpas produced by kamma, mind, temperature, and nutriment.

The temperature and nutriment in one kalāpa can generate new kalāpas. Temperature can produce new kalāpa directly. Nutriment regenerates by receiving help from the nutriment of other nutriment-born materiality and digestive heat. Thus, temperature and nutriments regenerate exponentially.

In this way an incredibly large number of them are regenerated. When practicing meditation on materiality, we observe materiality no matter what we do—whether sitting, walking, sitting, lying down, or eating. Nutriment-born materiality can be observed while we are eating too.

Kamma-born, mind-born, temperature-born, and nutriment-born materialities each may produce different numbers of generations of new kalāpas. The degree of regeneration varies according to many factors such as the strength of kamma, mind, temperature, and quality of food. Mind-born, temperature-born, nutriment-born materialities each comprise eight kinds of materiality. To discern materiality formed by the mind, all we have to do is see the materiality that is formed in the mind door when the mind operates. In order to discern materiality formed by temperature or nutriment, all we have to do is see materiality formed by the breaking apart of temperature or nutriment within kalāpas formed by kamma, the mind, temperature, and food.

When we see these materialities, we see how much they have been broken apart. Then we will be able to know that the degree of breaking apart depends on the type of materiality.

Materiality Formed by Kamma, the Mind, Temperature, and Nutriment

First we discern materiality formed by kamma, the mind, temperature, and nutriment at the six senses doors. Then we discern materiality formed by kamma, the mind, temperature, and nutriment from the thirty-two constituent parts of the body.

The first twenty of the thirty-two constituent parts are parts of the body in which the earth element is predominant: head hairs, body hairs, nails, teeth, skin, flesh, sinews, bones, bone marrow, kidneys, heart, liver, membrane, spleen, lungs, intestines, mesentery, contents of the stomach, feces, and the brain. The following twelve are parts of the body in which the water element is predominant: bile, phlegm, pus, blood, sweat, fat, tears, grease, spittle, snot, oil of the joints, and urine. After discerning the materiality of the thirty-two constituent parts of the body, we discern the four parts of the body in which fire element is predominant and the six parts of the body in which wind element is predominant, which aren't included in the original thirty-two constituent parts of the body. There are therefore altogether forty-two constituent parts of the body. These forty-two constituent parts of the body are mentioned in detail in the *Greater Discourse of Advice to Rāhula* in the Majjhima Nikāya (MN 62).

First we discern the materiality formed by kamma, the mind, temperature, and nutriment from the twenty parts of the body in which earth element is predominant. We do this through the kalāpas that are present in each of the twenty parts. (In the case of feces and the contents of the stomach, only materiality formed by temperature is present.) We now see the body not as head hairs, body hairs, nails, teeth, etc., but as materiality formed by kamma, the mind, temperature, and nutriment. We see it all as ultimate materiality. Rather than seeing the eye, for instance, we see the materialities of eye sensitivity, body sensitivity, earth, water, fire, wind, color, smell, taste, nutriment, and life faculty. They arise and perish very rapidly. We see them as they really are.

Once we finish discerning the twenty parts of the body in which the earth element is predominant, we discern materiality formed by kamma, the mind, temperature, and nutriment from the twelve parts of the body in which water element is predominant.

Afterward, we discern materiality from the four parts in which the fire element is predominant, which are as follows: heat that warms the body, heat that causes maturing and aging, heat of fever, and digestive heat. Other than digestive heat, the other types of heat comprise kalāpas where fire element is predominant and which are of all four origins—kamma-born (only life-nine materiality kalāpas), temperature-born, nutriment-born, and mind-born. For digestive heat, it comprises only kamma-born kalāpas with nine materiality including life faculty. Heat that warms the body is with us at all times. All we have to do is to discern the kalāpa in which heat is predominant and which makes our body warm. For heat that causes maturing and aging, we can examine the process of getting older and older day by day to determine the kalāpas in which fire element is predominant, too. For heat of fever, all we have to do is discern the kalāpa in which heat is predominant when we have a fever. If we don't currently have a fever, we can remember a time when we had a fever and discern materiality at that time. Kalāpas of digestive heat are kalāpas that contain the materiality of life faculty.

Next we discern materiality from the six parts in which the wind element is predominant. They are wind that rises, wind that falls, wind in the abdomen, wind in the intestines, wind in the entire body, and the in-breath and out-breath. We discern materiality among these kalāpas. In the first five of these parts (excluding the in-breath and out-breath), they comprise kalāpas where wind element is predominant and which is of all four origins—kamma-born (only life-nine materiality), temperature-born, nutriment-born, and mind-born. In contrast, in the in-breath and out-breath there are only mind-born kalāpas consisting of nine kinds of materiality including sound.

Discerning the Ten Kinds of Nonconcrete Materiality

To this point we have discerned materiality from the forty-two constituent parts of the body. Now we can discern the ten kinds of nonconcrete materiality. Since I have already talked about how to discern the materialities of bodily intimation and verbal intimation, I will just talk about discerning the remaining eight kinds of nonconcrete materiality.

In order to see the kalapas, we have already discerned the element of space. Kalāpas are separated by space. Whoever sees the space sees the kalāpas. Whoever sees the kalāpas sees the space.

The next three nonconcrete materialities are lightness, malleability, and wieldiness. There are times when we feel lightness of the body while practicing as well as in our daily activities. For instance, when we concentrate deeply, we feel a special kind of lightness.

When we are healthy, we can do whatever we like: we can walk the way we want, we can sit the way we want, we can easily walk up and down the stairs. All these are because of wieldiness.

If we can do all the activities with ease, there is also lightness and malleability; when malleability and lightness are present, we reach a wieldy state. When we are in the state of being light and soft, we can do anything easily.

The remaining nonconcrete materialities are production, continuity, decay, and impermanence. *Production* refers to materiality that is newly formed during the rebirth-linking process. The three kinds of materiality that form during rebirth-linking are formed by kamma and are kalāpas that have the heart base, kalāpas that have body sensitivity, and kalāpas that have materiality of sex. We can observe production only when we practice on dependent origination. *Continuity* is the arising phase of any materiality. *Decay* refers to the standing phase of the materiality. *Impermanence* is the perishing phase of the materiality.

Once we have finished discerning the ten kinds of nonconcrete materiality in this way, we have discerned all forms of materiality.

Phenomena in Which Concrete Materiality and Nonconcrete Materiality Are Both Present

Finally, we discern phenomena in which concrete materiality and nonconcrete materiality are present together. For example, we can discern materiality that arises when we act in a comfortable manner. In this case, twelve materialities—including the eight basic materialities of earth, water, fire, wind, color, smell, taste, and nutriment, as well as bodily intimation and the materialities of lightness, malleability, and wieldiness—are present. All we have to do is discern them. When we speak in a comfortable manner, it is the same twelve materialities except that we discern verbal intimation instead of bodily intimation. If we try discerning materiality when we feel happy while meditating, the materialities of lightness, malleability, and wieldiness will be present along with the eight basic materialities. If we discern materiality when talking, the materiality of verbal intimation and sound will be present along with the eight basic materialities. If we feel good when the weather is nice, the materialities of lightness, malleability, and wieldiness will be present along with the eight basic materialities. If we try discerning materiality when we eat suitable food in a good mood, the materialities of lightness, malleability, and wieldiness will be present along with the eight basic materialities. In this way materiality is present in any state, and we can discern it.

Escaping from Ego

Through the practice of discerning materiality, we learn definitively that the body is composed of ultimate materiality. We no longer see our hands, eyes, ears, nose, feet, and legs as we have seen them in the past, but rather as the ultimate materiality of the eighteen kinds of concrete materiality and nonconcrete materiality. And we actually see the arising and passing away of concrete materiality. Once we see ultimate materiality in this way, we no longer think that the body remains continuously as a static thing; instead we see the body as ultimate reality arising and passing away. We no longer think that our hands remain continuously as they are. We no longer see the hand as one lump but rather as the materiality inside of it.

Through this practice, we also know the functions of each materiality. We know that movement arises from the pushing of the wind element of mind-born materiality. We don't see things through our own thoughts, but rather as they actually are. And while doing so, we no longer think of the body as "ours." Instead, we know that the body is just ultimate materiality that arises according to its causes.

Once we also see the reality of mentality by practicing meditation on mentality (see the next chapter), we will know both the body and mind as they are. When that happens, we temporarily lose the perception that we exist as a "being," like a man or a woman.

This is the message that the Buddha has given to us. We will come to know this as our wisdom develops. And once we know this, we will live accordingly. For this reason, we complete meditation on materiality and begin meditation on mentality.

4. Meditation on Mentality

SEEING MENTALITY AS IT IS

If we don't see materiality as ultimate materiality, we see material phenomena as lumps and think about them in whatever way we like, rather than seeing their true form. So too if we don't see mentality as ultimate mentality, we see mental phenomena as one compact continuity (or one continuous whole) and we don't see what is really happening when mental phenomena arise. If we think about these things in whatever way we like, we won't be able to avoid suffering and harm.

For example, if we don't know what kinds of phenomena arise in our minds when we are angry, we may think that being angry is helpful to us. If we don't know what kinds of cognitive processes arise and what the consciousness and mental factors are when we are angry, we may start thinking about anger in whatever way we like. Once we practice meditation on mentality, we will see the cognitive process and the consciousness + mental factors that arise when we get angry, and we will know that they have a huge impact. Then we will try to not get angry again. The same goes for greed and ignorance. Once we practice meditation on mentality, we will see what kind of impact greed and ignorance actually have on us, and we will know why we should live wisely. In the following pages, I will talk in detail about what kind of consciousness + mental factors are present in anger, greed, and ignorance, and what kind of impact they have.

The practice of mentality meditation, in which we discern the ultimate reality of mentality, is discerning the cognitive processes of the mind as well as the consciousness + mental factors that are present in the cognitive processes.

Normally we think that the mind is made up of only consciousness. However, this isn't actually the case. It is made up of both a primary consciousness and various mental factors that operate by aiding that consciousness. Seeing mentality as the combination of consciousness and mental factors (referred to in this book by the phrase "consciousness + mental factors") is seeing mentality as it is. This appears clearly in the Abhidhamma and can be confirmed through practice.

THE COGNITIVE PROCESS OF JHĀNA

In order to discern consciousness + mental factors, we first need to discern the cognitive process in which the mentality arises. Generally speaking there are three kinds of cognitive processes that need to be discerned. The first starts with the cognitive process that arises in the eye, ear, nose, tongue, and body (the five doors) and then continues to the mind door. The second is the cognitive process that only arises in the mind door. The third is the cognitive process of jhāna, which is a kind of mind-door cognitive process but assumes a distinctive character and is therefore classified separately.

Among these, it's better to start practicing meditation on mentality by perceiving the cognitive process of jhāna. This is because it's easier to recognize the cognitive process of jhāna for the following two reasons: First, it isn't easy to discern consciousness and mental processes when we've just started practicing. However, since many javanas (impulsion consciousnesses) arise in the cognitive process of jhāna, there are many opportunities to discern consciousness + mental factors in the javanas. Second, the five jhānic factors, which we've discerned in the process of experiencing the first jhāna, refer to the mental factors that are present in the cognitive process of the first jhāna. Thus, we have already discerned jhānic factors as ultimate mentality. In jhāna, there are other mental factors aside from the five factors of jhāna, and so in meditation on mentality we discern the consciousness + mental factors that exist in the cognitive process of the state of jhāna in its entirety.

The cognitive process of the state of jhāna consists of mind-door adverting (*manodvārāvajjana*), preparation (*parikamma*), access (*upacāra*), conformity (*anuloma*), change-of-lineage (*gotrabhū*), and jhāna javana. In order to see cognitive processes, we need training. Therefore at first we only discern them as javanas and then, once we have been trained to a certain extent, we can distinguish them as preparation, access, conformity, change-of-lineage, and jhāna javana. The javanas of the cognitive process of jhāna arise much more frequently than javanas of the ordinary cognitive process. When we can see javanas arising and passing away, we are in the state of momentary concentration.

Before discerning the javanas of the cognitive process of the state of jhāna, we need to briefly discern the mind-door adverting that arises before javana, which is the moment of first turning attention to or orienting toward the object. But we discern the consciousness and mental factors present in the cognitive process of mind-door adverting only after we have become skilled at discerning the consciousness + mental factors present in javana. It's important to practice step by step. That way we can practice easily.

So before we begin discerning the javanas in the cognitive process of jhāna, we first need to study the consciousness + mental factors of the javanas of jhāna. There are thirty-four kinds of consciousness + mental factors in the javanas of the first jhāna. Since there are thirty-four kinds and they arise extremely quickly, it's necessary to memorize them ahead of time so that we can recall them quickly.

Consciousness and Mental Factors

The mind is composed of consciousness and mental factors. And consciousness and mental factors are inseparable. No mental factors can exist without consciousness, and consciousness can't exist without mental factors. They always exist together; they arise and pass away together. Also, the mind always has an object; a mind that hasn't taken an object can't exist. And finally, the mind arises dependent on a material base. Thus, there are three things that we must be able to discern: the mind itself, the object the mind has turned toward, and the material base of the mind.

Consciousness and mental factors are always present when there is a cognitive process, and they always have the same object. For example, in the jhānas, the object is the counterpart sign (*paṭibhāga-nimitta*). But the consciousness and mental factors are not equal; if we see consciousness as the king, then mental factors are the followers. At any point in time, there is one consciousness and its respective mental factors. The mental factors will differ depending on the type of consciousness. There are a total of fifty-two mental factors.

With every consciousness, the following seven mental factors are always present: contact (*phassa*), feeling (*vedanā*, which in this case includes happiness, suffering, and nonhappiness and nonsuffering), perception (*saññā*), volition (*cetanā*), concentration (*ekaggatā*), life faculty (*jīvitindriya*), and attention (*manasikāra*). These seven mental factors are called "the universals that arise together with all consciousnesses" (*sabbacittasādhāraṇa*). The functions of consciousness and these seven mental factors are as follows: *Consciousness* knows objects. *Contact* is coming into contact with an object. *Feeling* is the feeling toward an object, which is either pleasant, unpleasant, or neither pleasant nor unpleasant. *Perception* is either recalling "that object is this" when seeing something that is known or marking "that thing is this kind of thing" when seeing something that is unknown (so that we know what it is the next time we see it). *Volition* can be seen like a guide that stands at the very front of everything we do. *Concentration* is focusing on an object and bringing all of the present mental factors together. *Life faculty* sustains the consciousness + mental factors that are there together. *Attention* pays attention to an object.

The following six mental factors occasionally arise with consciousness: initial application (*vitakka*), sustained application (*vicāra*), decision (*adhimokkha*), energy (*viriya*), joy (*pīti*), and desire (*chanda*). They are called "the occasionals" (*pakiṇṇaka*). *Initial application* applies the mind to an object. *Sustained application* goes continuously toward the object. *Decision* determines what an object is. *Energy* is keeping the effort of what one is doing. *Joy* is delight. *Desire* is the will to do something.

Together, the universals and the occasionals are called "the ethically variable factors" (*aññasamānacetasika*). They can associate with both wholesome and unwholesome consciousness.

The fifty-two mental factors are outlined in table 4, but rather than elaborate all of them here, I will begin by explaining the consciousness + mental factors of the first jhāna; I'll explain the rest in their respective sections.

The seven "universals" and the six "occasionals" are present in the consciousness + mental factors of the first jhāna. In addition, they are accompanied by twenty of the beautiful mental factors. These twenty are wisdom plus the nineteen "universal beautiful mental factors": faith (*saddhā*), mindfulness (*sati*), shame of wrongdoing (*hiri*), fear of wrongdoing (*ottappa*), nongreed (*alobha*), nonhatred (*adosa*), neutrality of mind (*tatramajjhattatā*), tranquility of the mental body (*kāyapassaddhi*), tranquility of consciousness (*cittapassaddhi*), lightness of the mental body (*kāyalahutā*), lightness of consciousness (*cittalahutā*), malleability of the mental body (*kāyamudutā*), malleability of consciousness (*cittamudutā*), wieldiness of the mental body (*kāyakammaññatā*), wieldiness of consciousness (*cittakammaññatā*), proficiency of the mental body (*kāyapāguññatā*), proficiency of consciousness (*cittapāguññatā*), rectitude of the mental body (*kāyujjukatā*), and rectitude of consciousness (*cittujjukatā*).

Let's briefly look at the nineteen "universal beautiful mental factors" and then at wisdom in the first jhāna. *Faith* is having faith in the jhāna practice. *Mindfulness* is attentiveness to the nimitta. *Shame of wrongdoing* is being ashamed of doing bad things. *Fear of wrongdoing* is feeling afraid of doing bad things. *Nongreed* is the absence of greed when seeing the nimitta. *Nonhatred* is the absence of hatred when seeing the nimitta. *Neutrality of mind* is seeing the nimitta with equanimity. *Tranquility of the mental body* is the state in which all mental factors are tranquil when seeing the nimitta; in this case *body* means all mental factors. *Tranquility of consciousness* is the state in which the consciousness is tranquil when seeing the nimitta. *Lightness of the mental body* refers to all the mental factors being light. *Lightness of consciousness* is the consciousness being light. *Malleability of the mental body* is when all the mental factors are pliable. *Malleability of consciousness* is when the consciousness is pliable. *Wieldiness of the mental body* is a state in which all the mental factors are functioning successfully. *Wieldiness of consciousness* is when the consciousness is successful in making the nimitta an object. *Proficiency of the mental body* is the state in which the functions of all the mental factors are skillful. *Proficiency*

4. The Fifty-Two Mental Factors

Thirteen Ethically Variable Mental Factors	Seven Universals	contact, feeling, perception, volition, concentration, life faculty, attention
	Six Occasionals	initial application, sustained application, decision, energy, joy, desire
Twenty-Five Beautiful Mental Factors	Nineteen Universal Beautiful Mental Factors	faith, mindfulness, shame of wrongdoing, fear of wrongdoing, nongreed, nonhatred, neutrality of mind, tranquility of the mental body, tranquility of consciousness, lightness of the mental body, lightness of consciousness, malleability of the mental body, malleability of consciousness, wieldiness of the mental body, wieldiness of consciousness, proficiency of the mental body, proficiency of consciousness, rectitude of the mental body, rectitude of consciousness
	Three Abstinences	right speech, right action, right livelihood
	Two Illimitables	compassion, sympathetic joy
	Nondelusion	wisdom

Fourteen Unwholesome Mental Factors	Four Universal Unwholesome Mental Factors	delusion, shamelessness of wrongdoing, fearlessness of wrongdoing, restlessness
	Ten Occasional Unwholesome Mental Factors	greed, wrong view, conceit, hatred, envy, avarice, remorse, sloth, torpor, doubt

of consciousness is a state in which the consciousness is skillful. *Rectitude of the mental body* is a state in which all the mental factors are upright. *Rectitude of the mind* is a state in which the consciousness is upright. Finally, *wisdom* is seeing the nimitta with wisdom; it is seeing the nimitta as it is.

Mind-Door Adverting and Javana

After becoming completely proficient in discerning the consciousness + mental factors in the cognitive process of the first jhāna, we then discern the mind-door adverting that arises before the javanas of the cognitive process of jhāna. The mind-door adverting is turning attention toward the mental object. In this case, we determine, relative to the counterpart sign, that "this is the paṭibhāga-nimitta of ānāpānasati" after exiting the first jhāna of ānāpānasati and examining its five jhānic factors at the mind door. Then javanas arise after the mind-door adverting occurs.

While I was practicing, Sayadaw U Sīla told me to notice what kind of phenomena arose after the mind-door adverting discerned that "this is the paṭibhāga-nimitta of ānāpānasati." I observed that after the mind-door adverting, something arose continuously, "click, click, click." When I reported this in my interview, Sayadaw U Sīla told me that these were javana mind moments. Since they arose instantaneously, at first I only knew that, based on what he told me, "these must be javana mind-moments!" Though I only saw them to the extent that I noticed consciousnesses arising continuously, one after another, it was extremely surprising and amazing.

After clearly discerning the javana mind moments, I started to discern one by one the consciousness + mental factors of the mind moments. Consciousness + mental factors are present in each mind moment; the practice of meditation on mentality is discerning them. We discern the thirty-four consciousness + mental factors, starting with consciousness and going up to wisdom, for each mind moment that arises after the mind-door adverting consciousness that determines "this is the paṭibhāga-nimitta of ānāpānasati."

Upon exiting the first jhāna of ānāpānasati and examining the jhānic factors, at first we just discern the consciousness present in each javana mind moment. After having entered and exited jhāna once, during the time that the javana mind moments occur continuously we discern either just the consciousness or one mental factor. Then next time, after having entered and exited jhāna again, we discern the next mental factor in the javana mind moments of the cognitive process of jhāna. In this way we clearly discern the thirty-four kinds of consciousness + mental factors of the first jhāna one by one.

The number of javana mind moments that occur differs depending on the degree of jhāna. A great number of javana mind moments arise if the force of jhāna is powerful, and fewer javana mind moments arise if the force of jhāna is relatively less powerful. Actually, javana mind moments aren't only present in jhāna. They also occur after "determining" in the five-door cognitive process and also after mind-door adverting in a mind-door cognitive process. In cases that aren't jhāna, javana mind moments mostly arise seven times. In jhāna, powerful javana mind moments arise. But we discern the consciousness + mental factors of the javana mind moments of the cognitive process of jhāna after exiting jhāna. The javanas are so powerful in jhāna, their aftereffects continue even after exiting jhāna. Therefore the cognitive process of jhāna can still be discerned after we exit jhāna. But in the actual state of jhāna, more powerful javanas arise.

Once we can completely discern the thirty-four kinds of consciousness + mental factors of the first jhāna, we discern the consciousness + mental factors of the second jhāna, and then we move on to the third and fourth jhānas.

It is important to precisely discern consciousness and mental factors one by one. In the case of the second jhāna, there are thirty-two, since initial application and sustained application are absent. There are thirty-one in the third jhāna, because joy is also absent. There are also thirty-one in the fourth jhāna, because the mental factor of feeling has changed from happiness to equanimity. When we can precisely discern consciousness + mental factors one by one, we also discern consciousness and mental factors together.

We should perceive, one by one, the consciousness + mental factors of the cognitive processes of the jhāna mind moments of ānāpānasati, the kasiṇas, the immaterial jhānas, the four brahmavihāras, and the four protective meditations. Therein, we perceive the consciousness + mental factors of the cognitive processes of each of the first, second, third, and fourth jhānas where applicable.

THE MIND-DOOR COGNITIVE PROCESS: WHOLESOME SENSE-SPHERE CONSCIOUSNESS

After discerning the cognitive process of jhāna sufficiently, the next step is to discern the mind-door cognitive process that arises with *dhamma* (or experiential phenomena) as object.

We are instructed to start with the discernment of the mind-door cognitive process that arises with dhamma as object, as it is easier. When we become skillful in discerning the cognitive process, we can then proceed to discern the cognitive processes that arise both in the five doors (of the eye, ear, nose, tongue, and body) and in the mind-door process that arises afterward. There are more types of consciousness that arise in the five-door cognitive processes. (For example, in just the eye-door cognitive process alone there are eye-door adverting mind moments, eye consciousness mind moments, receiving mind moments, investigation mind moments, determining mind moments, and javana mind moments.) Therefore we discern the mind-door cognitive process that arises with dhamma as object first. Since dhamma is being taken as an object of the mind, it arises only in the mind-door cognitive process and not in the five-door cognitive processes.

There are six categories of dhammas that give rise only to the mind-door process—and not the five-door cognitive processes. They are sensitive materiality (*pasādarūpa*; eye, ear, nose, tongue, and body sensitivity), subtle

5. The Consciousness and Mental Factors of the Jhānas

Factor	First Jhāna	Second Jhāna	Third Jhāna	Fourth Jhāna
consciousness	■	■	■	■
contact	■	■	■	■
feeling	■	■	■	■
perception	■	■	■	■
volition	■	■	■	■
concentration	■	■	■	■
life faculty	■	■	■	■
attention	■	■	■	■
initial application	■			
sustained application	■			
decision	■	■	■	■
energy	■	■	■	
joy	■	■		
desire	■	■	■	■
faith	■	■	■	■
mindfulness	■	■	■	■
shame of wrongdoing	■	■	■	■
fear of wrongdoing	■	■	■	■
nongreed	■	■	■	■
nonhatred	■	■	■	■
neutrality of mind	■	■	■	■
tranquility of the mental body	■	■	■	■
tranquility of consciousness	■	■	■	■
lightness of the mental body	■	■	■	■
lightness of consciousness	■	■	■	■
malleability of the mental body	■	■	■	■
malleability of consciousness	■	■	■	■
wieldiness of the mental body	■	■	■	■

Factor	First Jhāna	Second Jhāna	Third Jhāna	Fourth Jhāna
wieldiness of consciousness				
proficiency of the mental body				
proficiency of consciousness				
rectitude of the mental body				
rectitude of consciousness				
wisdom				

matter (*sukhumarūpa*; sixteen kinds), consciousness (*citta*), mental factors (*cetasika*), nibbāna, and concepts. The sixteen kinds of subtle materiality are the water element, nutriment, the heart base, femininity, masculinity, life faculty, the space element, bodily intimation, verbal intimation, lightness of materiality, malleability of materiality, wieldiness of materiality, the characteristics of production, continuity, and decay of materiality, and impermanence.

Among the mind-door cognitive processes that arise with dhamma as object, we first perceive the wholesome sense-sphere consciousnesses that arise in javana mind moments. Although the wholesome sense-sphere consciousnesses are not consciousnesses of jhāna, they are wholesome states of mind. Wholesome consciousnesses occur together with two or three wholesome roots: nongreed, nonhatred, and wisdom.

The wholesome sense-sphere consciousnesses are divided into eight kinds depending on whether they are prompted, accompanied by joy or equanimity, and/or associated with knowledge. If we list these eight kinds, they are as follows: (1) accompanied by joy, associated with knowledge, unprompted, (2) accompanied by joy, associated with knowledge, prompted, (3) accompanied by joy, dissociated from knowledge, unprompted, (4) accompanied by joy, dissociated from knowledge, prompted, (5) accompanied by equanimity, associated with knowledge, unprompted, (6) accompanied by equanimity, associated with knowledge, prompted, (7) accompanied by equanimity, dissociated from knowledge, unprompted, and (8) accompanied by equanimity, dissociated from knowledge, prompted. (These, as well as the unwholesome sense-sphere consciousnesses, are reviewed in a table at the end of this section.) In this case *prompted* and *unprompted* refer to whether or not they were induced externally. For example, if we donated funds to a monastery by heeding our parents' advice, it is a prompted consciousness. If we had the desire to donate within ourselves, it is an unprompted consciousness.

The nineteen universal beautiful mental factors are also associated with wholesome sense-sphere consciousnesses. Therefore, if a wholesome sense-sphere consciousness is both accompanied by joy and associated with knowledge, there are thirty-four kinds of consciousness + mental factors. If there is no knowledge and only joy or vice versa, there are thirty-three kinds. If there is neither knowledge nor joy, there are thirty-two kinds.

So when do the wholesome sense-sphere consciousnesses arise? As I have mentioned above, wholesome consciousnesses are those that arise together with two or three wholesome roots: nongreed, nonhatred, and wisdom. They arise when we have wise attention (*yoniso manasikāra*). If, when coming in contact with objects through the eye, ear, nose, tongue, body, and mind, we see them as ultimate materiality or mentality, and we see them through their properties of impermanence, suffering, nonself, and repulsiveness, this is superior wise attention.

It isn't easy for someone who doesn't know the Buddha's teachings to have wise attention. I tried in my own way to live wisely before practicing meditation on mentality, but after learning when wholesome consciousnesses arise and what wise attention is while practicing meditation on mentality, I came to know that I had been living up to that point with more unwholesome consciousnesses than wholesome consciousnesses. If we live without being grounded in the truth, we will make the mistake of having unwise attention. As a result, the cognitive circuit of unwholesome consciousnesses will go round and round. Then those results will form in us.

When we attach adjectives or modifiers to a certain thing or phenomenon, it can be seen as the result of unwise attention. For example, we generally say that "there is a beautiful flower," but actually its true nature is materiality. "Delicious food" isn't truly present; rather there is simply nutriment. At Sayadaw U Sīla's birthday one year, people who were receiving his teachings offered him a meal to celebrate. When they encouraged him to eat a lot, enthusiastically naming the different kinds of delicious foods, Sayadaw U Sīla said simply that "today everyone has offered nutriment." We use a lot of modifiers while we live our lives. We say that "we did well" today, "we didn't do well" the next day, and so on.

To observe wholesome sense-sphere consciousness, we first do so by connecting it to all of the practices we have done up to that point. For example, when we reflect, "Life is uncertain, death is certain, I too will one day die, I can't avoid experiencing this" after seeing an external dead body, and we pay attention to the cessation of life faculty at the moment of our own death through the practice of "recollection of death," the mind-door adverting consciousness arises with this reflection. After the mind-door adverting consciousness, we can observe the wholesome sense-sphere consciousness javanas arise seven times. If joy and knowledge are present, we can discern the thirty-four kinds of consciousness + mental factors.

When we practice loving kindness, the mind-door cognitive process arises. Mind-door adverting arises followed by seven wholesome sense-sphere consciousness javana mind moments. Then, depending on whether there is joy or knowledge, there are thirty-two to thirty-four consciousness + mental factors.

Similarly, once we determine that "the Buddha has no defilements" after practicing meditation on "the recollection of the Buddha," mind-door adverting arises and the wholesome sense-sphere consciousness javanas arise seven times. After the wholesome sense-sphere javanas, the registration (*tadā-rammaṇa*) mind moment may arise twice, or it may not. Registration is a kind of consciousness that arises after javana. Depending on the nature of the object, the corresponding consciousness + mental factors of registration may vary. Registration arises when the object is ultimate reality, but it does not arise when the object is a concept. For example, when we observe eye sensitivity and determine that "this is materiality," registration arises twice after the wholesome sense-sphere consciousness javanas arise seven times. When we recall a flower as "beautiful," registration does not arise.

Once we have become used to this, we discern the wholesome sense-sphere consciousness javana mind moments that arise in daily life. If we determine that "the Buddha has no defilements" by recalling the Buddha's image while we are walking, that becomes the mind-door adverting consciousness and we can see that the wholesome sense-sphere consciousness javanas arise seven times afterward. When we see a dog on the street and intend "May that dog be free from danger," the wholesome sense-sphere consciousness javanas arise seven times.

I will move on after briefly explaining the rest of the beautiful mental factors. There are a total of twenty-five beautiful mental factors—nineteen universal beautiful mental factors and six others. I have already explained the nineteen universal beautiful mental factors in the above section on the consciousness + mental factors in the cognitive process of jhāna. Of the remaining six, I have also already explained the faculty of wisdom (paññindriya). The remaining five are the three abstinences (virati) of right speech, right action, and right livelihood and the two illimitables (appamaññā) of compassion and sympathetic joy. Right speech is abstaining from lying, slander, harsh speech, and frivolous talk. Right action is abstaining from killing, stealing, and sexual misconduct. Right livelihood has two meanings: The first meaning is not engaging in livelihood that harm others. For example, right livelihood means not trafficking human beings, sending animals for slaughter, smuggling weapons, or being involved with illegal terrorist organizations. The other meaning is simply having right speech and right action while making a living.

For example, the mental factor of right speech arises when we abstain from wrong speech.

When we decide to abstain from lying, mind-door adverting arises and afterward the wholesome sense-sphere consciousness javanas arise seven times. If joy and knowledge are present, there are thirty-five consciousness + mental factors. (It becomes thirty-five when we combine the mental factor of right speech with the thirty-four consciousness + mental factors of the wholesome sense-sphere consciousnesses that are accompanied by joy and associated with knowledge. Right action and right livelihood are also calculated in this way.)

When we see eye, ear, nose, tongue, and body sensitivities, the heart base, sex, life faculty, and the water element and determine that they are materiality, wholesome sense-sphere consciousnesses arise. If we determine "these are impermanent, suffering, nonself, and impure," wholesome sense-sphere consciousnesses arise. There are various cases in which wholesome sense-sphere consciousnesses arise, but they do so only when there is no greed, anger, or hatred and when there is wise attention.

Now we can discern the consciousness + mental factors of mind-door adverting. There are altogether twelve consciousness + mental factors of mind-door adverting: consciousness, the seven universals, and four of the six occasionals (initial application, sustained application, decision, and energy). When mind-door adverting arises, we discern these twelve kinds of consciousness + mental factors. It's a good idea to memorize the seven universals and the six occasionals in order—the table on the fifty-two mental factors (see page 98) can help with this. If, for example, there are eight consciousness + mental factors in the eye consciousness of the five-door consciousness, we count beginning with consciousness and through all seven universals, which adds up to eight. Likewise, the eleven consciousness + mental factors of receiving start with consciousness, include the seven universals, and include the first three of the six occasionals (up through decision).

Once we become skilled at discerning the cognitive processes in this way, we move on to the next step. We discern the consciousness + mental factors of the cognitive process of jhāna including the cognitive process of access concentration, after again entering and exiting the jhānas that we've experienced up to this point. When I engaged this practice, I discerned the consciousness of access concentration that I had not discerned from the cognitive process of jhāna.

After the mind-door adverting consciousness, the consciousnesses of preparation, access, conformity, and change-of-lineage arise, and after that the javana mind moments of jhāna arise. Thus we can discern the four consciousnesses of preparation, access, conformity, and change-of-lineage, which are themselves javana mind moments. There are altogether thirty-four consciousness + mental factors of these javana mind moments in the access concentration of the first, second, and third jhānas. However, there are only thirty-three for access concentration of the fourth jhāna and the immaterial jhānas, since joy is absent.

Whenever we practice meditation on mentality by discerning the consciousness + mental factors of the wholesome sense-sphere consciousnesses, we always do so after cultivating, in order, ānāpānasati jhāna, kasiṇa jhāna, and the immaterial jhānas and after exiting neither-perception-nor-nonperception and examining its jhānic factors. The reason we do this is because it is important to train ourselves to always be able to enter jhāna and for the discernment of consciousness and mental factors with the eye of wisdom that is developed through concentration. The stronger the concentration the better the penetration.

THE FIVE-DOOR COGNITIVE PROCESS

After becoming skilled at discerning the wholesome sense-sphere consciousnesses that form after practicing samatha and the wholesome sense-sphere consciousnesses that arise in daily life, we discern the five-door cognitive process, as well as the mind-door process that follows the five-door cognitive process. The five-door cognitive process is a cognitive process that arises by taking visible form, sound, smell, taste, and touch as objects from the eye, ear, nose, tongue, and body. The five-door cognitive process is usually followed by the mind-door process, but if the impact of the object on the respective sensitivities is weak, even the five-door cognitive process may not arise fully. In that case, the mind-door cognitive process does not arise.

First we will look at the eye-door cognitive process that arises taking visible form as object.

This process consists of mind moments of eye-door adverting, eye consciousness, receiving, investigation, determining, javana, and possibly registration.

Eye-door adverting arises when visible form impinges on eye sensitivity and attention goes to that object in order to see it. We don't necessarily have to see phenomena with our eyes open for the eye-door cognitive process to start. The eye-door cognitive process arises even if we pay attention to the color of the kalāpas nearby with our eyes closed. However, eye-door adverting doesn't arise just because a visible form impinges on eye sensitivity. We need to have the attention to see the visible form in order for eye-door adverting to arise. Once, when meditating, I was surprised when I experienced that the eye-door cognitive process didn't arise when I first looked at a tree, but rather it began when I turned my attention to see the tree. This attention is eye-door adverting. There are eleven consciousness + mental factors present in eye-door adverting: consciousness, contact, feeling, perception, volition, one-pointedness, life faculty, attention, initial application, sustained application, and decision. When there is eye-door adverting, the consciousness + mental factors operate on an object of visible form, but each performs its own functions.

Next eye-door adverting disappears and eye consciousness arises. There are eight consciousness + mental factors of eye consciousness: consciousness and the seven universals. When eye consciousness disappears, receiving arises. Receiving is the moment when the sensory object (in this case, visible form) is received by the sense door (in this case, the eye door). There are eleven consciousness + mental factors of receiving, the same as the consciousness + mental factors of eye-door adverting. When receiving disappears, investigation arises. Investigation is the moment when consciousness examines the sensory object (in this case, visible form). There are twelve consciousness + mental factors of investigation if the object is desirable and joy is present, and there are eleven if there is equanimity without joy. When investigation disappears, determining arises. Determining is the moment when the sense object (in this case, visible form) is identified by consciousness. There are twelve consciousness + mental factors of determining. Aside from the investigation mind moment, the rest (eye-door adverting, eye consciousness, receiving, and determining) are all mind moments of equanimity; the feeling of eye-door adverting, eye consciousness, receiving, and determining is neither pleasant nor unpleasant. The five-door cognitive process cannot determine as precisely as mind-door cognitive process; for example, the eye-door cognitive process can only pay attention to visible form as visible form, it cannot decide what kind of visible form it is, but the mind-door cognitive process can determine what kind of visible form it is. It can also know the impermanence, suffering, and nonself nature of that visible form.

When determining mind moment disappears, javana arises seven times. The consciousness + mental factors of javana differ depending on what kind of consciousness it is. If it is a wholesome consciousness, there are thirty-two to thirty-four consciousness + mental factors, depending on the presence of joy and knowledge. If it is an unwholesome consciousness, the consciousness + mental factors will differ depending on the type of unwholesome consciousness. I will talk about unwholesome mental factors in detail a little bit later. Following javana, registration may arise twice, or it may not arise. Registration can happen when consciousness takes ultimate reality as an object and if the impact of the object on the eye-sensitivity is strong. Registration cannot happen when consciousness takes a concept as an object.

To summarize the process described above: the eye-door cognitive process that rises from the eye taking visible form as object is made up of eye-door adverting, eye consciousness, receiving, investigation, determining, javana, and registration (which may or may not arise).

If the mind-door cognitive process arises after the eye-door cognitive process, *bhavaṅga* (life-continuum) arises, and then mind moments of mind-door adverting, javana, and registration arise. (Although, again, registration may or may not arise.) We do not need to think about bhavaṅga at this point; we can know it better when we practice meditation on dependent origination, after we finish practicing meditation on mentality. So when we discern the cognitive process of the mind, we do not discern bhavaṅga.

In the cognitive process for each of the rest of the five doors (the ear, nose, tongue, and body), there is the appropriate object and the specific form of adverting and consciousness, and the rest of the process is the same as described above for the eye-door cognitive process. In other words, in the case of the ear, the process is the same as above, but with the ear taking sound as object and beginning with ear-door adverting and ear consciousness. Likewise, in the case of the nose and smell, it becomes nose-door adverting and nose consciousness; in the case of the tongue and taste, it becomes tongue-door adverting and tongue consciousness; and in the case of the body and touch, it becomes body-door adverting and body consciousness.

The Fourteen Unwholesome Mental Factors

Unwholesome mental factors are mental factors that accompany unwholesome consciousnesses, which are consciousnesses rooted in greed, hatred, and delusion. There are altogether fourteen unwholesome mental factors. Among these, four are universal to all unwholesome consciousnesses—in other words, they are always present, whether it is a consciousness rooted in greed, a consciousness rooted in hatred, or a consciousness rooted in delusion. That is why they are called the "unwholesome universals." These four are delusion (*moha*), shamelessness of wrongdoing (*ahirika*), fearlessness of wrongdoing (*anottappa*), and restlessness (*uddhacca*).

Delusion has the characteristic of blindness; it is the covering up of the true nature of things. Delusion is not the same as the lack of worldly knowledge, but the ignorance of ultimate realities. Delusion is the root of all unwholesome consciousnesses. In delusion, we think only in our own way, we treat others only in our own way, and we handle things only in our own way. Since this is not in accordance with reality, we continuously clash with others and clash with reality. And to the extent we do that, we keep getting angry. More and more, we are unable to see reality as it is.

Shamelessness is not being shameful of performing unwholesome actions. *Fearlessness* is not being fearful of performing unwholesome actions. Shamelessness and fearlessness are explained through the simile of a princess and her attendants: A princess is shameful when she has performed an unwholesome action. However, an attendant feels fear toward performing an unwholesome action. Since shame and fear aren't present in an unwholesome consciousness, our thoughts or actions won't have any checks on them. Shame and fear are actually devices that help us avoid harm while we live our lives. However, since they are not present, our internal instincts or problems operate externally without restraint. When a problem arises, it actually isn't too late to look back at ourselves and fix our problems. But if we don't do that and instead merely resent others and the world, we fall into a vicious cycle. We become a car that has no brakes and we enter an extremely dangerous state.

And finally, *restlessness* is a state of not being calm. It is a state in which the mind is uneasy and is unable to go firmly toward an object. In this state, we cannot pay attention to the things that are happening, and therefore we are also unable to cope with them.

The remaining ten unwholesome mental factors are present or not depending on the type of unwholesome consciousness. Therefore they are called the "unwholesome occasionals." The ten are greed (*lobha*), wrong view (*diṭṭhi*), conceit (*māna*), hatred (*dosa*), envy (*issā*), avarice (*macchariya*), remorse (*kukkucca*), sloth (*thīna*), torpor (*middha*), and doubt (*vicikicchā*). Among these, greed, wrong view, and conceit are mental factors associated with greed; hatred, envy, avarice, and remorse are mental factors associated with hatred; sloth and torpor are associated with sluggishness; and doubt is associated with delusion.

Sloth and torpor are mental factors that form when there is an unwholesome prompted consciousness. The mental factors for prompted consciousnesses and unprompted consciousnesses are the same as for wholesome consciousnesses, but for unwholesome consciousnesses, the mental factors of sloth and torpor are added when the consciousness is prompted. If a consciousness is able to be engendered from the outside, it is a prompted consciousness. If someone lacks eagerness or initiative to do something, he is not enthusiastic with what he has to do. This is due to the effect of the mental factors of sloth and torpor. He acts under external or internal prompting. This is somewhat different from the sloth and torpor among the five hindrances, when meditators experience drowsiness.

Let's look briefly at each unwholesome mental factor. *Greed* is a mind that grasps; it is characterized by grabbing on to an object like a pitcher plant. In this state, we are unable to have a free mind that sees things in a balanced manner, and instead we focus on things that become the objects of greed and try to grasp on to them. If we are unable to easily grasp on to something, we suffer and become angry. We lose the stability of mind.

Wrong view refers to a view or idea that is mistaken. It is characterized by stubbornness that defies reason. Since we don't even know that we are seeing things in the wrong way, we can't fix it. We need to see things in the right way for there to be positive results, but since we see them in the wrong way, we don't know when they will collapse like a castle built on top of sand. Wrong view is the fundamental cause of suffering; the view that "I exist" (self-view) is an example of wrong view in Buddhism. All unwholesome things stem from self-view.

There is *conceit* or pride when we consider ourselves important. Because of conceit we may compare ourselves with others. There can be conceit when we think ourselves better, equal, or less than someone else. We may believe that there can be conceit only when we think ourselves better than someone else, but this is not so. There can be a kind of upholding of ourselves, of making ourselves important, when we compare ourselves with someone else, no matter in what way, and that is conceit. We need to do the things that help us and that we need, but this doesn't work properly when conceit operates because we compare ourselves with others.

Hatred is being angry.

Envy is being jealous of others' success. *Avarice* is the concealing and not sharing of our property, whether attained or about to be attained, whether wealth or psychological. Sharing what we have with others and celebrating the success of others is beneficial for us and brings us good results, but we don't do that; instead we pester our minds with avarice or envy.

Remorse is regretting or fretting over the things that have already passed. It has two forms: (1) regretting the unwholesome things we have done in the past, and (2) regretting the things we should have done but didn't do. When we observe carefully, the things we regret are actually things that are in a state that couldn't have gone any other way at that time. But with remorse we aren't able to see that, and instead we arouse desire by saying "I could have done things differently."

Sloth is indolence or laziness and *torpor* is the mind being slow and lethargic. In sloth and torpor we can't perceive the situation in the right way and thereby do what is needed.

Doubt is not being able to make clear decisions, being skeptical, and confused thinking without proper knowledge. When *doubt* is present, we doubt the things that are helpful to us and don't do them. Therefore they become our loss.

The Types of Unwholesome Consciousnesses

At this point, we have learned about all of the mental factors. When there is a wholesome consciousness in the javana of the five-door cognitive process, the corresponding mental factors are present. Likewise, when there is an unwholesome consciousness, the corresponding mental factors are present. All we have to do is discern them.

When practicing meditation on mentality by discerning the consciousness and mental factors of the five-door cognitive process, we always practice after cultivating (in order) ānāpānasati, the kasiṇas, and the immaterial jhānas that we have mastered up to this point, and after exiting neither-perception-nor-nonperception and examining its jhānic factors.

We see wholesome consciousnesses and unwholesome consciousnesses arising in the five-door cognitive processes and mind-door cognitive processes. For the sake of training, we initially start with a five-door cognitive process with a wholesome consciousness, and afterward we engage a five-door cognitive process with an unwholesome consciousness.

For example, in order to examine an eye-door cognitive process with a wholesome consciousness, we first pay attention to the color of a group of kalāpas as the ultimate materiality of color. When it impinges on our eye-sensitivity and bhavaṅga mind door, then wholesome eye-door cognitive process will arise, followed by mind-door process. If we enumerate the mind moments that arise in the cognitive processes in this case, they are as follows: bhavaṅga, eye-door adverting, eye consciousness, receiving, investigation, determining, seven (wholesome consciousness) javanas, two registrations, bhavaṅga, mind-door adverting, seven (wholesome consciousness) javanas, and two registrations.

Then, in order to examine an eye-door cognitive process with an unwholesome consciousness, when we see the kalāpas, we first see them with a conceited mind thinking, "I am practicing well enough to see the kalāpas." Then the consciousness + mental factors that correspond to the unwholesome consciousness of the eye-door cognitive process and the mind-door process will arise. If we enumerate the mind moments in the cognitive processes that arise in this case, they are as follows: bhavaṅga, eye-door adverting, eye consciousness, receiving, investigation, determining, seven (unwholesome consciousness) javanas, two registrations, bhavaṅga, mind-door adverting, seven (unwholesome consciousness) javanas, and two registrations.

When we practice discerning the consciousness + mental factors of all of the five-door cognitive processes and the mind-door cognitive processes that arise after each of the five-door cognitive processes, we do so by alternating between wholesome consciousnesses and unwholesome consciousnesses, as in the above two examples. We practice with each of the five doors of the eye, ear, nose, tongue, and body in the same way.

In the case of wholesome sense-sphere consciousnesses, we practiced with eight different cases depending on joy, knowledge, and prompting, as mentioned earlier. Unwholesome consciousnesses differ depending on greed, hatred, and ignorance, and there are several categories of unwholesome consciousness associated with each of these.

In the case of consciousnesses rooted in greed, the four unwholesome universal mental factors are present along with the unwholesome occasional mental factors of greed, wrong view, and conceit. However, wrong view and conceit cannot arise together. Greed and wrong view can arise together, and greed and conceit can arise together. Greed can also arise on its own without wrong view or conceit. Additionally, there are two further variables: whether they are accompanied by joy or by equanimity, and whether they are prompted or unprompted.

Therefore consciousnesses rooted in greed can be divided into the following eight categories: (1) a consciousness accompanied by joy, associated with greed and wrong view, prompted, (2) a consciousness accompanied by joy, associated with greed and wrong view, unprompted, (3) a consciousness accompanied by equanimity, associated with greed and wrong view, prompted, (4) a consciousness accompanied by equanimity, associated with greed and wrong view, unprompted, (5) a consciousness accompanied by joy, associated with greed but dissociated with wrong view, prompted, (6) a consciousness accompanied by joy, associated with greed but dissociated with wrong view, unprompted, (7) a consciousness accompanied by equanimity, associated with greed but dissociated with wrong view, prompted, and (8) a

consciousness accompanied by equanimity, associated with greed but dissociated with wrong view, unprompted. (For reference for this and the other
consciousnesses, please consult the table "Wholesome and Unwholesome
Consciousnesses," which is at the end of this section.) In the last four types,
those dissociated with wrong view, greed either arises on its own or together
with conceit.

Among these, as an example, we will look in detail at what kinds of consciousness and mental factors are present in a consciousness rooted in greed
that is accompanied by joy, associated with greed and wrong view, and
prompted. There are in total twenty-two consciousness + mental factors for
this consciousness, including the seven universals (contact, feeling, perception, volition, one-pointedness, life faculty, and attention), the six occasionals
(initial application, sustained application, decision, energy, joy, and desire),
the four unwholesome universals (delusion, shamelessness of wrongdoing,
fearlessness of wrongdoing, and restlessness), the two unwholesome occasionals (greed and wrong view), and the mental factors of sloth and torpor
associated with prompting. We can similarly calculate the total consciousness
+ mental factors for the other seven consciousnesses listed above, though we
have to be aware that in unwholesome consciousnesses that are unprompted,
the mental factors of sloth and torpor associated with prompting are absent.

In the case of consciousnesses rooted in hatred, the four unwholesome
universals and the unwholesome occasional mental factors of hatred, envy,
avarice, and remorse are present. Hatred may arise by itself or with envy, avarice, or remorse, but envy, avarice, and remorse cannot arise together because
their objects are all different. These consciousnesses may arise prompted in
some cases and unprompted in other cases.

Therefore we can divide consciousnesses rooted in hatred into the following eight kinds of consciousnesses: (1) a consciousness associated with
hatred, prompted, (2) a consciousness associated with hatred, unprompted,
(3) a consciousness associated with hatred and envy, prompted, (4) a consciousness associated with hatred and envy, unprompted, (5) a consciousness
associated with hatred and avarice, prompted, (6) a consciousness associated
with hatred and avarice, unprompted, (7) a consciousness associated with

hatred and remorse, prompted, and (8) a consciousness associated with hatred and remorse, unprompted.

Among these, as an example, we will look in detail at what kinds of consciousness + mental factors are present in a consciousness rooted in hatred that is prompted. There are in total twenty consciousness + mental factors for this consciousness, including the seven universals (contact, feeling, perception, volition, one-pointedness, life faculty, and attention), five of the occasionals (initial application, sustained application, decision, energy, and desire), the four unwholesome universals (delusion, shamelessness of wrongdoing, fearlessness of wrongdoing, and restlessness), the unwholesome occasional of hatred, and the mental factors of sloth and torpor associated with prompting. We can similarly calculate the total consciousness + mental factors for the remaining seven consciousnesses rooted in hatred in this way. Note that the ethically variable occasional mental factor of joy is absent in consciousnesses rooted in hatred. (Joy cannot be present in a consciousness rooted in hatred.) Also, in unwholesome consciousnesses that are unprompted, the mental factors of sloth and torpor associated with prompting are absent.

In the case of consciousnesses rooted in delusion, the four unwholesome universals and sometimes the mental factor of doubt are present. Restlessness and doubt are the mental factors associated with delusion, but restlessness is included as an unwholesome universal. The consciousnesses rooted in delusion are divided into the following two kinds of consciousness: (1) a consciousness associated with delusion and restlessness, and (2) a consciousness associated with delusion and doubt.

Among these, we will first look at what kinds of consciousness + mental factors are present in a consciousness associated with ignorance and restlessness. There are in total sixteen consciousness + mental factors for this consciousness, including the seven universals (contact, feeling, perception, volition, one-pointedness, life faculty, and attention), four of the occasionals (initial application, sustained application, decision, and energy), and the four unwholesome universals (delusion, shamelessness of wrongdoing, fearlessness of wrongdoing, and restlessness). Joy and desire are absent in a consciousness with restlessness.

For the consciousness associated with ignorance and doubt, there are again sixteen consciousness + mental factors, including the seven universals (contact, feeling, perception, volition, one-pointedness, life faculty, and attention), three of the occasionals (initial application, sustained application, and energy), the four unwholesome universals (delusion, shamelessness of wrongdoing, fearlessness of wrongdoing, and restlessness), as well as the unwholesome occasional of doubt. Decision, joy, and desire are absent in a consciousness with doubt.

At this point, we have looked into all the types of unwholesome consciousness and the mental factors that accompany them. So when unwholesome consciousness javanas arise in the five-door cognitive process and the mind-door process, all we have to do is discern their consciousness + mental factors as described above.

For example, when we are presented with a delicious kind of cake that we had eaten in the past, if we see that cake with the desire to eat it again (recalling the memory of how delicious it was in the past), an eye-door cognitive process begins. When eye-door adverting arises, eleven kinds of consciousness + mental factors arise. Immediately after eye-door adverting passes away, eye consciousness arises, which has eight kinds of consciousness + mental factors. When receiving arises immediately after eye consciousness passes away, eleven kinds of consciousness + mental factors arise. Immediately after receiving passes away, investigation arises and, in this case, there are twelve kinds of consciousness + mental factors because joy is present. Immediately after investigation passes away, determining arises, in which there are twelve kinds of consciousness + mental factors. Immediately after determining passes away, javana arises seven times. In this case, if we calculate as mentioned above, there are twenty consciousness + mental factors in the javana, because it is associated with greed and wrong view, accompanied by joy. Bhavaṅga arises without the arising of registration, and then the mind-door adverting consciousness mind moment arises, interrupting the bhavaṅga. The consciousness + mental factors of mind-door adverting are of twelve kinds. After mind-door adverting passes away, javana arises. The consciousness + mental factors are the same as the five-door cognitive process javanas. After this javana, bhavaṅga arises without registration arising. This is a summary example of the five-door cognitive process as well as the mind-door cognitive process that arises after the five-door cognitive process.

The Division of Wholesome and Unwholesome Consciousnesses

Wholesome and unwholesome consciousnesses are distinguished according to whether a decision occurs with wise attention or with unwise attention, respectively. If wise attention is operative, a wholesome consciousness arises and a cognitive process of a wholesome consciousness ensues. If unwise attention is operative, an unwholesome consciousness arises and a cognitive process of an unwholesome consciousness ensues. Therefore having wise attention is very important when we face objects with our eyes, ears, nose, tongue, body, and mind.

The wholesome consciousness produces many good materialities, which spread throughout the body, making us feel at ease. Whoever would like to have good health, should develop and sustain this wholesome state of mind most of the time.

In contrast, the unwholesome consciousness produces many bad materialities, which spread throughout the body, making us feel unease. It indirectly affects our physical health and well-being. Whoever would like to have good health should not allow themselves to have an unhealthy mind, which is unwholesome.

Furthermore, according to the *Visuddhimagga*, among the seven javanas, if they come to fruition, the first javana brings its kammic results in this life, the second through sixth javanas bring kammic results from the lives after the next life to future lives, and the seventh javana brings its kammic results in our immediate next life. Additionally, the five-door cognitive processes and mind-door cognitive processes don't just arise once, but rather they arise countless times in a very short period of time. As a result, countless javanas also arise. So the entire process affects us greatly, not only in our current life but also our future lives. Once we know this truth, we become very careful with our thoughts.

Actually, after we cultivate the jhānas, if we see the cognitive processes of wholesome consciousnesses and unwholesome consciousnesses, and know their effects, we will like to avoid such unwholesome consciousness.

But for the sake of our practice we do intentionally arouse cognitive processes of unwholesome consciousnesses. I didn't really want to have unwholesome consciousnesses, but I was obliged to have them for the sake of my practice. The mental factors that arise when an unwholesome consciousness is present have given me trouble, in contrast to when a jhānic or wholesome consciousness was present and the mental factors were quite pleasant. In some ways, we become more sensitive as we practice meditation. Just as a person who has lived in the mountains where the air is clean is more sensitive to the polluted air when he or she goes to the city, if we clearly perceive the mental factors of wholesome and unwholesome consciousnesses through the practice of meditation on mentality, we will become more sensitive to the mental factors of unwholesome consciousnesses and we will distance ourselves from them.

We train in the cognitive process that arises in the ear in the same way we did with the eye. We can either have a wholesome consciousness or an unwholesome consciousness toward the sounds that we hear while sitting. If we know sound as it is, as "sound," there will be wise attention. If we develop wise attention via saying "this is sound," ear-door adverting arises and subsequently ear consciousness, receiving, investigation, determining, javana, registration, bhavaṅga, mind-door adverting, javana, and registration arise. The consciousness + mental factors of a wholesome mind are present in javana and registration. But if we decide "this is such a pleasant sound, I want to keep listening to it," unwise attention will operate and the consciousness + mental factors of a consciousness associated with greed and wrong view will arise. If we have thoughts of disliking a certain sound, a consciousness associated with hate will arise. In the latter case, the consciousness + mental factors of a consciousness associated with hate will be present in javanas of the ear-door cognitive process.

There are also many ways of discerning the cognitive process that arises in the nose. If we breathe in fresh air and determine "this is smell," there will be wise attention. Wholesome consciousness + mental factors are present in the javanas of the nose-door cognitive process and the javanas of the mind-door process that subsequently arise. On the other hand, if we arouse attachment while breathing in fresh air, it becomes a consciousness of greed. If we have thoughts of disliking when we smell an unpleasant smell, it becomes a consciousness of hatred. As another example, if we know the unpleasant smell as it is saying "this is smell," it becomes a wholesome consciousness. But if we spray something in our nose because it is clogged but then regret doing so, saying we shouldn't have sprayed it and asking why we sprayed it, then a mind of hatred and remorse has arisen.

We discern the cognitive process that arises in the tongue in the same way. When we taste something, a wholesome consciousness or an unwholesome consciousness may arise depending on what kind of attention we have toward it. When we taste disgusting food and have thoughts of disliking that food, a consciousness associated with hate arises, but if we think "that taste is impermanent," our attention will become wise and a wholesome consciousness will arise along with the cognitive process that follows it.

We discern the body-door cognitive process in the same way as in the eye, ear, nose, and tongue. The objects of the body-door cognitive process are tangible objects: the earth, fire, and wind elements. The six properties of the earth element that we have discussed in meditation on materiality, the properties of heat and cold of the fire element, and the properties of pushing and supporting of the wind element are tangible objects. When any of them impinge on the body sensitivity, body-door cognitive process arises. When smoothness is felt on the body and we feel good and try to continue feeling that, then a consciousness associated with greed has arisen. If we think of softness as materiality, then wise attention operates and a wholesome consciousness arises.

If we have self-conceit while practicing, thinking "I am practicing well," our attention will become unwise and an unwholesome consciousness associated with greed and conceit arises. We can discern this from the mind-door cognitive process.

6. Wholesome and Unwholesome Consciousnesses

Eight Wholesome Consciousnesses		consciousness accompanied by joy, associated with knowledge, unprompted
		consciousness accompanied by joy, associated with knowledge, prompted
		consciousness accompanied by joy, dissociated from knowledge, unprompted
		consciousness accompanied by joy, dissociated from knowledge, prompted
		consciousness accompanied by equanimity, associated with knowledge, unprompted
		consciousness accompanied by equanimity, associated with knowledge, prompted
		consciousness accompanied by equanimity, dissociated from knowledge, unprompted
		consciousness accompanied by equanimity, dissociated from knowledge, prompted
Eighteen Unwholesome Consciousnesses	Eight Consciousnesses Rooted in Greed	consciousness accompanied by joy, associated with greed and wrong view, prompted
		consciousness accompanied by joy, associated with greed and wrong view, unprompted
		consciousness accompanied by equanimity, associated with greed and wrong view, prompted
		consciousness accompanied by equanimity, associated with greed and wrong view, unprompted

Eighteen Unwholesome Consciousnesses *(continued)*	Eight Consciousnesses Rooted in Greed *(continued)*	consciousness accompanied by joy, associated with greed but dissociated with wrong view, prompted
		consciousness accompanied by joy, associated with greed but dissociated with wrong view, unprompted
		consciousness accompanied by equanimity, associated with greed but dissociated with wrong view, prompted
		consciousness accompanied by equanimity, associated with greed but dissociated with wrong view, unprompted
	Eight Consciousnesses Rooted in Hatred	consciousness associated with hatred, prompted
		consciousness associated with hatred, unprompted
		consciousness associated with hatred and envy, prompted
		consciousness associated with hatred and envy, unprompted
		consciousness associated with hatred and avarice, prompted
		consciousness associated with hatred and avarice, unprompted
		consciousness associated with hatred and remorse, prompted
		consciousness associated with hatred and remorse, unprompted
	Two Consciousnesses Rooted in Ignorance	consciousness associated with delusion and restlessness
		consciousness associated with delusion and doubt

Wholesome consciousnesses will arise if we develop wise attention, and unwholesome consciousnesses will arise if we develop unwise attention. Meditation is a way of knowing this and making the effort that makes this knowledge helpful to us. Meditation on mentality, specifically, is about discerning the consciousness + mental factors from the cognitive process.

Once we become skilled in the cognitive processes that arise in the six doors, we discern the five aggregates.

DISCERNING THE FIVE AGGREGATES

On the basis of being able to discern materiality through meditation on materiality and discern consciousness and mental factors through meditation on mentality, we will now practice discerning the five aggregates. Up to this point we have practiced discerning materiality and mentality separately, but in discerning the five aggregates we will practice discerning materiality and mentality at the same time.

The five aggregates are material form (*rūpa*), feeling (*vedanā*), perception (*saññā*), mental formations (*saṅkhāra*), and consciousness (*viññāṇa*). They are the five aggregates that make up existence. The aggregate of form is materiality, and the aggregates of feeling, perception, mental formations, and consciousness are mentality. The aggregates of feeling, perception, and mental formations are mental factors and the aggregate of consciousness is consciousness. We have discerned all of these through the practices of meditation on materiality and mentality.

Discerning the five aggregates is very important. When we discern the five aggregates, we are seeing the true form of beings. Beings are none other than the five aggregates. Materiality arises quickly depending on its conditions and then passes away quickly depending on its conditions. Mentality also arises quickly depending on its conditions and then passes away quickly depending on its conditions. If we see the five aggregates made up of materiality and mentality, arising quickly and passing away quickly depending on their conditions, we can temporarily remove the self-view that "I exist" as a being and that this being continues.

After entering and exiting the first jhāna through ānāpānasati, seeing the paṭibhāga-nimitta of ānāpānasati that is in the mind door, and determining "this is the paṭibhāga-nimitta of ānāpānasati," mind-door adverting arises. Then the cognitive process of jhāna arises: mind-door adverting, preparation, access, conformity, and change-of-lineage, as well as the absorption javanas arise. When discerning the five aggregates, we don't discern consciousness and mental factors one by one, but in the case of mind-door adverting we see twelve kinds, in the case of preparation, access, conformity, and change-of-lineage we see thirty-four kinds each, and in the case of absorption javanas we see thirty-four kinds altogether, along with the materiality of the heart base.

The materialities in the mind door are composed of the following six categories of materiality: the ten kinds of material kalāpas present with the materiality of heart base, the ten kinds of material kalāpas present with the materiality of body sensitivity, the ten kinds of material kalāpas present with the materiality of sex (all three of these originate from kamma), the eight kinds of material kalāpas originating from the mind, the eight kinds of material kalāpas originating from temperature, and the eight kinds of material kalāpas originating from food. Altogether there are fifty-four kinds of materiality. These materialities are all the aggregate of rūpa, material form. Seeing the five aggregates is seeing these fifty-four materialities and consciousness and the mental factors of feeling, perception, and intention (or else all the mental factors in the mind excluding feeling, perception, and consciousness). The material base, the mind, and the objects of the mind are always present together. Materiality is the base upon which the mind arises.

The five aggregates do not arise separately; they arise together. We discern the aggregates of material form, feeling, perception, mental formations, and consciousness together. The five aggregates are present in each and every mind moment of cognitive process. This is how the five aggregates arise and pass away. Existence is not something that goes on continuously as one thing, but rather it arises and passes away depending on conditions. In order for a new set of five aggregates to arise, the previous set of five aggregates must pass away.

We discern the five aggregates for both wholesome and unwholesome cognitive processes. We observe the five aggregates not only in jhāna but also in daily life. When we see a dog on the road and intend "May that dog be free from danger," mind-door adverting and javanas arise. If we see consciousness + mental factors arising and the materiality of the mind door that is their base, we are seeing the five aggregates. When we are walking somewhere, the materiality that arises originating from kamma, the mind, temperature, and food are seen as the aggregate of material form; the intention to walk is seen as the aggregate of mental formations; the feeling that arises then is the aggregate of feeling; we recall the place we are going through the aggregate of perception; and knowing that we are going is the aggregate of consciousness. The materiality, feelings, perceptions, intentions, and consciousness that arise in whatever we do are the five aggregates, and seeing them as described above is discerning the five aggregates.

THE PSYCHOTHERAPEUTIC IMPLICATIONS OF MEDITATION ON MENTALITY

As a psychiatrist engaging in psychotherapy, I have been greatly helped by the practice of meditation on mentality in understanding psychological problems and psychological symptoms. I came to understand the concrete effects of listening, seeing, experiencing, and thinking about something with a consciousness rooted in greed, hatred, and delusion. Greed, hatred, and delusion are unwholesome consciousnesses. When unwholesome consciousnesses operate, cognitive processes that have javanas of unwholesome consciousnesses arise. The mental factors that are present in the javanas of an unwholesome consciousness affect us negatively.

On the other hand, there are nineteen beautiful universal mental factors in wholesome consciousnesses that are devoid of greed, hatred, and delusion. These nineteen kinds make us feel at ease, make us calm, and are pleasant. Among the nineteen kinds, lightness, malleability, wieldiness, proficiency, and rectitude of consciousness and mental factors make us feel light, malleable, and comfortable, and help us gain the confidence of being able to do anything. Through the effects of these mental factors, we look cheerful, confident, and trustworthy to others.

While we perceive the objects of visible form, sound, smell, taste, and touch, and the mental objects through the sense organs of the eye, ear, nose, tongue, and body, as well as the mind, the javanas of a wholesome consciousness or an unwholesome consciousness will arise, depending on whether the consciousness is wholesome or unwholesome. These arise along with the corresponding mental factors, and the phenomena that we previously mentioned arise and affect us. If many good cognitive processes occur through wholesome consciousnesses, and as a result many wholesome mental factors perform their functions, positive effects will come to our bodies and minds. If many harmful cognitive processes occur through unwholesome consciousnesses, and as a result many unwholesome mental factors perform their functions, negative effects will come to our bodies and minds. When positive effects are accumulated, our bodies and minds will become healthy, filled with energy, and happy, and our lives will become successful. However, if negative effects are accumulated, our lives will become difficult and miserable, and this may lead to psychological problems.

It's very important for our own mental health to try and maximize wholesome consciousnesses such that their beautiful mental factors arise frequently. And it's important to prevent the vicious cycle of unwholesome consciousnesses bringing about further unwholesome consciousnesses.

5. Meditation on Dependent Origination

Meditation on dependent origination is the practice that gets us to see cause and effect as it is. When a certain phenomenon arises, meditation on dependent origination thoroughly investigates how the phenomenon is present through its causes and effects. When we thoroughly know cause and effect, or causes and conditions, we won't have thoughts that are different from reality. The world and phenomena operate completely through their own laws; they don't operate in accordance with our thoughts. But we generally want reality to operate in accordance with our own thoughts, and thus we suffer when it doesn't. The practice of meditation on dependent origination offers one solution, by bringing our thoughts into accord with reality. When this happens, we are able to live in the world without difficulty.

Even our thoughts and intentions cannot occur without causes and conditions. We can know this through practicing meditation on dependent origination. Our ability to see things as they are becomes deeper and much more precise.

The Five Methods of Seeing Dependent Origination

Once the eye of wisdom opens by cultivating jhāna, we can discern materiality and mentality by practicing meditation on materiality and mentality. Then, on the basis of discerning the five aggregates, we can practice meditation on dependent origination.

Dependent origination refers to the arising of phenomena in accordance with cause and effect. Meditation on dependent origination is seeing the causes and effects of any particular phenomenon. It is seeing the causes and effects of the materiality and mentality that makes up existence.

There are five forms of meditation on dependent origination. In his book *Knowing and Seeing*, Pa-Auk Sayadaw said, "the Buddha taught four ways of discerning dependent origination according to the character of his listeners, and there is a fifth method taught by the Venerable Sāriputta recorded in the *Paṭisambhidāmagga*."

The first through fourth methods all appear in the Majjhima Nikāya in the *Greater Discourse on the Destruction of Craving*. It is a sutta in which a wrong view arose in a bhikkhu named Sāti who was reciting the *jātakas* (tales of the Buddha's previous births). He said, "As I understand the Dhamma taught by the Blessed One, it is this same consciousness that runs and wanders through the round of rebirths, not another." Other bhikkhus told him, "Do not say so. . . . The Blessed One has stated consciousness to be dependently arisen, since without a condition there is no origination of consciousness." But to no avail. Hereupon they reported this to the Buddha, who then directly summoned the bhikkhu Sāti, pointed out that his view was wrong, and gave the proper teaching. (MN 38)

The first method of meditation on dependent origination goes in the forward order of dependent origination, beginning with ignorance and leading to old age and death. The second method is also one that proceeds in the forward order of dependent origination, but beginning with feeling and leading to old age and death. The third approach goes in the reverse order of dependent origination, beginning with old age and death and leading to ignorance. The fourth method is also in the reverse order of dependent origination, but it begins with the four nutriments in the middle of the cycle (physical food, contact, intention, and consciousness) and leads to ignorance. The fifth method simply discerns how the five past causes lead to the arising of the five present effects, and the five present causes lead to the five future effects.

In the Pa-Auk Center, we usually practice the first and fifth methods as a requisite course for dependent origination. We begin by practicing with the fifth method and then we practice with the first method afterward. Then, if meditators are interested and want to practice other methods, they can do them without difficulty.

I suspect that the reason for this is because the fifth method is simpler than the first, and because practitioners can understand the basic framework of dependent origination by seeing how the causes in their past lives are connected to effects in their present lives. Once that understanding is formed, it is easier to thoroughly comprehend the first method of seeing dependent origination in the forward order.

According to the Buddha, there are two ways of seeing our past lives. One is seeing our past lives through vipassanā insight knowledge, and the other is seeing them through supernatural powers. If we see our past lives through supernatural powers, we can know all the details of each past life, including our name, race, food, happiness, and suffering. In contrast, seeing our past lives through vipassanā insight knowledge is seeing them simply as the five aggregates.

The Buddha referred to seeing past lives as the five aggregates by saying:

> Bhikkhus, those ascetics and brahmins who recollect their manifold past abodes all recollect the five aggregates subject to clinging or a certain one among them. What five?
>
> When recollecting thus, bhikkhus: "I had such form in the past," it is just form that one recollects. When recollecting: "I had such feeling in the past," it is just feeling that one recollects. When recollecting: "I had such perception in the past," it is just perception that one recollects. When recollecting: "I had such volitional formations in the past," it is just volitional formations that one recollects. When recollecting: "I had such consciousness in the past," it is just consciousness that one recollects.
>
> *Khajjaniya Sutta,* SN 22:79; trans. Bhikkhu Bodhi

In the Pa-Auk Center, we see our past lives based on this sutta.

1. The Fifth Method
Discerning the Five Aggregates Internally and Externally

In the fifth method of meditation on dependent origination, we see that the five past causes (past ignorance, craving, clinging, formations, and kamma) lead to the five present effects (present consciousness, mentality-materiality, the six sense bases, contact, and feeling) and that the five present causes (present ignorance, craving, clinging, formations, and kamma) lead to the five future effects (future consciousness, mentality-materiality, the six sense bases, contact, and feeling).

In order to discern dependent origination through the fifth method, we have to be able to actually see the five past causes of ignorance, craving, clinging, formations, and kamma. The past causes are the causes in our past lives. Therefore we have to be able to see our past lives.

Here *past lives* refers to the life before our present life, or in other words our immediate past life.

We have to be able to see the ignorance, craving, clinging, formations, and kamma of our immediate past life and the consciousness, mentality-materiality, six sense bases, contact, and feeling of our present life. And we have to see their connection.

In order to do this, we must train ourselves to see our past lives.

Up to this point we have only practiced seeing the five aggregates inside of ourselves. In order to see our immediate past life, we have to see the five aggregates of our past lives, so we have to be able to see the five aggregates outside of ourselves.

We train ourselves in this as follows.

After exiting each jhāna of ānāpānasati, the kasiṇas, and the immaterial jhānas and seeing the mentality and materiality (in other words, the five aggregates) of the jhānas inside ourselves, if we have the thought that "there is mentality and materiality outside" and intend to see mentality and materiality outside, materiality and mentality will appear in the same way as when we saw them on the inside. In this way, we discern mentality and materiality from the outside.

Discerning mentality and materiality inside and outside of us is called "discerning mentality and materiality internally and externally." Note that *internally* and *externally* are used a little differently than their typical meaning: *internally* means "that which is ours" and *externally* means "that which is others."

Let's look at this method in more detail. In my case, after exiting the first jhāna of ānāpānasati and discerning the mentality and materiality—that is, the five aggregates—of the first jhāna, if we intend to send mentality and materiality outside, mentality and materiality will move outside. They move straight through and then they stop on their own. This phenomenon arises even though we aren't doing anything. After the first jhāna, mentality and materiality stop after moving just a little bit. When they stop, mentality and materiality unfold in the same way as from the inside. This phenomenon arises naturally without our will intervening at all.

If I move mentality and materiality outside after exiting the second jhāna and discerning the five aggregates of the second jhāna, mentality and materiality move farther than they did in the first jhāna. Then at a certain point they stop. Again, the mentality and materiality unfold on the outside automatically, in the same way as was seen from the inside.

If I enter and exit the third jhāna, discern the five aggregates of the third jhāna, and move them outside, they will move even farther than in the second jhāna and stop. And then the five aggregates of the third jhāna can be discerned from the outside exactly as they had been seen on the inside. It now feels automatic, as if I had activitated a setting. It feels like the eye of wisdom is functioning.

Finally, I enter and exit the fourth jhāna, discern its aggregates from the inside, and then move and discern mentality and materiality from the outside. In this case, when they go outside they sometimes go far.

In this way, I discern the five aggregates internally and externally concerning the first, second, third, and fourth kasiṇa jhānas, and then proceed to the immaterial jhānas (infinite space, infinite consciousness, nothingness, and neither-perception-nor-nonperception). When I enter and exit neither-perception-nor-nonperception, discern the five aggregates at the mind door, and move them outside, mentality and materiality will move for a very long time and then stop. After they stop, the discerning of mentality and materiality will arise.

We train to see external mentality and materiality in all the cognitive processes of wholesome and unwholesome consciousnesses that arise in the six sense doors of the eye, ear, nose, tongue, body, and mind, internally and externally. Regardless of what kind of cognitive process it is, we strive to be able to see it internally and externally. That way there will be no difficulty in discerning any cognitive process that occurs in our past lives. This experience was an extremely surprising one for me.

We see our past and future lives in the same way.

Seeing Our Past Lives

There are two ways of seeing past lives: we can see our past life by moving from this present moment to the past, or we can see it by moving directly to our past life.

Although the two methods are the same once we become skilled, we first try both methods one by one. Depending on the circumstances, one method may be a bit more useful than the other.

Let's first look at the method of going incrementally from this present moment to the past. If it is night time now, for example, we reflect on the afternoon and discern the five aggregates of that time. Then we move to yesterday and discern the five aggregates of that time. In this way we move progressively to last week, last month, last year, and so on, discerning the five aggregates of each time. We move to when we were born and see our form and cognitive process at that time. Then we see when we were inside our mothers' wombs, and if we want to know the causes of the five aggregates that we discerned in the womb, we move to our past life.

Now let's look into the method of moving to our past lives directly. After entering and exiting ānāpānasati, the kasiṇas, and the immaterial jhānas in order, and discerning mentality and materiality internally and externally, if we contemplate, "mentality and materiality are truly suffering; what are the past causes of this present mentality and materiality?" we can directly see our past mentality and materiality.

My Six Past Lives

After listening to Sayadaw U Sīla's explanation of the two methods, I first tried the method of moving to the past incrementally. After discerning the mentality and materiality of ānāpānasati, the kasiṇas, and the immaterial jhānas internally and externally, I moved to yesterday, a few days ago, and so on to when I was young. As cognitive processes, I saw my childhood body and what I saw at that time, which I normally wasn't able to remember. I felt the feelings I had at that time. After passing through my infancy and seeing my birth and then being inside my mother's womb as cognitive processes, I felt the existence of my past life, but I could only feel the presence of mentality and materiality and I wasn't able to see anything specific.

During my next meditation session, I tried the method of moving directly to my past life. After discerning the mentality and materiality of ānāpānasati, the kasiṇas, and the immaterial jhānas internally and externally, when I contemplated, "mentality and materiality are truly suffering; what are the past causes of this present mentality and materiality?" the mentality and materiality that was outside began to move toward the past. They moved continuously and then stopped. At that point I saw my previous life. I saw a large being.

Then the mentality and materiality moved again. But this time, strangely enough, there was a somewhat unpleasant consciousness. Again the mentality and materiality stopped moving. And then I saw a different past life. This past life was not a good past life; it was a past life as a dog. The dog looked like a very fair Korean Jindo dog, and it looked very clear and not greedy. As I looked at that dog, tears flowed continuously. Once I heard a story about a certain practitioner who was practicing meditation on dependent origination at the Pa-Auk Center and who, when he tried to look at his past lives, was at first too afraid and couldn't do it. But one day he saw his past life and said that it was a past life in hell. What happened to me seemed similar to that experience.

Again the mentality and materiality started to move. After moving for some time it stopped again and a different past life unfolded itself. I saw an Indian man who was good-looking and seemed to be without much greed.

Afterward the mentality and materiality moved again, and this time it moved for a long time. And then another past life unfolded itself. A heavenly being appeared. There is a relationship between the time of movement and each being's lifespan. If the lifespan is long, mentality and materiality move for a long time.

After that life unfolded itself, the mentality and materiality moved again. After stopping, another past life unfolded itself. It seemed like a prince in Nepal, whose form shone and was good-looking, and who also looked very wise. Again the mentality and materiality's movement began, and after a lot of time passed, it stopped. The past life that unfolded looked like a heavenly being that was wise.

In this way, I saw altogether six past lives by the time my meditation session was over. If I had continued to sit and retained the practice, it seemed like I might have been able to continue seeing my past lives. During this session, I only saw the general picture that allowed me to check the connection between the mentality and materiality of the past lives and the present and so know that my present life and my past lives were connected. I was able to know the specifics, including the five past causes, when I turned my attention to them afterward.

When I reported this to Sayadaw U Sīla, he said that I had to practice the fifth method of meditation on dependent origination with my six past lives. He said that I should begin by designating the first of my six past lives as "past" and my present life as "present." After seeing the effects of the present life through the first past life's causes, I should then see the second past life as the past and the first past life as the present. In this way I would see the causes and effects of all six past lives. For my first task, I discerned the five past causes of ignorance, craving, clinging, formations, and kammic force in my first past life.

Seeing the Five Past Causes

After having entered the ānāpānasati, the kasiṇas, and the immaterial jhānas, I discerned mentality and materiality both internally and externally. Then I moved to my first past life and searched for ignorance, craving, clinging, formations, and kamma there. *Ignorance* is not seeing reality and knowing falsely. *Craving* is arousing greed on the basis of ignorance. *Clinging* is the continuation of craving. (That is, the initial indication of liking something is craving, and when it becomes strong it is clinging.) *Formations* are volitions. And *kammic force* is the force or potentiality that has been left behind after we have done either good or bad deeds. It is the reason why we can remember our past events in life and why they are able to appear as objects of the near-death moment in any existence. Ignorance, craving, and clinging are called "rounds of defilement" (*kilesa vaṭṭa*) and formations and kamma are called "rounds of kamma" (*kamma vaṭṭa*). I searched for all of these in my first past life.

When I focused on asking what ignorance was in my first past life, I found the thought "I want to become a person who studies Buddhism." I must have seen a monk at some point in my first past life and had this thought. Seeing myself as a person who studies Buddhism is seeing falsely. It is seeing through self-view. It is not being able to see things as they are. This was the ignorance of my first past life. This ignorance was the cause of the continuance of saṃsāra. I saw the mind-door cognitive process at the time this ignorance arose. Greed and wrong view were present in the javanas of the mind-door cognitive process, and as a consciousness accompanied by joy that was unprompted, there were twenty consciousness + mental factors. Seeing in this way, I discerned ignorance.

Although there are some cases in which these things are seen clearly, generally they aren't.

For instance, the being of my first past life felt extremely large, to the point that I first thought it might be a heavenly being. But during an interview, I was told by Sayadaw U Sīla that it isn't possible to be reborn as a brahma among the heavenly beings immediately following birth as an animal, and my second past life was as a dog. And so I had to look closer. I discerned the mentality and materiality of my first past life, and it was a human being that was like a soldier or policeman. He had short hair. It seems like he felt big because he had a high rank. Each being has its own inherent mentality and materiality. By discerning them, we can know for sure what kind of being it is. I knew, from practicing meditation on materiality and mentality before practicing meditation on dependent origination, that there is no materiality of masculinity or femininity in the realm of brahmas, and I discerned masculinity from the first past life. So that confirmed that the first past life was a human being.

Craving in my first past life was having attachment toward the life of a person who studies Buddhism. It was the attachment toward wanting to be that kind of person. Clinging was the continuing of that attachment. Greed and wrong view were also present in the javanas of the mind-door cognitive process of craving and clinging, and as consciousnesses accompanied by joy that were unprompted, there were twenty consciousness + mental factors.

When discerning formations, it is important to discern the mind's formations at the near-death moment. There are many formations during one lifetime, and the formations at the near-death moment don't always have to be the formations of that lifetime; they can also be the formations of the lifetime before. But the formation that is connected to the next life is the formation in the mind at the near-death moment. If we see the mind's formations at the near-death moment, we understand the formations that are the cause of the next life. Having moved to the near-death moment of the first past life, we see the signs that were the objects of the mind, consciousness, and mental factors at that time.

In the case of my first past life, the sign at the near-death moment was a temple. The formation had thirty-four kinds of consciousness + mental factors as a wholesome consciousness accompanied by joy and wisdom. When I turned my attention to what the formations and kamma of my first past life were, I saw that I was restoring a temple that was destroyed by a disaster. The formations and kamma that were present in my first past life appeared as the formation at the near-death moment.

The sign at the near-death moment, the sign of the rebirth-linking consciousness of the next life, the sign of bhavaṅga of the next life, and the sign of the consciousness of death of the next life (which is the last consciousness of a given lifetime) are all the same. These are all signs of the mind, and they are of three types: First, kamma sometimes becomes the sign. For example, where the kamma is helping others, the act of helping others becomes the sign. Second, the object of kamma sometimes becomes the sign. For example, when the kammic action of restoring a temple is done, the temple becomes the sign, or in the case of offering robes to a monk, the robes become the sign. Lastly, the place of future rebirth becomes the sign. Heaven becomes the sign.

In order to examine these four consciousnesses and signs, we (1) go to the near-death moment of our first past life and examine the consciousness and sign, (2) see the consciousness and sign of rebirth-linking of our present life, (3) see the consciousness and sign of the bhavaṅga that arises subsequently, and (4) discern the consciousness and sign of death, the last mind, of our present life. Rebirth-linking is the first mind of our present life, and fifteen or sixteen bhavaṅga consciousnesses arise immediately afterward. Once the cognitive process begins while being in the consciousness of bhavaṅga, bhavaṅga disappears and the consciousness of the cognitive process arises. There are bhavaṅga consciousnesses before the cognitive process begins.

The consciousness and mental factors of rebirth-linking, bhavaṅga, and the consciousness of death are the same. Consciousness arises and passes away very quickly and then another consciousness arises.

Kamma is the force or potentiality that has been left behind after we have done either good or bad deeds; different formations are causes to leave different kammic forces behind to affect our lives even at the present.

Once, out of curiosity regarding the cause of a present matter, I turned my attention to my past life by thinking, "What is that cause?" To my surprise, I was able to discover the cases in which there was such a cause in my past life.

Many different people may come up when looking for causes in our past lives. If we aren't able to tell which person we were, we have to discern which people are associated with us now. We find this out by observing the mentality and materiality of the two people: The mentality and materiality of a person connected to us will connect with us. The mentality and materiality of a person not connected to us will not connect with us.

Materiality formed by kamma and resultant mind moments caused by kamma in every cognitive process arise continuously throughout the entire life. Therefore I once asked Sayadaw U Sīla how kamma that was accumulated in the past can continuously effect the present. He explained it to me using a simile. Kamma functions continuously in the sense that if we have money saved in the bank, we will always be able to find it "continuously," until that money runs out.

As I was practicing comfortably and quickly, Sayadaw U Sīla said that he thought I had practiced meditation in my past lives and told me to search for when I practiced in past lives. It wasn't clear whether I'd practiced in the six past lives I have mentioned previously. So I turned my attention to specifically look at past lives that were related to the practice of meditation. I saw that I practiced vipassanā meditation as a bhikkhu during the time of the Buddha Vipassī. At that time the Buddha's form was that of a holy man, as told in the scriptures. After that I practiced vipassanā twice as a bhikkhu, and I saw one past life in which I even practiced vipassanā as a lay person. There was also another past lifetime as a bhikkhuni. As I looked into the meditation I practiced in my past lives in my next sitting session, in addition to the past lives in which I practiced vipassanā as a householder and meditation as a renunciate, I also saw past lives in which I practiced loving-kindness meditation, cultivated the immaterial jhānas, and saw kalāpas.

Once the five past causes are discerned, we must look at the five present effects. The five present effects are consciousness, mentality-materiality, the six sense bases, contact, and feeling. I see the five present effects of consciousness, mentality-materiality, the six sense bases, contact, and feeling as being included in the five aggregates.

When we look at what kinds of effects the five past causes produce in the five aggregates, we are discerning dependent origination through the fifth method. Pa-Auk Sayadaw says that when we discern dependent origination according to the fifth method, we have to discern by way of five aggregates.

We find the causes and effects in each moment of consciousness. Consciousnesses can be divided into two groups: process-freed and cognitive process. Process-freed are rebirth-linking consciousness, bhavaṅga which flows on through the course of existence until the termination of the life-process at death, and the consciousness of death. Cognitive process are consciousness of the five-door cognitive process and of the mind-door cognitive process. We connect and discern the causes and effects by way of the five aggregates both in the consciousnesses of cognitive process and in the consciousnesses of the process-freed. First we discern the causes and effects of the five aggregates of rebirth-linking and bhavaṅga. Then we discern the causes and effects of the five aggregates that are in the consciousnesses of the cognitive process.

The Five Aggregates of Rebirth-Linking

We search for the causes and effects in the five aggregates of form, feeling, perception, mental formations, and consciousness of rebirth-linking upon exiting the jhānas of ānāpānasati, the kasiṇas, and the immaterial jhānas. Since there are both past and present causes, we have to find both the past causes and their effects and the present causes and their effects.

We will first look into the aggregate of material form in rebirth-linking. There are only thirty kinds of materiality in the first moment of the formation of the embryo of rebirth-linking, which have been formed by kamma and by the five past causes: the ten element kalāpas of the heart, the ten element kalāpas of the body, and the ten element kalāpas of sex. The five past causes are summarized as follows, using my own experience as an example:

1. As ignorance arises, materiality formed by the kamma of rebirth-linking arises. Ignorance is the cause, and the materiality formed by the kamma of rebirth-linking is the effect. The ignorance of my first past life was seeing myself as a person when I thought, "I also want to become someone who studies Buddhism." Ignorance is seeing myself as a person instead of as the ultimate realities of materiality and mentality.

2. As craving arises, materiality formed by the kamma of rebirth-linking arises. Craving is the cause, and the materiality formed by the kamma of rebirth-linking is the effect. The craving of my first past life was having attachment toward the life of a person who studies Buddhism.

3. As clinging arises, materiality formed by the kamma of rebirth-linking arises. Clinging is the cause, and materiality formed by the kamma of rebirth-linking is the effect. The clinging of my first past life was the continuation of my craving. Initial indication of liking something is craving, and when it becomes strong it is clinging.

4. As formations arise, materiality formed by the kamma of rebirth-linking arises. Formations are the cause, and materiality formed by the kamma of rebirth-linking is the effect. The formations of my first past life, as a consciousness accompanied by joy and wisdom, were the thirty-four consciousness + mental factors. The sign of this consciousness was the temple.

5. As kamma arises, materiality formed by the kamma of rebirth-linking arises. Kamma is the cause, and the materiality formed by the kamma of rebirth-linking is the effect. The kamma of my first past life was restoring the temple that was destroyed by a disaster. At that time there were thirty-four consciousness + mental factors in the javanas of the cognitive process, as it was a wholesome consciousness accompanied by joy and wisdom.

Discerning in this manner is discerning the aggregate of material form of rebirth-linking through cause and effect. All of the causes of material form of rebirth-linking are past causes. The body of my present life was formed by the five causes of my past life without having anything to do with my own will.

Now we will look at the aggregate of feeling of rebirth-linking. Feeling is the effect of both past and present causes. It cannot just have past causes nor can it just have present causes. The aggregate of feeling of rebirth-linking in the present life won't arise if the five past causes from the first past life aren't there. However, it can't arise solely from the five past causes. There must also be three present causes.

As I emphasized earlier, since feeling is a mental factor, there must be a present material base, an object, and consciousness and other mental factors in order for feeling to be present. Feeling cannot exist without consciousness and other mental factors. This material base, object, and consciousness + mental factors, which arise with feeling, are the present causes of the feeling of rebirth-linking.

The past and present causes of the aggregate of feeling of rebirth-linking and their effects are summarized as follows.

Five Past Causes

1. The feeling of rebirth-linking arises because ignorance arises. Ignorance is the cause, and the feeling of rebirth-linking is the effect.
2. The feeling of rebirth-linking arises because craving arises. Craving is the cause, and the feeling of rebirth-linking is the effect.
3. The feeling of rebirth-linking arises because clinging arises. Clinging is the cause, and the feeling of rebirth-linking is the effect.
4. The feeling of rebirth-linking arises because formations arise. Formations are the cause, and the feeling of rebirth-linking is the effect.
5. The feeling of rebirth-linking arises because kamma arises. Kamma is the cause, and the feeling of rebirth-linking is the effect.

Three Present Causes

1. The feeling of rebirth-linking arises because the material base (the thirty materialities of the heart base) arises. The material base is the cause, and the feeling of rebirth-linking is the effect.
2. The feeling of rebirth-linking arises because objects arise. The object is the cause, and the feeling of rebirth-linking is the effect.

3. The feeling of rebirth-linking arises because contact (the thirty-
three kinds of consciousness + mental factors aside from feeling)
arises. Contact is the cause, and the feeling of rebirth-linking is the
effect.

Now we will look at the aggregate of perception of rebirth-linking, which
also has past and present causes. They are summarized as follows:

Five Past Causes
1. Ignorance is the cause, and the perception of rebirth-linking is the
effect.
2. Craving is the cause, and the perception of rebirth-linking is the
effect.
3. Clinging is the cause, and the perception of rebirth-linking is the
effect.
4. Formations are the cause, and the perception of rebirth-linking is
the effect.
5. Kamma is the cause, and the perception of rebirth-linking is the
effect.

Three Present Causes
1. The material base (the thirty materialities of the heart base) is the
cause, and the perception of rebirth-linking is the effect.
2. The object is the cause, and the perception of rebirth-linking is the
effect.
3. Contact (the thirty-three kinds of consciousness + mental factors
aside from perception) is the cause, and the perception of rebirth-
linking is the effect.

Now we will look at the aggregate of mental formations of rebirth-linking.
This aggregate is twofold. We can see it only as intention, or we can see it as

everything in the mind aside from the aggregates of feeling, perception, and consciousness. If we summarize the past and present causes of the aggregate of mental formations of rebirth-linking, they are as follows:

Five Past Causes
1. Ignorance is the cause, and the mental formation of rebirth-linking is the effect.
2. Craving is the cause, and the mental formation of rebirth-linking is the effect.
3. Clinging is the cause, and the mental formation of rebirth-linking is the effect.
4. Formations are the cause, and the mental formation of rebirth-linking is the effect.
5. Kamma is the cause, and the mental formation of rebirth-linking is the effect.

Three Present Causes
1. The material base (the thirty materialities of the heart base) is the cause, and the mental formation of rebirth-linking is the effect.
2. The object is the cause, and the mental formation of rebirth-linking is the effect.
3. Contact (the thirty-three kinds of consciousness + mental factors aside from formations or the remaining mentalities excluding the aggregates of feeling, perception, and consciousness: if we take intention/volition as formations, this would refer to the thirty-three kinds of consciousness + mental factors aside from volition; or if we take all remaining mentalities excluding the aggregates of feeling, perception, and consciousness as formations, then it refers to consciousness, and the mental factors of feeling and perception) is the cause, and the mental formation of rebirth-linking is the effect.

Now we will look at the aggregate of consciousness, which also has past and present causes:

Five Past Causes
1. Ignorance is the cause, and the consciousness of rebirth-linking is the effect.
2. Craving is the cause, and the consciousness of rebirth-linking is the effect.
3. Clinging is the cause, and the consciousness of rebirth-linking is the effect.
4. Formations are the cause, and the consciousness of rebirth-linking is the effect.
5. Kamma is the cause, and the consciousness of rebirth-linking is the effect.

One Present Cause
1. Mentality (the thirty-three mental factors that accompany consciousness) and materiality (base materiality and object materiality) are the cause, and the consciousness of rebirth-linking is the effect.

The Five Aggregates of Bhavaṅga

Once we can discern the causes and effects of the five aggregates of rebirth-linking, we have to discern the causes and effects of the five aggregates of bhavaṅga (life-continuum), which arises after rebirth-linking.

In order to do that, all we have to do is discern the past and present causes in the same way we did for the five aggregates of rebirth-linking. Just as for rebirth-linking, the first past life is taken as the past and the present life as the present. The five past causes are the ignorance, craving, clinging, formations, and kamma we discern from our first past life. We see how these five past causes function as causes of the five aggregates of bhavaṅga. And then we discern the present causes.

We will start with the aggregate of material form of bhavaṅga. In contrast to rebirth-linking, there are present causes of material form of bhavaṅga; there is materiality formed by the mind and temperature, and while initially there isn't any materiality formed by nutriment, materiality formed by nutriment is there as time passes.

Five Past Causes
1. Ignorance is the cause, and the form (materiality formed by kamma) of bhavaṅga is the effect.
2. Craving is the cause, and the form (materiality formed by kamma) of bhavaṅga is the effect.
3. Clinging is the cause, and the form (materiality formed by kamma) of bhavaṅga is the effect.
4. Formations are the cause and the form (materiality formed by kamma) of bhavaṅga is the effect.
5. Kamma is the cause and the form (materiality formed by kamma) of bhavaṅga is the effect.

Three Present Causes
1. The mind is the cause, and the form (materiality formed by the mind) of bhavaṅga is the effect.
2. Temperature is the cause, and the form (materiality formed by temperature) of bhavaṅga is the effect.
3. Nutriment is the cause, and the form (materiality formed by nutriment) of bhavaṅga is the effect.

Next we will look at the aggregate of feeling of bhavaṅga.

Five Past Causes
1. Ignorance is the cause, and the feeling of bhavaṅga is the effect.
2. Craving is the cause, and the feeling of bhavaṅga is the effect.
3. Clinging is the cause, and the feeling of bhavaṅga is the effect.

4. Formations are the cause, and the feeling of bhavaṅga is the effect.
5. Kamma is the cause, and the feeling of bhavaṅga is the effect.

Three Present Causes
1. Material base (six kinds of kalāpas, or the fifty-four kinds of materiality) is the cause, and the feeling of bhavaṅga is the effect.
2. The object is the cause, and the feeling of bhavaṅga is the effect.
3. Contact:
   a. The contact of the mind of the preceding bhavaṅga (thirty-four kinds of consciousness + mental factors) is the cause, and the feeling of bhavaṅga is the effect.
   b. The contact of the mind of the subsequent bhavaṅga (thirty-three kinds of consciousness + mental factors excluding feeling) is the cause, and the feeling of bhavaṅga is the effect.

Now we will look at the aggregate of perception of bhavaṅga.

Five Past Causes
1. Ignorance is the cause, and the perception of bhavaṅga is the effect.
2. Craving is the cause, and the perception of bhavaṅga is the effect.
3. Clinging is the cause, and the perception of bhavaṅga is the effect.
4. Formations are the cause, and the perception of bhavaṅga is the effect.
5. Kamma is the cause, and the perception of bhavaṅga is the effect.

Three Present Causes
1. Material base is the cause, and the perception of bhavaṅga is the effect.
2. The object is the cause, and the perception of bhavaṅga is the effect.
3. Contact:
   a. The contact of the mind of the preceding bhavaṅga (thirty-four

kinds of consciousness + mental factors) is the cause, and the perception of bhavaṅga is the effect.

b. The contact of the mind of the subsequent bhavaṅga (thirty-three kinds of consciousness + mental factors excluding perception) is the cause, and the perception of bhavaṅga is the effect.

Now we will look at the aggregate of mental formations of bhavaṅga.

Five Past Causes

1. Ignorance is the cause, and the mental formation of bhavaṅga is the effect.

2. Craving is the cause, and the mental formation of bhavaṅga is the effect.

3. Clinging is the cause, and the mental formation of bhavaṅga is the effect.

4. Formations are the cause, and the mental formation of bhavaṅga is the effect.

5. Kamma is the cause, and the mental formation of bhavaṅga is the effect.

Three Present Causes

1. Material base is the cause, and the mental formation of bhavaṅga is the effect.

2. The object is cause, and the mental formation of bhavaṅga is the effect.

3. Contact:

a. The contact of the mind of the preceding bhavaṅga (thirty-four kinds of consciousness + mental factors) is the cause, and the mental formation of bhavaṅga is the effect.

b. The contact of the mind of the subsequent bhavaṅga (thirty-three kinds of consciousness + mental factors excluding mental formations, which is volition) is the cause, and the mental formation of bhavaṅga is the effect.

Finally, we will look at the aggregate of consciousness of bhavaṅga.

Five Past Causes
1. Ignorance is the cause, and the consciousness of bhavaṅga is the effect.
2. Craving is the cause, and the consciousness of bhavaṅga is the effect.
3. Clinging is the cause, and the consciousness of bhavaṅga is the effect.
4. Formations are the cause, and the consciousness of bhavaṅga is the effect.
5. Kamma is the cause, and the consciousness of bhavaṅga is the effect.

Two Present Causes
1. The contact of the mind of the preceding bhavaṅga (thirty-four kinds of consciousness + mental factors) is the cause, and the consciousness of bhavaṅga is the effect.
2. Mentality (the thirty-three mental factors that accompany consciousness) and materiality (base and object) are the cause, and the consciousness of bhavaṅga is the effect.

The Mind-Door-Only Cognitive Process

A mind-door cognitive process that arises without the prior arising of a five-door cognitive process is called a "mind-door-only cognitive process." Examples are the cognitive process of jhāna and the mind-door cognitive process. They arise taking dhamma as object. First we will discern the past and present causes of the cognitive process of jhāna (including mind-door adverting and the javanas of access concentration and of the cognitive process of jhāna; registration does not arise in this process). Then we will discern the past and present causes of the five aggregates of mind-door adverting, javana, and registration of the mind-door-only cognitive process.

The Cognitive Process of Jhāna:
The Five Aggregates of Mind-Door Adverting

Mind-door adverting arises when we exit jhāna and decide that the nimitta has become the object of jhāna by saying, "This is the nimitta that has become the object of jhāna." This decision becomes mind-door adverting. Examples include when we decide after exiting the first jhāna of ānāpānasati that "this is the paṭibhāga-nimitta of ānāpānasati" or we decide in the case of the white kasiṇa that "this is the white kasiṇa." These become mind-door adverting.

When we discern the cognitive process of jhāna, we take all of the jhānas we have experienced up to now as objects. After experiencing the jhānas of ānāpānasati, the kasiṇas, the immaterial jhānas, the four sublime abidings, and the four protective meditations, mind-door adverting occurs after each jhāna. After mind-door adverting, the javanas of access concentration arise four times, and after that the javanas of jhāna arise many times. Since the mentality of mind-door adverting doesn't arise dependent on past causes and only arises dependent on present causes, there are no past causes and only present causes of the mentality of mind-door adverting. In other words, there are only present causes of the aggregates of feeling, perception, mental formations, and consciousness of mind-door adverting.

In contrast, there are both past and present causes of the aggregate of form of mind-door adverting. They are the same as we saw earlier in the form of bhavaṅga. There is materiality formed by kamma in the past causes, and there is materiality formed by the mind, temperature, and nutriment in the present causes. For reference, we can review the past and present causes of the aggregate of form of bhavaṅga.

Let's look at the present causes of the aggregate of feeling of mind-door adverting.

Three Present Causes

1. Material base (the heart base: the six kinds of kalāpas, or the fifty-four kinds of materiality) is the cause, and the feeling of mind-door adverting is the effect.
2. The object is the cause, and the feeling of mind-door adverting is the effect.
3. Contact:
   a. The contact of the mind of bhavaṅga (thirty-four kinds of consciousness + mental factors) is the cause, and the feeling of mind-door adverting is the effect.
   b. The contact of the mind of mind-door adverting (eleven kinds of consciousness + mental factors excluding feeling) is the cause, and the feeling of mind-door adverting is the effect.

If we look at the aggregate of perception of mind-door adverting, there are almost no differences between that and the aggregate of feeling of mind-door adverting. Numbers 1–3a are the same as for the aggregate of feeling. But in 3b it changes to "eleven kinds of consciousness + mental factors excluding perception."

It is the same for the aggregate of mental formations of mind-door adverting. Numbers 1–3a are the same as for the aggregate of feeling, and in 3b it changes to "eleven kinds of consciousness + mental factors excluding mental formations, which is volition."

The aggregate of consciousness of mind-door adverting is as follows:

Two Present Causes

1. The contact of the mind of bhavaṅga (thirty-four kinds of consciousness + mental factors) is the cause, and the consciousness of mind-door adverting is the effect.
2. The mentality of mind-door adverting (the eleven mental factors that accompany consciousness) and materiality (base and object) are the cause, and the consciousness of mind-door adverting is the effect.

The Cognitive Process of Jhāna:
The Five Aggregates of the Javanas of Access Concentration

After mind-door adverting occurs upon exiting jhāna, in the case of all of the jhānas we have experienced up to now, the javanas of access concentration arise four times. The four consciousnesses of preparation, access, conformity, and change-of-lineage arise. The javanas of access concentration have the same consciousness + mental factors as the javanas of the jhāna. There is only a difference in *number*. Although there are thirty-four kinds of consciousness + mental factors in the javanas of access concentration for the first, second, and third jhānas, there are only thirty-three kinds of consciousness + mental factors in the javanas of access concentration for the fourth jhāna because joy is absent. The mentality of the javanas of access concentration does not arise dependent on past causes, but rather only dependent on present causes. In other words, there are only present causes of the aggregates of feeling, perception, mental formations, and consciousness of access concentration. In contrast, there are both past and present causes of the aggregate of form of access concentration.

We discern the causes and effects for the five aggregates of the javanas of the four access concentrations, beginning with those of the first access concentration.

There are both past and present causes of the aggregate of form of the javanas of the first access concentration. Since they are the same as the past and present causes of the form of bhavaṅga and the form of mind-door adverting, we can refer to the previous discussions.

Let's look at the aggregate of feeling of the javanas of the first access concentration.

Three Present Causes
1. Material base (the heart base: six kinds of kalāpas, or the fifty-four kinds of materiality) is the cause, and the feeling of the javanas of the first access concentration is the effect.
2. The object is the cause, and the feeling of the javanas of the first access concentration is the effect.

3. Contact:

   a. The contact of the mind of the javanas of the first access
   concentration (thirty-three kinds of consciousness + mental
   factors excluding feeling) is the cause, and the feeling of the
   javanas of the first access concentration is the effect.

   b. Wise attention (mind-door adverting: twelve consciousness +
   mental factors) is the cause, and the feeling of the javanas of the
   first access concentration is the effect.

If we look at the aggregate of perception of the javanas of the first access
concentration, there are almost no differences between that and the aggregate
of feeling of the javanas of the first access concentration. Numbers 1, 2, and
3b are the same as for the aggregate of feeling, but 3a changes to "thirty-three
kinds of consciousness + mental factors excluding perception."

It is the same for the aggregate of mental formations of the javanas of
the first access concentration. Numbers 1, 2, and 3b are the same as for the
aggregate of feeling, but 3a changes to "thirty-three kinds of consciousness
+ mental factors excluding mental formations, which is volition."

The aggregate of consciousness of the javanas of the first access concentration is as follows:

Two Present Causes

   1. Mentality of the javanas of the first access concentration (the
   thirty-three mental factors that accompany consciousness) and
   materiality (base and object) are the cause, and the consciousness
   of the javanas of the first access concentration is the effect.

   2. Wise attention (mind-door adverting: twelve kinds of
   consciousness + mental factors) is the cause, and the consciousness
   of the javanas of the first access concentration is the effect.

The method of discerning the javanas of the second through fourth access
concentrations is almost the same as the method of discerning the javanas of
the first access concentration. The only difference is that in addition to 1, 2,

and 3b of the three present causes of the javanas of the first access concentration, they add the contact of the mind of the javanas of the preceding access concentrations (the number of consciousness + mental factors) as 3c, and 3a changes to the javanas of the relevant access concentration.

In other words, in the case of the javanas of the second access concentration, 3a changes to refer to the javanas of the second access concentration and "the contact of the mind of the javanas of the first access concentration" is added as 3c. In the case of the javanas of the third access concentration, 3a changes to refer to the javanas of the third access concentration and "the contact of the mind of the javanas of the second access concentration" is added as 3c. In the case of the javanas of the fourth access concentration, 3a changes to refer to the javanas of the fourth access concentration and "the contact of the mind of the javanas of the third access concentration" is added as 3c.

The Cognitive Process of Jhāna:
The Five Aggregates of the Javanas of the Cognitive Process of Jhāna

Following the javanas of access concentration, we discern the causes and effects of the five aggregates of the javanas of the cognitive process of jhāna.

The javanas of the cognitive process of jhāna arise many times. Since the mentality of the javanas of the cognitive process of jhāna does not arise dependent on past causes and only arises dependent on present causes, there are only present causes of the mentality of the javanas of the cognitive process of jhāna. In other words, there are only present causes of the aggregates of feeling, perception, mental formations, and consciousness of the javanas of the cognitive process of jhāna. In contrast, there are both past and present causes of the aggregate of form of the cognitive process of jhāna.

Let's look first at the aggregate of form of the first javana of the cognitive process of jhāna.

There are past and present causes of the form of the first javana of the cognitive process of jhāna. They are the same as the past and present causes of the form of bhavaṅga, mind-door adverting, and access concentration that we have looked earlier, so we can refer to the previous listings for details.

Now let's look at the aggregate of feeling of the first javana of the cognitive process of jhāna. The attainment of jhāna is caused by present training. Therefore when the causes and effects of the first javana of the cognitive process of jhāna are discerned, there need be no past causes. The feeling of the first javana of the cognitive process of jhāna is summarized as follows:

Three Present Causes

1. Material base (the heart base: six kinds of kalāpas, or the fifty-four kinds of materiality) is the cause, and the feeling of the first javana of the cognitive process of jhāna is the effect.
2. The object is the cause, and the feeling of the first javana of the cognitive process of jhāna is the effect.
3. Contact:
   a. The contact of the mind of bhavaṅga (thirty-four kinds of consciousness + mental factors) is the cause, and the feeling of the first javana of the cognitive process of jhāna is the effect.
   b. The contact of the mind of the first javana (thirty-three kinds of consciousness + mental factors excluding feeling) is the cause, and the feeling of the first javana of the cognitive process of jhāna is the effect.
   c. Wise attention (mind-door adverting: twelve consciousness + mental factors) is the cause, and the feeling of the first javana of the cognitive process of jhāna is the effect.

If we look at the aggregate of perception of the first javana of the cognitive process of jhāna, numbers 1–3a and 3c are the same as for the aggregate of feeling of the first javana of the cognitive process of jhāna, and 3b changes to "thirty-three kinds of consciousness + mental factors aside from perception."

It is the same for the aggregate of mental formations of the first javana of the cognitive process of jhāna. Numbers 1–3a and 3c are the same as for the aggregate of feeling of the first javana of the cognitive process of jhāna, and 3b changes to "thirty-three kinds of consciousness + mental factors aside from mental formations, which is volition."

The aggregate of consciousness of the first javana of the cognitive process of jhāna is as follows:

Three Present Causes

1. The contact of the mind of bhavaṅga (thirty-four kinds of consciousness + mental factors) is the cause, and the consciousness of the first javana of the cognitive process of jhāna is the effect.
2. Mentality of the first javana (the thirty-three mental factors that accompany consciousness) and materiality (base and object) are the cause, and the consciousness of the first javana of the cognitive process of jhāna is the effect.
3. Wise attention (mind-door adverting, and twelve kinds of consciousness + mental factors) is the cause, and the consciousness of the first javana of the cognitive process of jhāna is the effect.

The method of discerning the second through the last javanas of the cognitive process of jhāna is almost the same as the method of discerning the first javana of the cognitive process of jhāna. Numbers 1–3a and 3c of the three present causes of the aggregate of feeling of the first javana of the cognitive process of jhāna are the same, and the only differences are that 3b changes to the relevant javana of the cognitive process of jhāna and "the consciousness + mental factors of the preceding javana of the cognitive process of jhāna" is added as 3d.

They are summarized like this: In the case of the second javana of the cognitive process of jhāna, 3b changes to "the second javana," and "the consciousness + mental factors of the first javana of the cognitive process of jhāna" is added as 3d. In the case of the third javana of the cognitive process of jhāna, 3b changes to "the third javana," and "the consciousness + mental factors of the second javana of the cognitive process of jhāna" is added as 3d. In the case of the fourth javana of the cognitive process of jhāna, 3b changes to "the fourth javana," and "the consciousness + mental factors of the third javana of the cognitive process of jhāna" is added as 3d. This progression continues through the last javana of the cognitive process of jhāna.

The Five Aggregates of the Javanas of Wholesome Consciousnesses of the Mind-Door Cognitive Process

To this point, we have discerned the causes and effects of the five aggregates of mind-door adverting of the cognitive process of jhāna, the javanas of access concentration, and the javanas of the cognitive process of jhāna. Now we will discern the causes and effects of the five aggregates of the mind-door adverting, the javanas, and registration that arises after the javanas of the mind-door-only cognitive process. However, since we have discerned the causes and effects of the five aggregates of mind-door adverting in the cognitive process of jhāna, I have omitted that discussion here.

We will first look at the javanas of wholesome consciousnesses. Wholesome consciousnesses arise if we develop wise attention while seeing dhammas, and unwholesome consciousnesses arise if we develop unwise attention. For example, a wholesome consciousness arises if we determine while seeing eye-sensitive materiality that "this is materiality," and an unwholesome consciousness associated with greed and conceit arises if we determine that "I can see eye-sensitive materiality."

Although I have already mentioned wise attention and unwise attention while explaining meditation on mentality, in order to help us understand, I will point out one thing further about wise attention and then move on. There is wise attention when greed, hatred, and delusion are absent in the javana consciousness. To express it differently, wise attention is knowing materiality and mentality as they are and seeing them as impermanent, suffering, nonself, and impure.

Wholesome consciousness javanas arise seven times after mind-door adverting that has wise attention. Registration arises twice if it takes ultimate reality as its object, and registration doesn't arise if it doesn't take ultimate reality as an object. The javana mind moments of wholesome cognitive process have wholesome consciousness + mental factors. Since the mentality of the javana mind moments of wholesome cognitive process does not arise dependent on past causes and only arises dependent on present causes, there are no past causes and only present causes of the mentality of the javana mind moments of wholesome cognitive process. In other words, there are only present causes of the aggregates of feeling, perception, mental formations, and consciousness of the javana mind moments of wholesome cognitive process. In contrast, there are both past and present causes of the aggregate of form of the javana mind moments of wholesome cognitive process.

Now we discern the causes and effects of the five aggregates of the javana mind moments of wholesome consciousnesses that arise seven times.

There are past and present causes of the aggregate of form of the first javana of a wholesome consciousness. They are the same as the past and present causes of the form of bhavaṅga, mind-door adverting, and the javanas that we examined earlier.

Let's look into the aggregate of feeling of the first javana of a wholesome consciousness. As I explained in meditation on mentality, there are eight kinds of wholesome consciousnesses. Among these eight, let's look at a wholesome consciousness accompanied by joy and associated with knowledge as an example. There are thirty-four consciousness + mental factors in a wholesome consciousness accompanied by joy and associated with knowledge. The feeling of the javanas of this consciousness is summarized as follows:

Three Present Causes

1. Base (the heart base: six kinds of kalāpas, or the fifty-four kinds of materiality) is the cause, and the feeling of the first javana of the wholesome consciousness is the effect.
2. The object is the cause, and the feeling of the first javana of the wholesome consciousness is the effect.
3. Contact:
   a. The contact of the mind of bhavaṅga (thirty-four kinds of consciousness + mental factors) is the cause, and the feeling of the first javana of the wholesome consciousness is the effect.
   b. The contact of the mind of the first javana of the wholesome consciousness (thirty-three kinds of consciousness + mental factors excluding feeling) is the cause, and the feeling of the first javana of the wholesome consciousness is the effect.

c. Wise attention (mind-door adverting, and twelve consciousness
+ mental factors) is the cause, and the feeling of the first javana
of the wholesome consciousness is the effect.

If we look at the aggregate of perception of the first javana of the wholesome consciousness, numbers 1–3a and 3c are the same as for the aggregate of feeling of the first javana of the wholesome consciousness. In 3b
it changes to "thirty-three kinds of consciousness + mental factors aside
from perception."

It is the same for the aggregate of mental formations of the first javana of
the wholesome consciousness. Numbers 1–3a and 3c are the same as for the
aggregate of feeling of the first javana of the wholesome consciousness, and it
changes to "thirty-three kinds of consciousness + mental factors aside from
mental formations" in 3b.

The aggregate of consciousness of the first javana of the wholesome consciousness is as follows:

Three Present Causes
1. The contact of the mind of bhavaṅga (thirty-four kinds
   of consciousness + mental factors) is the cause, and the
   consciousness of the first javana of the wholesome cognitive
   process is the effect.
2. Mentality of the first javana of the wholesome cognitive process
   (the thirty-three mental factors that accompany consciousness)
   and materiality (base and object) are the cause, and the
   consciousness of the first javana of the wholesome cognitive
   process is the effect.
3. Wise attention (mind-door adverting, and twelve kinds of
   consciousness + mental factors) is the cause, and the consciousness
   of the first javana of the wholesome cognitive process is the effect.

The method of discerning the second through seventh javanas of a
wholesome cognitive process is almost the same as the method of discern-

ing the first javana of a wholesome cognitive process. The only differences are that 3b of the three present causes of the aggregate of feeling of the first javana of the wholesome consciousness changes to the relevant javana of the wholesome consciousness, and the consciousness + mental factors of the preceding javana of the wholesome consciousness is added as 3d. For example, in the case of the second javana of a wholesome consciousness, 3b changes to "the second wholesome consciousness," and "the consciousness + mental factors of the first javana of the wholesome consciousness" is added as 3d. In the case of the third javana of a wholesome consciousness, 3b changes to "the third wholesome consciousness," and "the consciousness + mental factors of the second javana of the wholesome consciousness" is added as 3d. It progresses this way through the seventh javana of a wholesome consciousness.

This happens because in order for a certain consciousness to arise, the preceding consciousness must always pass away. In other words, the first javana of a wholesome cognitive process must pass away in order for the second javana of a wholesome cognitive process to arise, eye consciousness must pass away in order for receiving to arise, and receiving must pass away in order for investigation to arise. This is why the consciousness + mental factors of a preceding consciousness are there as the present causes.

The javanas of the remaining seven kinds of wholesome consciousnesses can be discerned in the same way as with a wholesome consciousness accompanied by joy and associated with knowledge.

The Five Aggregates of the Javanas of the Unwholesome Consciousnesses of the Mind-Door Cognitive Process

Next we discern the causes and effects of the five aggregates of the javanas of unwholesome consciousnesses. Unwholesome consciousnesses arise dependent on unwise attention. Unwholesome consciousnesses are consciousnesses associated with greed, hatred, and delusion. As I explained in meditation on mentality, consciousnesses associated with greed are divided into eight kinds depending on whether they are associated with greed and wrong view or with greed and conceit, or greed alone, whether each of those are accompanied by joy or by equanimity, and whether or not they are prompted. Consciousnesses associated with hatred are divided into eight kinds depending on whether they are only associated with hatred, associated with hatred and envy, associated with hatred and avarice, associated with hatred and remorse, and whether or not each of these are prompted. Consciousnesses associated with delusion are divided into two kinds depending on whether or not they are associated with doubt. The consciousness and mental factors of each of these are different. The specific details are explained in the section "The Five-Door Cognitive Process" and table 6 "Wholesome and Unwholesome Consciousnesses" in chapter 4.

If we develop unwise attention taking dhamma as object, mind-door adverting and the javanas of an unwholesome consciousness arise seven times, and sometimes registration arises twice and sometimes it doesn't. Discerning the causes and effects of the five aggregates of mind-door adverting is the same as explained above. Discerning the causes and effects of the five aggregates of the seven javanas of an unwholesome consciousness is also the same as discerning the causes and effects of the five aggregates of the javanas of a wholesome consciousness explained above. The only thing that is different is the number of consciousness + mental factors.

The Five Aggregates of Registration of the Mind-Door Cognitive Process

Once the javanas of the mind-door cognitive process pass away, registration sometimes arises and sometimes doesn't. Registration arises in the case of objects of ultimate reality. Registration doesn't arise for concepts. When it does arise, registration arises twice. The registration is either registration of a wholesome consciousness or registration of an unwholesome consciousness. In the case where registration arises, we discern the causes and effects of the five aggregates of registration.

Registration is a resultant consciousness. Therefore there are past and present causes of all of the five aggregates of registration.

The past and present causes of the aggregate of form of the first registration are the same as the past and present causes of the form of bhavaṅga, mind-door adverting, and the javanas that we have already looked at. We can refer to those previous discussions.

Let's look into the causes and effects of the aggregate of feeling of the first registration.

There are both past and present causes of the feeling of the first registration, and we will look at them taking a wholesome consciousness accompanied by joy and associated with knowledge as an example. (When seeing an unwholesome consciousness, all we have to do is change the consciousness + mental factors to those of an unwholesome consciousness.)

Five Past Causes
1. Ignorance is the cause, and the feeling of the first registration is the effect.
2. Craving is the cause, and the feeling of the first registration is the effect.
3. Clinging is the cause, and the feeling of the first registration is the effect.
4. Formations are the cause, and the feeling of the first registration is the effect.
5. Kamma is the cause, and the feeling of the first registration is the effect.

Three Present Causes
1. Material base (six kinds of kalāpas, or the fifty-four kinds of materiality) is the cause, and the feeling of the first registration is the effect.
2. The object is the cause, and the feeling of the first registration is the effect.
3. Contact:
   a. The contact of the mind of bhavaṅga (thirty-four kinds of consciousness + mental factors) is the cause, and the feeling of the first registration is the effect.
   b. The contact of the mind of the seventh javana (thirty-four kinds

of consciousness + mental factors) is the cause, and the feeling
of the first registration is the effect.

c. The contact of the mind of the first registration (thirty-three
kinds of consciousness + mental factors excluding feeling) is the
cause, and the feeling of the first registration is the effect.

If we look at the aggregate of perception of the first registration, it is almost
the same as the aggregate of feeling of the first registration. Everything is the
same except 3c changes to "the thirty-three kinds of consciousness + mental
factors excluding perception."

Likewise, for the aggregate of mental formations of the first registration,
everything is the same except 3c changes to "the thirty-three kinds of consciousness + mental factors excluding mental formations, which is volition."

The five past causes of the aggregate of consciousness of the first registration are the same as for the aggregate of feeling of the first registration.
However, the three present causes change as follows:

Three Present Causes
1. The contact of the mind of bhavaṅga (thirty-four kinds of
consciousness + mental factors) is the cause, and the consciousness
of the first registration is the effect.
2. The contact of the mind of the seventh javana (thirty-four kinds of
consciousness + mental factors) is the cause, and the consciousness
of the first registration is the effect.
3. The mentality of the first registration (the thirty-three kinds of
mental factors that accompany consciousness) and materiality
(base and object) is the cause, and the consciousness of the first
registration is the effect.

The method of discerning the second registration is almost the same as the
method of discerning the first registration. The only differences are that
among the three present causes 3b changes to "the contact of the mind of
the first registration (thirty-four kinds of consciousness + mental factors)"

and 3c changes to "the contact of the mind of the second registration (the thirty-three kinds of consciousness + mental factors [excluding the appropriate mental factor])."

The Five-Door Cognitive Process

The Five Aggregates of Five-Door Adverting

Up to this point we have discerned the causes and effects of the five aggregates in the mind-door-only cognitive process: mind-door adverting; the javanas of the cognitive process of jhāna and of wholesome and unwholesome consciousnesses; and registration.

Now we discern the causes and effects of the five aggregates in the five-door cognitive process and the mind-door cognitive process that arises following the five-door cognitive process. I will omit the things that overlap with what we've already discerned in the mind-door-only cognitive process, and focus only on the differences. We begin with discerning the aggregates of five-door adverting.

If we take the eye-door cognitive process as an example from the five-door cognitive process, when a visible form impinges on eye sensitivity and the attention that intends to see that visible form forms, eye-door adverting arises as bhavaṅga passes away. The ear-door, nose-door, tongue-door, body-door, and mind-door cognitive processes also work in the same way.

The mentality of five-door adverting doesn't arise through past causes but rather as a functional consciousness; it is a consciousness that simply performs its function. In other words, there are no past causes of the aggregates of feeling, perception, mental formations, and consciousness of five-door adverting. Since they arise through present causes, there are only present causes. In contrast, there are past and present causes of the aggregate of form of five-door adverting. They are the same as for the form of bhavaṅga, mind-door adverting, javanas, and registration that we have seen earlier. Therefore, when we discern the form of five-door adverting, all we have to do is refer to the method of discerning the past and present causes of the aggregate of form described previously.

Now let's look at the present causes of the aggregate of feeling of five-door adverting, still using eye-door adverting as an example, and see what is different about the aggregates of perception, mental formations, and consciousness.

Three Present Causes

1. Base (the heart base: six kinds of kalāpas, or the fifty-four kinds of materiality) is the cause, and the feeling of eye-door adverting is the effect.

2. The object (visible form) is the cause, and the feeling of eye-door adverting is the effect.

3. Contact:

   a. The contact of the mind of bhavaṅga (thirty-four kinds of consciousness + mental factors) is the cause, and the feeling of eye-door adverting is the effect.

   b. The contact of the mind of eye-door adverting (ten kinds of consciousness + mental factors excluding feeling) is the cause, and the feeling of eye-door adverting is the effect.

If we look at the aggregate of perception of eye-door adverting, it is almost the same as the aggregate of feeling of eye-door adverting. The only difference is that 3b changes to "ten kinds of consciousness + mental factors excluding perception."

It is the same for the aggregate of mental formations of eye-door adverting. Numbers 1–3a are the same as the aggregate of feeling and 3b changes to "ten kinds of consciousness + mental factors excluding mental formations."

The aggregate of consciousness of eye-door adverting is as follows:

Two Present Causes

1. The contact of the mind of bhavaṅga (thirty-four kinds of consciousness + mental factors) is the cause, and the consciousness of eye-door adverting is the effect.

2. The mentality of eye-door adverting (the ten kinds of mental factors that accompany consciousness) and materiality (base and object) are the cause, and the consciousness of eye-door adverting is the effect.

The five-door adverting that arises in the ear door, nose door, tongue door, and body door only differs from the five-door adverting that arises in the eye door in terms of objects. Thus, the object becomes sound for the ear consciousness, smell for the nose consciousness, taste for the tongue consciousness, and touch for the body consciousness. The rest is the same as the five-door adverting that arises in the eye door described above.

The Five Aggregates of the Five Consciousnesses

Following five-door adverting, we discern the causes and effect of the five aggregates of eye consciousness, ear consciousness, nose consciousness, tongue consciousness, and body consciousness. Again I will look in detail at eye consciousness and then mention only the differences for the others.

The five sense consciousnesses of the five-door cognitive process, along with the following processes of receiving and investigation, all arise as resultant consciousnesses. Eye consciousnesses arise as resultant consciousnesses. Therefore there are both past and present causes of an eye consciousness.

Since the past and present causes of the aggregate of form of eye consciousness are the same as those of the aggregate of form of bhavaṅga, mind-door adverting, javanas, registration, and five-door adverting, all we have to do is discern them by referring to what has been explained previously.

Now we will look at the aggregate of feeling of eye consciousness, which as both past and present causes.

Five Past Causes
1. Ignorance is the cause, and the feeling of eye consciousness is the effect.
2. Craving is the cause, and the feeling of eye consciousness is the effect.
3. Clinging is the cause, and the feeling of eye consciousness is the effect.
4. Formations are the cause, and the feeling of eye consciousness is the effect.

5. Kamma is the cause, and the feeling of eye consciousness is the effect.

Five Present Causes

1. Material base (eye base: six kinds of kalāpas, or the fifty-four kinds of materiality) is the cause, and the feeling of eye consciousness is the effect.

2. The object (visible form) is the cause, and the feeling of eye consciousness is the effect.

3. The contact of the eye (seven kinds of consciousness + mental factors excluding feeling) is the cause, and the feeling of eye consciousness is the effect.

4. Light is the cause, and the feeling of eye consciousness is the effect.

5. Attention (eye-door adverting, eleven kinds of consciousness + mental factors) is the cause, and the feeling of eye consciousness is the effect.

Next we will look at the aggregate of perception of eye consciousness, which is almost the same as the aggregate of feeling of eye consciousness. The only difference is that among the five present causes, number 3 changes to "seven kinds of consciousness + mental factors excluding perception."

It is the same for the aggregate of mental formations of eye consciousness. The only difference is that among the five present causes, number 3 changes to "seven kinds of consciousness + mental factors excluding mental formations."

The aggregate of consciousness of eye consciousness is as follows. The five past causes are the same as for the aggregate of feeling of eye consciousness, and the present causes are as follows:

Three Present Causes:

1. Mentality (seven kinds of mental factors that accompany consciousness) and materiality (base and visible form) are the cause, and the consciousness of eye consciousness is the effect.

2. Light is the cause, and the consciousness of eye consciousness is the effect.

3. Attention (eye-door adverting, eleven kinds of consciousness
    + mental factors) is the cause, and the consciousness of eye
    consciousness is the effect.

When the consciousnesses that arise in the ear, nose, tongue, and body doors are compared with the eye consciousness that arises in the eye door, only the object and the cause of the arising of that consciousness are different; the rest is the same. Sound is the object and space is the cause of ear consciousness, smell is the object and the element of wind is the cause of nose consciousness, taste is the object and the element of water is the cause of tongue consciousness, and touch is the object and the element of earth is the cause of body consciousness.

The Five Aggregates of Receiving

Then we discern the causes and effects of the five aggregates of receiving that arises after the five consciousnesses. Again I will look in detail at receiving that arises after eye consciousness and then only mention the differences for receiving that arises after ear, nose, tongue, body, and mind consciousness.

Receiving arises as a resultant consciousness. Therefore receiving has both past and present causes. We will look at the past and present causes of the five aggregates of receiving.

First, there are past and present causes of the aggregate of form of receiving. Since they are the same as the past and present causes of the aggregate of form of bhavaṅga, mind-door adverting, javanas, registration, five-door adverting, and eye consciousness, all we have to do is discern them by referring to what has been explained previously.

Now we will look at the past and present causes of the aggregate of feeling of receiving. The five past causes are the same as the five past causes of the aggregate of feeling of eye consciousness, and the three present causes are as follows:

Three Present Causes
1. Material base (the heart base: six kinds of kalāpas, or the fifty-four

kinds of materiality) is the cause, and the feeling of receiving is the effect.

2. The object (visible form) is the cause, and the feeling of receiving is the effect.

3. Contact:

    a. The contact of the eye (eight kinds of consciousness + mental factors excluding feeling) is the cause, and the feeling of receiving is the effect.

    b. The contact of the mind of receiving (ten kinds of consciousness + mental factors excluding feeling) is the cause, and the feeling of receiving is the effect.

If we look at the aggregate of perception of receiving, everything is the same as the aggregate of feeling of receiving except that 3b changes to "ten kinds of consciousness + mental factors excluding perception."

It is the same for the aggregate of mental formations of receiving. Everything is the same as for aggregate of feeling of receiving except that 3b changes to "ten kinds of consciousness + mental factors excluding mental formations."

The five past causes of the aggregate of consciousness of receiving are the same as the aggregate of feeling of receiving, and the present causes are the following:

Two Present Causes

1. The contact of the eye (eight kinds of consciousness + mental factors) is the cause, and the consciousness of receiving is the effect.

2. The mentality of receiving (the ten kinds of mental factors that accompany consciousness) and materiality (base and visible form) is the cause, and the consciousness of receiving is the effect.

Receiving that arises in the ear, nose, tongue, and body doors is the same as the receiving that arises in the eye door except for their objects and consciousnesses. For the ear door, sound is the object and ear consciousness is the consciousness; for the nose door, smell is the object and nose consciousness is the consciousness; for the tongue door, taste is the object and tongue consciousness is the consciousness; and for the body door, touch is the object and body consciousness is the consciousness.

The Five Aggregates of Investigation

Then we discern the causes and effects of the five aggregates of investigation that arises following receiving. Again, after looking in detail at investigation that arises after eye consciousness, I will only mention the differences for investigation that arises after ear, nose, tongue, and body consciousness.

Investigation arises as a resultant consciousness. Therefore there are both past and present causes of investigation. We will look at the past and present causes of the five aggregates of investigation.

First we will look at the past and present causes of the aggregate of form of investigation. Since they are the same as the aggregate of form of receiving, and of all the other processes before, all we have to do refer to the previous discussions.

The aggregates of feeling, perception, mental formations, and consciousness of investigation are similar to those of receiving. The only difference that can be distinguished is that the number of mental factors differs depending on whether or not joy is present in the consciousness of investigation. The five past causes of the aggregate of feeling of investigation are the same as the five past causes of the aggregate of feeling of receiving, and the five present causes are as follows:

Five Present Causes
1. Material base (the heart base: six kinds of kalāpas, or the fifty-four kinds of materiality) is the cause, and the feeling of investigation is the effect.
2. The object (visible form) is the cause, and the feeling of investigation is the effect.
3. Contact:
   a. The contact of the eye (eight kinds of consciousness + mental factors) is the cause, and the feeling of investigation is the effect.

b. The contact of the mind of receiving (eleven kinds of consciousness + mental factors) is the cause, and the feeling of investigation is the effect.

c. The contact of the mind of investigation (ten or eleven kinds of consciousness + mental factors excluding feeling) is the cause, and the feeling of investigation is the effect.

The aggregate of perception of investigation is the same as the aggregate of feeling of investigation except that 3c changes to "ten or eleven kinds of consciousness + mental factors excluding perception."

It is the same for the aggregate of mental formations of investigation. Everything is the same as for the aggregate of feeling of investigation except that 3c changes to "ten or eleven kinds of consciousness + mental factors excluding mental formations."

The five past causes of the aggregate of consciousness of investigation are the same as for the feeling of investigation, and the present causes are the following:

Three Present Causes

1. The contact of the eye (eight kinds of consciousness + mental factors) is the cause, and the consciousness of investigation is the effect.

2. The contact of the mind of receiving (eleven kinds of consciousness + mental factors) is the cause, and the consciousness of investigation is the effect.

3. The mentality of investigation (the ten or eleven kinds of mental factors that accompany consciousness) and materiality (base and visible form) are the cause, and the consciousness of investigation is the effect.

Investigation that arises in the ear, nose, tongue, and body doors is the same as investigation that arises in the eye door except for their objects and consciousness. For the ear door, sound is the object and ear consciousness is the consciousness; for the nose door, smell is the object and nose consciousness is the consciousness; for the tongue door, taste is the object and tongue consciousness is the consciousness; and for the body door, touch is the object and body consciousness is the consciousness.

The Five Aggregates of Determining

We next discern the causes and effects of the five aggregates of determining that arises following investigation. The mentality of determining doesn't arise through past causes but simply performs its function. Therefore there are only present causes of the aggregates of feeling, perception, mental formations, and consciousness of determining. Again, after looking in detail at determining that arises after eye consciousness, I will only mention the differences for determining that arises after ear, nose, tongue, and body consciousness.

First, in contrast to the other aggregates of determining, there are both past and present causes of the aggregate of form of determining. Since they are the same as in the case of the aggregate of form of all the other processes we have covered, all we have to do is discern them by referring to the previous discussions.

Now let's look at the present causes of the aggregate of feeling of determining and then see what is different about the aggregates of perception, mental formations, and consciousness.

Three Present Causes
1. Material base (the heart base: six kinds of kalāpas, or the fifty-four kinds of materiality) is the cause, and the feeling of determining is the effect.
2. The object (visible form) is the cause, and the feeling of determining is the effect.
3. Contact:
   a. The contact of the eye (eight kinds of consciousness + mental factors) is the cause, and the feeling of determining is the effect.
   b. The contact of the mind of investigation (eleven or twelve kinds

of consciousness + mental factors) is the cause, and the feeling of determining is the effect.

c. The contact of the mind of determining (eleven kinds of consciousness + mental factors excluding feeling) is the cause, and the feeling of determining is the effect.

If we look at the aggregate of perception of determining, everything is the same as for the aggregate of feeling of determining except that 3c changes to "eleven kinds of consciousness + mental factors excluding perception."

It is the same for the aggregate of mental formations of determining. Everything is the same as for the aggregate of feeling of determining except that 3c changes to "eleven kinds of consciousness + mental factors excluding mental formations."

The aggregate of consciousness of determining is as follows:

Three Present Causes
1. The contact of the eye (eight kinds of consciousness + mental factors) is the cause, and the consciousness of determining is the effect.
2. The contact of the mind of investigation (eleven or twelve kinds of consciousness + mental factors) is the cause, and the feeling of determining is the effect.
3. The mentality of determining (the eleven mental factors that accompany consciousness) and materiality (base and object) are the cause, and the consciousness of determining is the effect.

Determining that arises in ear, nose, tongue, and body doors is the same as determining that arises after eye door except for their objects and consciousnesses. For the ear door, sound is the object and ear consciousness is the consciousness; for the nose door, smell is the object and nose consciousness is the consciousness; for the tongue door, taste is the object and tongue consciousness is the consciousness; and for the body door, touch is the object and body consciousness is the consciousness.

The Five Aggregates of the Javanas of the Five-Door Cognitive Process

Javana mind moments of the five-door cognitive process arise following determining. Javana mind moments of the five-door cognitive process arise seven times. Since the mentality of javanas does not arise dependent on past causes and only arises dependent on present causes, there are no past causes of the mentality of javanas. In other words, although there are past and present causes of the form of javanas, there are only present causes of the feeling, perception, mental formations, and consciousness of javanas.

As an example, we will look in detail at the five aggregates of the first javana in the eye-door cognitive process, using a wholesome consciousness accompanied by joy and associated with knowledge. When seeing unwholesome consciousnesses, all we have to do is turn the consciousnesses + mental factors of wholesome consciousnesses into the consciousnesses + mental factors of unwholesome consciousnesses. This is a case where there are thirty-four consciousness + mental factors. We will then look at the differences for the other six javanas.

There are past and present causes of the aggregate of form of the first javana. Since they are the same as the past and present causes of the aggregate of form of all the other processes we have looked at, all we have to do is discern them by referring to the explanations given previously.

Now let's look at the aggregate of feeling of the first javana. We will look at the present causes of the feeling of the first javana and then see what's different about the aggregates of perception, mental formations, and consciousness.

Three Present Causes
1. Material base (the heart base: six kinds of kalāpas, or the fifty-four kinds of materiality) is the cause, and the feeling of the first javana is the effect.
2. The object (visible form) is the cause, and the feeling of the first javana is the effect.
3. Contact:
    a. The contact of the eye (eight kinds of consciousness + mental factors) is the cause, and the feeling of the first javana is the effect.

b. The contact of the mind of the first javana (thirty-three kinds of consciousness + mental factors excluding feeling) is the cause, and the feeling of the first javana is the effect.

c. Wise attention (determining, twelve kinds of consciousness + mental factors) is the cause, and the feeling of the first javana is the effect.

If we look at the aggregate of perception of the first javana, everything is the same as for the aggregate of feeling of the first javana except number 3b changes to "thirty-three kinds of consciousness + mental factors excluding perception."

For the aggregate of mental formations of the first javana, everything is the same as for the aggregate of feeling of the first javana except number 3b changes to "thirty-three kinds of consciousness + mental factors excluding mental formations."

The aggregate of consciousness of the first javana is as follows:

Three Present Causes

1. The contact of the eye (eight kinds of consciousness + mental factors) is the cause, and the consciousness of the first javana is the effect.

2. The mentality of the first javana (the thirty-three kinds of mental factors that accompany consciousness) and materiality (base and visible form) are the causes, and the consciousness of the first javana is the effect.

3. Wise attention (determining, twelve kinds of consciousness + mental factors) is the cause, and the consciousness of the first javana is the effect.

The method of discerning the second through seventh javanas is almost the same as the method of discerning the first javana. The only differences are that 3b of the three present causes of the aggregate of feeling of the first javana of the wholesome consciousness changes to the contact of the mind of the relevant javana (thirty-three kinds of consciousness + mental factors excluding the relevant mental factor), and for each javana the contact of the mind of the previous javana (the number of consciousness + mental factors) is added as 3d. In other words, for example, in the case of the second javana, 3b changes to "the contact of the mind of the second javana (thirty-three kinds of consciousness + mental factors excluding [the relevant mental factor])," and "the thirty-four kinds of consciousness + mental factors of the first javana" is added as 3d. In the case of the third javana, 3b changes to "the contact of the mind of the third javana (thirty-three kinds of consciousness + mental factors excluding [the relevant mental factor])," and "the thirty-four kinds of consciousness + mental factors of the second javana" is added as 3d. All we have to do is discern each successive javana this way through the seventh javana.

This happens because in order for a certain consciousness to arise, the preceding consciousness must always pass away. The first javana must pass away in order for the second javana to arise, eye consciousness must pass away in order for receiving to arise, and receiving must pass away in order for investigation to arise. This is why the consciousness + mental factors of a preceding consciousness are there as the present causes.

The seven javanas that arise in ear, nose, tongue, and body consciousness are the same as the seven javanas that arise in eye consciousness except for their objects and consciousnesses. For the ear door, sound is the object and ear consciousness is the consciousness; for the nose door, smell is the object and nose consciousness is the consciousness; for the tongue door, taste is the object and tongue consciousness is the consciousness; and for the body door, touch is the object and body consciousness is the consciousness.

The Five Aggregates of Registration of the Five-Door Cognitive Process

When the javanas of the five-door cognitive process pass away, sometimes registration of the five-door cognitive process arises and sometimes it doesn't. When registration does arise, it arises twice. Since registration arises in the case of objects of ultimate reality and when the force of impact of the object on the respective sense sensitivity is strong, registration can arise if the ultimate reality of the color of a group of kalāpas is taken as the object of eye consciousness. Registration doesn't arise for concepts. The registration is either of a wholesome consciousness or of an unwholesome consciousness.

In the case where registration arises, we discern the causes and effects of the five aggregates of registration. Registration is a resultant consciousness. Therefore there are past and present causes of all of the five aggregates of registration. We will look at registration that occurs in an eye-door cognitive process as an example.

The past and present causes of the aggregate of form of the first registration are the same as the past and present causes of the aggregate of form of all the other processes we have examined previously.

There are also past and present causes of the aggregate of feeling of the first registration. As an example, we will look at the past and present causes of the feeling of the first registration in a wholesome cognitive process accompanied by joy and associated with knowledge. (When we see unwholesome cognitive processes, all we have to do is change the consciousness + mental factors of wholesome consciousnesses to those of unwholesome consciousnesses.) The past causes of the feeling of the first registration are the same as the past causes of investigation. The five present causes of the feeling of the first registration are as follows.

Five Present Causes

1. Material base (the heart base: six kinds of kalāpas, or the fifty-four kinds of materiality) is the cause, and the feeling of the first registration is the effect.

2. The object (visible form) is the cause, and the feeling of the first registration is the effect.

3. Contact:
    a. The contact of the eye (eight kinds of consciousness + mental factors) is the cause, and the feeling of the first registration is the effect.
    b. The contact of the mind of the seventh javana (thirty-four kinds

of consciousness + mental factors) is the cause, and the feeling
of the first registration is the effect.

c. The contact of the mind of the first registration (thirty-three
kinds of consciousness + mental factors excluding feeling) is the
cause, and the feeling of the first registration is the effect.

If we look at the aggregate of perception of the first registration, everything
is the same as for the aggregate of feeling of the first registration except 3c
changes to "thirty-three kinds of consciousness + mental factors excluding
perception."

For the aggregate of mental formations of the first registration, everything
is the same as for the aggregate of feeling of the first registration except 3c
changes to "thirty-three kinds of consciousness + mental factors excluding
mental formations."

The past causes of the aggregate of consciousness of the first registration
are the same as the past causes of investigation. The three present causes of
the consciousness of the first registration are as follows:

Three Present Causes
1. The contact of the eye (eight kinds of consciousness + mental
factors) is the cause, and the consciousness of the first registration
is the effect.
2. The contact of the mind of the seventh javana (thirty-four kinds of
consciousness + mental factors) is the cause, and the consciousness
of the first registration is the effect.
3. The mentality of the first registration (the thirty-three kinds of
consciousness + mental factors that accompany consciousness)
and materiality (base and visible form) are the causes, and the
consciousness of the first registration is the effect.

The method of discerning the second registration is almost the same as
the method of discerning the first registration. The only differences are that
3b of the five present causes changes to "the contact of the mind of the first

registration (thirty-four kinds of consciousness + mental factors)" and 3c changes to "the contact of the mind of the second registration (thirty-three kinds of consciousness + mental factors excluding [the relevant mental factor])."

Registration that arises after ear, nose, tongue, and body consciousness is the same as registration that arises after eye consciousness except for their objects and consciousnesses. For the ear door, sound is the object and ear consciousness is the consciousness; for the nose door, smell is the object and nose consciousness is the consciousness; for the tongue door, taste is the object and tongue consciousness is the consciousness; and for the body door, touch is the object and body consciousness is the consciousness.

The Five Aggregates of the Mind-Door Cognitive Process that Arises after the Five-Door Cognitive Process

The causes and effects of the five aggregates of mind-door adverting, javanas, and registration that arise after the five-door cognitive process differ from those of the five aggregates in the mind-door-only cognitive process, in that they add the following one present cause to the causes and effects listed above: in the case of the eye door, the contact of the eye (eight kinds of consciousness + mental factors); in the case of the ear door, the contact of the ear (eight kinds of consciousness + mental factors); in the case of the nose door, the contact of the nose (eight kinds of consciousness + mental factors); in the case of the tongue door, the contact of the tongue (eight kinds of consciousness + mental factors); and in the case of the body door, the contact of the body (eight kinds of consciousness + mental factors).

Discerning the Causes and Effects of Five Previous Existences

By taking our first past life as the past and our present life as the present, we have discerned the five past causes (ignorance, craving, clinging, formations, kamma) and the five present causes (consciousness, mentality-materiality, the six sense bases, contact, feeling) in all of the cognitive processes. We have discerned the five present effects through the five aggregates.

Now we will discern the five past causes and the five present causes of all of the cognitive processes by taking our second past life as the past and our first past life as the present. The method of discerning is the same as before. All we have to do is discern the causes and effects in the five aggregates of the cognitive process of the first past life by discerning the five past causes of ignorance, craving, clinging, formations, and kamma in our second past life.

First we discern the ignorance, craving, clinging, formations, and kamma of our second past life. My second past life was as a dog. The ignorance, craving, and clinging of this life was that I wanted to become a human being. The craving and clinging of wanting to be a human being was on the basis of the ignorance of presuming a "human being" existed as such. Ignorance, craving, and clinging were "consciousnesses of greed associated with wrong view." When I saw the formations at the time of death of my second past life, the sign was the image of a person who practiced meditation in past lives, and there were thirty-four kinds of consciousness + mental factors including wisdom and joy. The sign of rebirth-linking of my first past life was the same as the sign at the time of death of my second past life.

We discern how the five causes of our second previous life operated as the causes in all of the cognitive processes of our first past life. And then we also discern the present causes of our first past life. We do it in the same way as when we take our first past life as the past and our present life as the present. Although our first past life and obviously our second past life are actually both the past, we take the first past life as the present as a reference point for discerning effects.

After discerning the causes and effects of the five aggregates of all of the cognitive processes by taking our second past life as the past and our first past life as the present, we discern the causes and effects by taking our third past life as the past and our second past life as the present. In order to do that, we have to discern the five past causes of ignorance, craving, clinging, formations, and kamma in our third past life.

My third past life was as an Indian man. I had wrong view in a religious context as a Hindu. I performed sacrificial ceremonies on animals, and I incorrectly believed that I would attain something if I performed these ceremonies. These are unwholesome. Wrong view is ignorance. Because of ignorance, craving and clinging arose. The sign at the time of death was a dog.

The formations were twenty kinds of consciousness + mental factors including ignorance and wrong view. The kamma was performing sacrificial ceremonies on animals, and greed and wrong view were also present. The sign of rebirth-linking of my second past life was also a dog. As an investigating consciousness accompanied by equanimity, there were eleven kinds of consciousness + mental factors for rebirth-linking of a dog. By taking these five past causes, I discerned the causes and effects of the five aggregates of all of the cognitive processes of my second past life.

After discerning the causes and effects of the five aggregates of all of the cognitive processes by taking our third past life as the past and our second past life as the present, we can then discern the causes and effects by taking our fourth past life as the past and our third past life as the present. In order to do that we have to discern the five past causes of ignorance, craving, clinging, formations, and kamma in our fourth past life.

My fourth past life was as a heavenly being. The sign at the time of death was the image of a practitioner. The ignorance, craving, and clinging were related to human existence. Wrongly thinking that there is human life; this is ignorance. Because of ignorance, craving and clinging arose. The formations were thirty-four kinds of consciousness + mental factors including joy and wisdom. By taking these five past causes I discerned the causes and effects of the five aggregates of all of the cognitive processes of my third past life.

Then we can discern the causes and effects by taking our fifth past life as the past and our fourth past life as the present. In order to do that, we have to discern the five past causes of our fifth past life.

My fifth past life was as a prince of Nepal. I helped many people with lots of loving-kindness, and I had thoughts of wanting to be reborn in heaven. I had the ignorance of presuming "a heavenly being" existed as such and the craving and clinging of wanting to be reborn in heaven. The sign at the time of death was heaven, and there were thirty-four kinds of consciousness + mental factors including joy and wisdom. The kamma was helping others. By taking these five past causes of ignorance, craving, clinging, formations, and kamma, I discerned the causes and effects of the five aggregates of all of the cognitive processes of my fourth past life.

With this we conclude discerning the cause and effects of our present life and five past lives through the fifth method of seeing dependent origination. Before going into the first method of seeing dependent origination, let's look at future lives.

Future Lives

The method of seeing future lives is the same as the method of seeing past lives. The only difference is that since future lives are not fixed, if the present state changes the future may also change.

Before seeing future lives, we discern the five aggregates externally, as we discussed earlier, after discerning the five aggregates at the mind door upon exiting each of the jhānas of ānāpānasati, the kasiṇas, and the immaterial jhānas. Then the five aggregates are discerned externally in the same way as they were discerned internally. Finally, we discern the five aggregates externally after discerning the five aggregates at the mind door upon exiting neither-perception-nor-nonperception. And then if we turn our attention by thinking, "how is our present life related to our future lives in terms of cause and effect?" our attention moves to mentality and materiality, the five aggregates of our future lives.

There are also two methods for seeing future lives: the method of moving slowly from the present moment and the method of moving directly to our future lives.

First I used the method of moving directly to my future lives. After discerning the mentality and materiality of the jhānas of ānāpānasati, the kasiṇas, the immaterial jhānas, and finally neither-perception-nor-nonperception, and then discerning the mentality and materiality externally, when I turned my attention thinking, "how will my future lives come to be through the causes of this present life?" my attention began moving to the future mentality and materiality, which moved continuously without stopping. Unlike when I discerned my past lives, I could not manage to see my future lives by way of moving directly to the future. When I saw my past lives, once one life ended the mentality and materiality stopped and that life unfolded itself to me, but this time the mentality and materiality moved continuously. It seemed like they wouldn't stop no matter how long I waited.

Therefore I used the other method. I moved gradually from my present life to the time of death of my present life. The ignorance, craving, and clinging of my present life was that I was going to become a monk in my next life. The sign at the time of death was that of a practitioner, and there were thirty-four kinds of consciousness + mental factors including joy and wisdom. Likewise, the sign of rebirth-linking of my first future life was also a practitioner and there were thirty-four kinds of consciousness + mental factors including joy and wisdom. In my first future life, I became a monk by ordaining early. As a monk I practiced much samatha and vipassanā meditation. There was light when practicing meditation. The sign at the time of death was heaven.

My second future life was as a heavenly being. The mentality and materiality moved for a long time. Masculinity was present in that heavenly being. I practiced much samatha meditation. The formations were the practice. My third future life was as a brahma, who had no materiality of sex. I practiced much samatha meditation. Again the mentality and materiality moved for a really long time, and I wonder whether that was because the life was very long. The ignorance was wanting to be reborn as a human in order to practice. The sign at the time of death was a practitioner. The formations were the practice. My fourth future life was that of a monk. I became a monk by ordaining early. As a monk I cultivated the jhānas, my nimitta was light, and I practiced vipassanā as well. After that I could not discern my fifth future life any more. The mentality and materiality reached their end. The mentality and materiality that were moving suddenly stopped and disappeared. There were no existences. I saw no more causal relationships. It must be because of cessation of ignorance, craving, and attachment.

Just as we have done for our past lives, we can also discern the causes and effects of the five aggregates of our future lives by connecting them to their preceding lives.

2. The First Method
The Forward Order of the Twelve Links of Dependent Origination

As discussed previously, the first method of seeing dependent origination is going in the forward order of the twelve links of dependent origination. It is seeing formations arising dependent on ignorance (*avijjāpaccayā saṅkhāra*), consciousness arising dependent on formations (*saṅkhārapaccayā viññāṇam*), mentality-materiality arising dependent on consciousness (*viññāṇapaccayā nāmarūpam*), the six sense bases arising dependent on mentality-material-ity (*nāmarūpapaccayā saḷāyatanam*), contact arising dependent on the six sense bases (*saḷāyatanapaccayā phasso*), feeling arising dependent on contact (*phassapaccayā vedanā*), craving arising dependent on feeling (*vedanāpaccayā taṇhā*), clinging arising dependent on craving (*taṇhāpaccayā upādānam*), existence arising dependent on clinging (*upādānapaccayā bhavo*), birth aris-ing dependent on existence (*bhavapaccayā jāti*), and old age, death, sorrow, lamentation, pain, dissatisfaction, and despair arising dependent on birth (*jātipaccayā jarāmaraṇamsokaparidevadukkhadomanassaupāyāsam*).

In this method, which is the most widely known among the methods of seeing dependent origination, we discern the twelve links of dependent origination one by one in terms of their causes and effects. First we see the twelve links of dependent origination by taking our first past life as the past, our current life as the present, and our first future life as the future. Once this is completed, we see the twelve links of dependent origination by tak-ing our second past life as the past, our first past life as the present, and our present life as the future. Through this method we see the twelve links of dependent origination by taking all five of our past lives as objects. Just as we did in the fifth method detailed above, we always discern dependent origi-nation through the first method after practicing the jhānas of ānāpānasati, the kasiṇas, and the immaterial jhānas.

Formations Arise Dependent on Ignorance

Taking our first past life as the past, we see the ignorance of our first past life and also the formations of our first past life. The formations of our first past life arose with ignorance of our first past life being the cause. Ignorance of our first past life is the cause, and formations of our first past life are the effect. Thus we discern both ignorance and formations of the first past life from the javanas of the mind-door cognitive process.

The ignorance of my first past life was "I want to become someone who studies Buddhism."

I discerned the ignorance of my first past life when I saw a monk in the eye-door cognitive process and the mind-door cognitive process. I discerned twenty kinds of consciousness + mental factors including greed and wrong view in the javanas of the mind-door cognitive process. This ignorance brought about the result of the formations of my first past life.

We see the formations at the time of death. The formations at the time of death become the formations that are connected to our next life.

The sign of the formations at the time of death in my first past life was a temple. They were the formations of the kamma of restoring and repairing that temple. I discerned thirty-four kinds of consciousness + mental factors including joy and wisdom in the javanas of the mind-door cognitive process. These were the formations of my first past life.

In this way we discern "formations arise dependent on ignorance," the first of the twelve links of dependent origination.

Consciousness Arises Dependent on Formations

Taking our first past life as the past, we see the formations that arose dependent on ignorance. In my case, they were the wholesome consciousness that has thirty-four consciousness + mental factors including joy and wisdom. This gives rise to the resultant consciousness of the present life.

There are two types of resultant consciousnesses: (1) the consciousnesses of rebirth-linking and bhavaṅga and the consciousness of the mind at the time of death, which are process-freed, and (2) the resultant consciousnesses in the five sense-door cognitive processes (eye, ear, nose, tongue, and body consciousness). They are, for eye-door cognitive process, seeing consciousnesses, receiving consciousnesses, investigating consciousnesses, and registration.

Consciousness arises dependent on formations, as the result of formations. Formations are the cause, and the resultant consciousness that appears as the result of formations is the effect. We discern the consciousness that arises as the result in the five-door cognitive process, the mind-door cognitive process that arises following the five-door cognitive process, and the mind-door cognitive process that arises taking dhamma as object. We discern them together with consciousness and mental factors. We discern all of the cognitive processes of the javanas of wholesome consciousnesses and the javanas of unwholesome consciousnesses. We discern the consciousness of rebirth-linking, the consciousness of bhavaṅga, the consciousness of the mind at the time of death, the five sense consciousnesses, receiving, investigating, and registration.

Mentality-Materiality Arises Dependent on Consciousness

When we say "mentality-materiality arises dependent on consciousness," there are two types of consciousness implied: consciousness that appears as a result and consciousness that is not resultant. Both of these consciousnesses cause mentality-materiality to arise. The consciousnesses that appear as results are rebirth-linking, bhavaṅga, the mind at the time of death, the five sense consciousnesses, receiving, investigating, and registration. The consciousnesses that are not resultant are wholesome consciousnesses, unwholesome consciousnesses, and functional consciousnesses. Among the latter, wholesome consciousnesses and unwholesome consciousnesses are sometimes called "kamma formations" (*abhisaṅkhāra*) or "kamma consciousnesses" because they can cause new states of existence to arise. Kamma consciousnesses are the kamma that bring about results. The consciousnesses that bring about mentality-materiality are kamma consciousnesses and consciousnesses that appear as resultants.

First let's look at how kamma-consciousnesses cause mentality-materiality to arise. Kamma consciousnesses are those that are accompanied by formations of our previous life. All we have to do is discern the consciousness among the consciousness + mental factors of the formations of our first past life. This kamma-consciousness causes the mentality-materiality of rebirth-linking, bhavaṅga, the mind at the time of death, the five sense consciousnesses, receiving, investigating, and registration to arise. Therefore the kamma-consciousness of the past is the cause, and the mentality-materiality of rebirth-linking, bhavaṅga, the mind at the time of death, the five sense consciousnesses, receiving, investigating, and registration is the effect. In this case mentality is consciousness and mental factors, and materiality is materiality formed by kamma. We discern these in all of the wholesome and unwholesome cognitive processes.

Now we will look at how consciousness that appears as a result causes mentality-materiality to arise. As stated above, the consciousnesses that appear as resultant are rebirth-linking, bhavaṅga, the mind at the time of death, the five sense consciousnesses, receiving, investigating, and registration. Pa-Auk Sayadaw said that five-door adverting, determining, javana, mind-door adverting, and the consciousnesses of javana should also be included in the discernment of causes and their effects. The second book of the Mahāṭīkā says this: "According to the method taught in the scriptures, consciousness, mentality-materiality, the six sense bases, contact, and feeling are all dhammas that only appear as resultants. However, among the dhammas that appear as resultants, the five sense consciousnesses, receiving, and investigation cannot arise without five-door adverting and registration cannot arise without javana."

The way this second kind of consciousness brings about mentality-materiality is expressed as follows: mentality-materiality that is formed together arises dependent on the arising of consciousness that is formed together. The consciousness in this case is consciousness, the mentality of mentality-materiality are mental factors, and the materiality is materiality formed by consciousness. However, the materiality of rebirth-linking and of the five consciousnesses is materiality formed by kamma.

The above is summarized as follows:

As the past kamma-consciousness arises, the mentality-materiality of rebirth-linking (bhavaṅga, the mind at the time of death, the five sense consciousnesses, receiving, investigating, and registration) arise.

The past kamma-consciousness is the cause, and the mentality-materiality of rebirth-linking (bhavaṅga, the mind at the time of death, the five sense consciousnesses, receiving, investigating, and registration) is the effect.

As the consciousness of rebirth-linking (bhavaṅga, the mind at the time of death, the five-door adverting, the five consciousnesses, receiving, investigating, determining, javana, registration, mind-door adverting, javana, and registration) arises, the mentality-materiality of rebirth-linking (bhavaṅga, the mind at the time of death, the five-door adverting, the five consciousnesses, receiving, investigating, determining, javana, registration, mind-door adverting, javana, and registration) arise.

The consciousness of rebirth-linking (bhavaṅga, the mind at the time of death, the five-door adverting, the five sense consciousnesses, receiving, investigating, determining, javana, registration, mind-door adverting, javana, and registration) is the cause, and the mentality-materiality of rebirth-linking (bhavaṅga, the mind at the time of death, the five-door adverting, the five sense consciousnesses, receiving, investigating, determining, javana, registration, mind-door adverting, javana, and registration) is the effect.

The Six Sense Bases Arise Dependent on Mentality-Materiality

Let's look at how the presence of mentality-materiality is connected to the formation of the six sense bases. Sometimes mentality becomes the cause of the sense bases, sometimes materiality becomes the cause of the sense bases, and sometimes mentality-materiality becomes the cause of the sense bases. Regardless, the sense bases cannot form without mentality-materiality. In order to know this clearly we need see them by dividing them into five cases as follows:

1. The mind base arises dependent on mentality.
2. Sense-base materiality arises dependent on mentality.
3. Sense-base materiality arises dependent on materiality.
4. The mind base arises dependent on materiality.
5. The mind base arises dependent on mentality and materiality.

1. The Mind Base Arises Dependent on Mentality (Mentality Supports the Mind Base)

In this case, mentality is the mental factors that accompany each mind base, and the base refers to each consciousness that arises with the mental factors. In other words, the consciousness that performs the function of the mind base is present because mental factors are present. Knowing the relationship between mentality, materiality that is the base of mentality, and the object that mentality turns toward is very important for understanding dependent origination. Mentality, its material base, and its object are always present together (for beings of the five aggregates realm). One of them cannot be absent. These three become the causes and effects of each other. Mentality becomes the cause of its material base, and material base becomes the effect of mentality. Material base also becomes the cause of mentality, and mentality also becomes the effect of material base.

Meditation on dependent origination is distinguishing all of the factors (in terms of cause and effect) that function when a certain phenomenon is present. After practicing meditation on dependent origination, when we see a phenomenon, we will thoroughly see it in terms of cause and effect. We will no longer be able to see phenomena outside the perspective of cause and effect.

By observing my body and mind, I knew the true nature of the body and mind even before practicing meditation on dependent origination. But by practicing meditation on dependent origination, I was able to clearly know why the things I had experienced previously were the way that they were. For example, before I even practiced meditation on dependent origination I clearly knew, by observing mental phenomena moment-to-moment, that my thoughts and volitions aren't caused by me but arise dependent on their conditions. However, as I practiced meditation on dependent origination, I was able to know that thoughts and volitions are all connected with other mental processes, material base, and objects via cause and effect, and I was able to understand that I couldn't control them, as they arose extremely quickly. In this way my understanding of phenomena became more fine-tuned and accurate.

The above can be summarized as follows:

As the mentality of rebirth-linking (bhavaṅga, the mind at the time of death, five-door adverting, the five consciousnesses, receiving, investigating, determining, javana, registration, mind-door adverting, javana, and registration) arises, the mind base of rebirth-linking (bhavaṅga, the mind at the time of death, five-door adverting, the five consciousnesses, receiving, investigating, determining, javana, registration, mind-door adverting, javana, and registration) arises.

The mentality of rebirth-linking (bhavaṅga, the mind at the time of death, five-door adverting, the five consciousnesses, receiving, investigating, determining, javana, registration, mind-door adverting, javana, and registration) is the cause, and the mind base of rebirth-linking (bhavaṅga, the mind at the time of death, five-door adverting, the five consciousnesses, receiving, investigating, determining, javana, registration, mind-door adverting, javana, and registration) is the effect.

2. The Sense-Base Materiality Arises Dependent on Mentality

According to the *Paṭṭhāna*, excluding the four immaterial resultant consciousnesses, there are eighty-five kinds of consciousness and fifty-two mental factors that arise to support the four kinds of materiality that have arisen in the preceding mental moments. Here, saying that consciousness and mental factors (mentality) support sense-base materiality means that the materiality that is the effect arises first, and the mentality that is the cause arises afterward. After materiality arises once, mentality arises sixteen times. In other words, if we add the past bhavaṅga, materiality receives the support of seventeen consciousnesses. The mentality we refer to when we say "sense-base materiality arises dependent on mentality" is both consciousness and mental factors.

To summarize, using eye consciousness as an example:

With the arising of the mentality of the agitation of bhavaṅga (the cutting off of bhavaṅga, five-door adverting, eye consciousness, receiving, investigating, determining, the first through seventh javanas, the first registration, and the second registration), the eye base (eye sensitivity) arises.

The mentality of the agitation of bhavaṅga (the cutting off of bhavaṅga, five-door adverting, eye consciousness, receiving, investigating, determining, the first through seventh javanas, the first registration, and the second registration) is the cause, and the eye base (eye sensitivity) is the effect.

It is also the same case for ear consciousness, nose consciousness, tongue consciousness, and body consciousness.

3. The Sense-Base Materiality Arises Dependent on Materiality

This means that the four great elements, life faculty, and nutriment inside the kalāpas support the eye, ear, nose, tongue, and body bases (sensitive materiality) in the same kalāpas. Thus, for example, the eye sensitivity (sensitive materiality) of the same kalāpas is supported by the power of the four great elements, the power of protection of life faculty, and the power of nutriment in the same kalāpas. It is the same for ear, nose, tongue, and body bases.

To summarize:

As the four great elements (or life faculty or nutriment) inside the kalāpas of eye (or ear, nose, tongue, or body) sensitivity arise, eye (or ear, nose, tongue, or body) sensitivity arises.

The four great elements (or life faculty or nutriment) inside the kalāpas of eye (or ear, nose, tongue, or body) sensitivity are the cause, and eye (or ear, nose, tongue, or body) sensitivity is the effect.

4. The Mind Base Arises Dependent on Materiality

Mentality cannot arise without a material base (for beings in the five aggregates realms).

The five consciousnesses are mind bases that arise dependent on material bases, such as the material base of the eye and so on. Mind bases excluding the five consciousnesses depend on the heart base.

To summarize:

With the arising of the heart base, the mind base of rebirth-linking (bhavaṅga, the mind at the time of death, five-door adverting, receiving, investigating, determining, the first through seventh javanas, the first registration, the second registration, and mind-door adverting) arises.

The heart base is the cause, and the mind base of rebirth-linking (bhavaṅga, the mind at the time of death, five-door adverting, receiving, investigating, determining, the first through seventh javanas, the first registration, the second registration, and mind-door adverting) is the effect.

With the arising of the eye (or ear, nose, tongue, or body) base, the mind base of eye (or ear, nose, tongue, or body) consciousness arises.

The eye (or ear, nose, tongue, or body) base is the cause, and eye (or ear, nose, tongue, or body) consciousness is the effect.

5. The Mind Base Arises Dependent on Mentality and Materiality

In this case mentality is the mental factors. In other words, it means that the mind base is present because mental factors and material bases are present.

To summarize this using eye consciousness as an example:

As the mentality-materiality of rebirth-linking (bhavaṅga, the mind at the time of death, eye-door adverting, eye consciousness, receiving, investigating, determining, the first through seventh javanas, the first registration, the second registration, and mind-door adverting) arises, the mind base of rebirth-linking (bhavaṅga, the mind at the time of death, eye-door adverting, eye consciousness, receiving, investigating, determining, the first through seventh javanas, the first registration, the second registration, and mind-door adverting) arises.

The materiality-mentality of rebirth-linking (bhavaṅga, the mind at the time of death, eye-door adverting, eye consciousness, receiving, investigating, determining, the first through seventh javanas, the first registration, the second registration, and mind-door adverting) is the cause, and the mind base of rebirth-linking (bhavaṅga, the mind at the time of death, eye-door adverting, eye consciousness, receiving, investigating, determining, the first through seventh javanas, the first registration, the second registration, and mind-door adverting) is the effect.

The ear, nose, tongue, and body consciousnesses are the same as the eye consciousness. In this way, we also discern all of the cognitive processes of wholesome consciousness javanas and unwholesome consciousness javanas.

Contact Arises Dependent on the Six Sense Bases

There are actually six internal sense bases and six external sense bases. These twelve sense bases together are generally called "the six sense bases."

The six internal sense bases are eye sense base, ear sense base, nose sense base, tongue sense base, body sense base, and mind base. The six external sense bases are the base of visible form, the base of sound, the base of smell, the base of taste, the base of touch, and the base of dhamma. The fifty-two kinds of mental factors and the sixteen kinds of subtle matter are included in these twelve sense bases. All consciousnesses are called the mind base, and all mental factors that accompany consciousness as well as the heart base are called the base of dhamma. All mental factors that accompany each consciousness, especially each mental factor that accompanies contact, are called the accompanying bases of dhamma.

There are six kinds of contact: contact of the eye, contact of the ear, contact of the nose, contact of the tongue, contact of the body, and contact of the mind. All forms of contact that accompany rebirth-linking—bhavaṅga, the mind at the time of death, five-door adverting, receiving, investigating, determining, javana, registration, and mind-door adverting—are called contact of the mind.

Contact is something that is accompanied by mentality (consciousness and mental factors), base, and objects. Therefore consciousness, mental factors, base, and objects must be present in order for contact to arise. Consciousness, mental factors, base, and objects are the cause, and contact is the effect.

To summarize:

1a. With the arising of the heart base (a base of dhamma), the contact of the mind of rebirth-linking (bhavaṅga, the mind at the time of death, five-door adverting, receiving, investigating, determining, the first through seventh javanas, the first registration, the second registration, and mind-door adverting) arises.

The heart base (a base of dhamma) is the cause, and the contact of the mind of rebirth-linking (bhavaṅga, the mind at the time of death, five-door adverting, receiving, investigating, determining, the first through seventh javanas, the first registration, the second registration, and mind-door adverting) is the effect.

1b. With the arising of the eye (or ear, nose, tongue, or body) sensitivity (the eye, ear, nose, tongue, or body base), the contact of the eye (or ear, nose, tongue, or body) arises.

The eye (or ear, nose, tongue, or body) sensitivity (the eye, ear, nose, tongue, or body base) is the cause, and the contact of the eye (or ear, nose, tongue, or body) is the effect.

2. With the arising of an external sense base (object), the contact of the mind base of rebirth-linking (bhavaṅga, the mind at the time of death, five-door adverting, the five consciousness, receiving, investigating, determining, the first through seventh javanas, the first registration, the second registration, and mind-door adverting) arises.

The external sense base (object) is the cause, and the contact of the mind base of rebirth-linking (bhavaṅga, the mind at the time of death, five-door adverting, the five consciousness, receiving, investigating, determining, the first through seventh javanas, the first registration, the second registration, and mind-door adverting) is the effect.

3a. With the arising of the consciousness (the mind base) of rebirth-linking (bhavaṅga, the mind at the time of death, five-door adverting, receiving, investigating, determining, the first through seventh javanas, the first registration, the second registration, and mind-door adverting), the contact of the mind of rebirth-linking (bhavaṅga, the mind at the time of death, five-door adverting, receiving, investigating, determining, the first through seventh javanas, the first registration, the second registration, and mind-door adverting) arises. The consciousness (the mind base) of rebirth-linking (bhavaṅga, the mind at the time of death, five-door adverting, receiving, investigating, determining, the first through seventh javanas, the first registration, the second registration, and mind-door adverting) is the cause, and the contact of the mind of rebirth-linking (bhavaṅga, the mind at the time of death, five-door adverting, receiving, investigating, determining, the first through seventh javanas, the first registration, the second registration, and mind-door adverting) is the effect.

3b. With the arising of the mind base of eye (or ear, nose, tongue, or body) consciousness , the contact of the eye (or ear, nose, tongue, or body) arises.

The mind base of eye (or ear, nose, tongue, or body) consciousness is the cause, and the contact of the eye (or ear, nose, tongue, or body) is the effect.

4. With the arising of the accompanying bases of dhamma, the contact of the mind of rebirth-linking (bhavaṅga, the mind at the time of death, five-door adverting, receiving, investigating, determining, the first through seventh javanas, the first registration, the second registration, and mind-door adverting) arises.

The accompanying bases of dhamma are the cause, and the contact of the mind of rebirth-linking (bhavaṅga, the mind at the time of death, five-door adverting, receiving, investigating, determining, the first through seventh javanas, the first registration, the second registration, and mind-door adverting) is the effect.

In this way we discern all of the cognitive processes of wholesome consciousness javanas and unwholesome consciousness javanas.

Feeling Arises Dependent on Contact

The following six kinds of feeling arise because of the six kinds of contact: feeling formed by the contact of the eye, feeling formed by the contact of the ear, feeling formed by the contact of the nose, feeling formed by the contact of the tongue, feeling formed by the contact of the body, and feeling formed by the contact of the mind.

We have to know the difference between "feeling formed by contact of the eye (or ear, nose, tongue, body, or mind)" and "feeling that is dependent on contact of the eye (or ear, nose, tongue, body, or mind)." The feeling formed by contact of the eye (or ear, nose, tongue, body, or mind) is powerful in respect to the contact of the eye (or ear, nose, tongue, body, or mind), and the feelings formed as a result are also powerful. On the other hand, feelings dependent on contact of the eye (or ear, nose, tongue, body, or mind) are those in which contact of the eye (or ear, nose, tongue, body, or mind) arises and affects all consciousnesses, and as a result feeling is formed due to contact in all consciousnesses. Therefore feeling dependent on contact of the eye (or ear, nose, tongue, body, or mind) is weaker than feeling formed by contact of the eye (or ear, nose, tongue, body, or mind). We discern these two feelings when we practice meditation. All we have to do is discern contact of the mind as contact of mind-door adverting.

To summarize:

As contact of the eye (or ear, nose, tongue, body, or mind) arises, feeling formed by contact of the eye (or ear, nose, tongue, body, or mind) arises.

Contact of the eye (or ear, nose, tongue, body, or mind) is the cause, and feeling formed by contact of the eye (or ear, nose, tongue, body, or mind) is the effect.

We discern these in the five-door cognitive process, the mind-door cognitive process that arises following the five-door cognitive process, and the mind-door cognitive process that arises taking dhamma as object. In this way we discern all of the cognitive processes of wholesome consciousness javanas and unwholesome consciousness javanas.

Craving Arises Dependent on Feeling

Here *feeling* is a specific feeling concerning our first future life. Craving concerning our future life arises dependent on the specific feeling concerning our first future life. Many feelings that we experience while living give rise to craving. Some cravings that arise on the basis of these feelings end in our present life and don't connect to our next life. In contrast, other cravings that arise on the basis of feelings in our present life may connect to our next life. Since the twelve links of dependent origination concern the causes and effects of continuous existence in saṃsāra, the craving that we take as object in meditation on dependent origination has to be one that connects with our next life. This craving gives rise to clinging, clinging gives rise to existence, and existence gives rise to birth.

In order to discern feeling in this way, we have to be able to see our first future life.

For example, I discerned that my first future life was the life of a monk. If there is a feeling toward those things that I see about my future life and I arouse attachment toward that feeling by delighting in it, it soon becomes craving. So if a pleasant feeling occurs when I see that people are delighting in my future-life dhamma talk and I arouse attachment toward that feeling, craving arises. Also if I feel happy with the lifestyle of a monk and attachment toward that feeling forms, craving arises.

We can see "arising of craving with the arising of feeling." In this case six kinds of attachment arise: craving toward visible form, sound, smell, taste, touch, and dhamma form. We discern craving through the objects and consciousness + mental factors in the mind-door cognitive process. We see unwholesome consciousnesses with the mental factors of greed and wrong view or conceit arising in javanas.

To summarize:

As feeling formed by contact of the eye (or ear, nose, tongue, body, or mind) arises, craving toward visible form (or sound, smell, taste, touch, or dhamma) arises.

Feeling formed by contact of the eye (or ear, nose, tongue, body, or mind) is the cause and craving toward visible form (or sound, smell, taste, touch, or dhamma) is the effect.

We discern these in the five-door cognitive process, the mind-door cognitive process that arises following the five-door cognitive process, and the mind-door cognitive process that arises taking dhamma as object. In this way we discern all of the cognitive processes of wholesome consciousness javanas and unwholesome consciousness javanas.

Clinging Arises Dependent on Craving

Craving is the first attachment that arises for which feeling is the cause, but the continuation of that craving is called "clinging." In other words, clinging is additional, continued craving for the same object. If we see other cravings that arise following the first craving, we are seeing clinging. All we have to do is see them in the mind-door cognitive process. We see the javanas of unwholesome consciousnesses that are associated with greed, such as craving and wrong view or conceit.

Existence Arises Dependent on Clinging

There are two kinds of existence: (1) existence as kamma (*kammabhava*) and (2) the resultant process of existence (*upapattibhava*). Resultant existence is rebirth-linking. So existence as kamma is the cause of arising, and existence as rebirth-linking is arising (production).

The wholesome kamma and unwholesome kamma that we are accumulating in our present life through our desire for future lives is all called "existence as kamma." The materiality formed by kamma (the aggregate of form) and the resultant mentality (the aggregates of feeling, perception, mental formations, and consciousness) that arises due to those wholesome and unwholesome kammas are called "resultant existence."

To discern existence as kamma, all we have to do is see the formations at the time of death. The formations at the time of death and kamma can be seen as the same. We discern these in the javanas of the mind-door cognitive process. To discern resultant existence, all we have to do is discern the five aggregates of rebirth-linking.

Birth Arises Dependent on Existence

As stated above, existence as kamma is the formations at the time of death, and we can discern it in the javanas of the mind-door cognitive process. Similarly, to discern birth, all we have to do is discern the five aggregates of rebirth-linking of the first future life.

Old Age and Death Arise Dependent on Birth

We can discern old age and death of the first future life in two ways. The first is the method of conventional reality, and the other is the method of ultimate reality. The method of conventional reality is seeing the experience of old age, death, sorrow, lamentation, physical pain, mental pain, and despair after rebirth-linking like a panorama. Although old age and death are present for everyone, the other experiences listed above from sorrow through despair are present or absent depending on the specific being. The method of ultimate reality is seeing the continuous connection of mentality and materiality after rebirth-linking until the mind at the time of death.

The Effect Dependent Origination Meditation Has on Our Outlook on Life

We have now completed our review of the practice of meditation on dependent origination by discerning the twelve links of dependent origination concerning our five past lives. As we live in an age of science, we have the tendency to think that the things that we can't perceive through our senses aren't there. Therefore we think that past lives don't exist. But once we actually see our past lives through the practice of meditation, we no longer have those thoughts. However, that doesn't mean that we are able to prove the existence of past lives scientifically.

When we practice, we develop faith in the things that many practitioners have experienced since the Buddha himself experienced and taught them. At the very least we no longer think that past lives don't exist. Rather, we learn to believe that lives are connected and understand that our present life is but a short life among all of our connected lives. On this basis we no longer try to explain the problems in our lives solely based on our present life's experiences.

In psychoanalysis there is a tendency to explain everything as being affected by our parents when we were young. Since we can see things mistakenly on the basis of this view, we need to let go of this tendency and instead try to see what is actually arising. We also need to admit when we don't know something. Admitting that we don't know when we don't know is wisdom. All we have to do is make an effort to know the things we don't know and to see reality. If we live with this kind of attitude, we will not clumsily make conclusions, our lives will become well grounded, and we will stand on a firm base. Although it takes a long time, we establish a base of life that doesn't easily falter.

Once we know that beings pass through various realms when undergoing rebirth in saṃsāra, we will escape from a human-centered life. Our attitude toward animals will also change. When we know that if we harm others the result of that action will definitely come back to us, we will never harm others.

We will gladly help other beings. We will also understand that this world is one that we can come back to and live in again.

If we look at the people around us who are eager in their practice of Buddhist meditation, the majority of them believe in rebirth. Once we believe in rebirth, our point of view toward our present life changes. Rather than enjoying ourselves in our present life, our biggest priority becomes preparing for our next life. The factors that we consider to be important in life change, and as our practice becomes thus urgent, we always practice without looking elsewhere.

Also, once we believe that rebirth exists, we will never end our own lives. Freud said that humans have the drive of seeking pleasure and the drive of death. Whenever people undergo hardship they long to be at ease. They wish that the hardships would disappear. And so they have thoughts of dying. There is probably not a single person who hasn't ever thought about wanting to die at least once. However, once we believe in rebirth, no matter what kind of situation we are in we will understand that we must practice meditation to control the mind in every moment that we are alive.

Once we practice meditation on materiality, mentality, and dependent origination, our view of death also changes. Rather than fearing death, we fear what state we will die in. In the Pa-Auk "meditation on death" practice, we see when we will die in our present life. Of course the future can change. But when the time comes our present life will certainly end. When our present life is over, our next life will unfold itself based on the law of cause and effect. If lives continue on and on, we don't need to cling too much to our present life. And if our future life is better than our present life, we have no reason to be sad that our present life will end.

6. Vipassanā Meditation

ENTERING VIPASSANĀ MEDITATION

At the time of writing this book, I am practicing vipassanā meditation. I haven't completed it yet. And in this book I intend to write only about the things that I have experienced. I will look at how to actually practice vipassanā meditation on the basis of my experiences.

Vipassanā meditation focuses on seeing the characteristics of impermanence, suffering, and nonself in materiality, mentality, and dependent origination. Actually, we can say that we are practicing vipassanā meditation even while we are practicing meditation on materiality or mentality. This is because we see ultimate materiality and the ultimate mentalities of consciousness and mental factors arising and passing away, and we thus see their characteristics of impermanence, suffering, and nonself. Nevertheless, meditation on materiality, mentality, and dependent origination is separate from vipassanā meditation. This is because the focus of meditation on materiality, mentality, and dependent origination is not on seeing impermanence, suffering, and nonself but rather clearly knowing what materiality, mentality, and dependent origination are.

Before practicing vipassanā meditation we practice understanding the factors of materiality, mentality, and dependent origination in terms of four aspects: characteristics, functions, manifestation, and proximate cause. *Characteristics* are the marked characteristics of a phenomenon. *Function* is the function that operates specifically and tries to achieve a goal. *Manifestation* is the way an experience manifests, the form in which it manifests, or the form it results in. *Proximate cause* is the most important cause that a phenomenon depends upon. Below, we define and understand materiality, mentality, and dependent origination in light of these four aspects.

THE FOUR ASPECTS OF MATERIALITY

Among the five aggregates that constitute existence, materiality is the aggregate of form, and there are altogether twenty-eight kinds. If we list these twenty-eight kinds of materiality, they are as follows: the earth element, the water element, the fire element, the wind element, visible form, sound, smell, taste, nutriment, eye sensitivity, ear sensitivity, nose sensitivity, tongue sensitivity, body sensitivity, the heart base, femininity, masculinity, life faculty, the element of space, bodily intimation, verbal intimation, the lightness of materiality, the malleability of materiality, the wieldiness of materiality, the production of concrete materiality, the continuity of concrete materiality, the decay of concrete materiality, and the impermanence of concrete materiality. We define and understand all of these materialities in terms of the four aspects.

As an example, let's look at defining and understanding the earth element in terms of the four aspects:

- Characteristic: The earth element is hard.
- Function: The earth element is the base of other great elements and the derived materiality that accompanies it within its own kalāpa.
- Manifestation: The earth element receives the materialities that accompany it within its own kalāpa.
- Proximate cause: The other three great elements (water, fire, and wind) within its own kalāpa are the proximate causes.

In this way we can define and understand the characteristics, functions, manifestations, and proximate causes of all materialities in terms of the four aspects.

THE FOUR ASPECTS OF MENTALITY

Mentality consists of mental factors and the aggregate of consciousness. There are fifty-two kinds of mental factors, but these can be divided into the aggregates of feeling, perception, and mental formations; all of the mental factors excluding feeling and perception are the aggregate of mental formations. We define the consciousness + mental factors that are included in each aggregate by dividing mentality into the aggregates of feeling, perception, mental formations, and consciousness in this way. We will first look at the aggregate of consciousness.

The types of consciousness are as follows: rebirth-linking, bhavaṅga, five-door adverting, the five consciousnesses, receiving, investigating, determining, wholesome javanas, unwholesome javanas, registration, mind-door adverting, and the consciousness of death. We define and understand these consciousnesses from the four aspects.

- Characteristic: Consciousnesses are aware of objects, such as the paṭibhāga-nimitta of ānāpānasati.
- Function: Consciousnesses are the forerunners of mental factors. They preside over mental factors and are always present with them.
- Manifestation: Consciousnesses arise as the continuity of the process.
- Proximate cause: Mentality and materiality, mental factors and materiality that is the base of mentality, and base and object are the proximate causes. This is because consciousness cannot arise on its own without mental factors and the materiality that is their base.

Now we'll look at the aggregate of feeling. Feeling is fivefold, consisting of physical pleasure, physical suffering, mental pleasure, mental suffering, and equanimity. We also define and understand feeling in terms of the four aspects.

If we take physical pleasure as an example, it is as follows:

· Characteristic: Physical pleasure experiences desirable contact.
· Function: Physical pleasure invigorates its accompanying
mentalities.
· Manifestation: It manifests as physical pleasure.
· Proximate cause: The faculty of the body is its proximate cause.

We also define the other elements of feeling in terms of the four aspects
in this way. If we define the aggreggate of perception in terms of the four
aspects, it is as follows:

· Characteristic: Perception recognizes the characteristics of objects.
· Function: Perception brings to mind things that have been
perceived in the past. In addition, it creates a sign that becomes the
cause for an object to be perceived again, just as a carpenter marks
the back of lumber.
· Manifestation: Since perception is unable to pierce like lightning
through objects, it appears as the act of trying to understand things
that have been previously sensed in a simple manner depending on
their characteristics, like a blind man touching an elephant.
· Proximate cause: Just as a fawn sees a scarecrow and perceives
it to be a human, the object that appears is the proximate cause,
regardless of how it appears.

The mental factors that constitute the aggregate of mental formations are
all of the mental factors excluding consciousness, feeling, and perception.
If we enumerate these mental factors, they are as follows: the fifty mental
factors of contact, volition, concentration, mental life faculty, attention,
initial application, sustained application, decision, energy, joy, desire, faith,
mindfulness, shame of wrongdoing, fear of wrongdoing, nongreed, nonhatred, neutrality of mind, tranquility of mental body, tranquility of consciousness, lightness of mental body, lightness of consciousness, malleability
of mental body, malleability of consciousness, wieldiness of mental body,
wieldiness of consciousness, proficiency of mental body, proficiency of

consciousness, rectitude of mental body, rectitude of consciousness, right speech, right action, right livelihood, compassion, sympathetic joy, wisdom faculty, delusion, shamelessness of wrongdoing, fearlessness of wrongdoing, restlessness, greed, wrong view, conceit, hatred, envy, avarice, remorse, sloth, torpor, and doubt.

If we define contact among these in terms of the four aspects, it is as follows:

- Characteristic: Contact has the characteristic of touching.
- Function: Contact performs the action of making consciousness come in touch with its object.
- Manifestation: Contact appears as consciousness, the sense doors, and an object come together.
- Proximate cause: The object that has entered the domain of contact is its proximate cause.

We also define the other elements of mental formations in terms of the four aspects in this way.

The Four Aspects of Dependent Origination

Finally, we look at the factors of dependent origination. In other words, ignorance, formations, consciousness, mentality-materiality, the six sense bases, contact, feeling, craving, clinging, existence, birth, old age and death, sorrow, lamentation, physical pain, mental suffering, and despair.

Among these, we will take ignorance as an example and look at defining it in terms of the four aspects.

- Characteristic: Ignorance is not knowing ultimate reality.
- Function: Ignorance has the function of delusion.
- Manifestation: Ignorance appears as the concealment of the true nature of dhammas.
- Proximate cause: Defilement is the proximate cause of ignorance.

We also define the remaining factors of dependent origination in terms of the four aspects in this way.

VIPASSANĀ: SEEING IMPERMANENCE, SUFFERING, AND NONSELF

By defining materiality, mentality, and dependent origination in terms of the four aspects, we can clearly understand the materiality, mentality, and dependent origination that become the objects of vipassanā. We practice vipassanā after completing this task.

Vipassanā is observing the characteristics of impermanence, suffering, and nonself of the ultimate realities of materiality, consciousness, mental factors, and dependent origination. I practiced vipassanā by starting with materiality.

In this practice, we see the materiality, or in other words the properties or characteristics, within kalāpas that arises and passes away. Kalāpas are not ultimate materiality. Kalāpas are materiality gathered together. There are kalāpas where eight kinds of materiality are gathered together, kalāpas where nine kinds of materiality are gathered together, and kalāpas where ten kinds of materiality are gathered together. We have to discern the characteristics of impermanence, suffering, and nonself in the materialities of earth, water, fire, wind, visible form, smell, taste, nutriment, life faculty, materiality of sex, sensitive materiality, heart base, and sounds.

For example, we see the property of hardness of the earth element arising and passing away. We observe it until we clearly see it arising and passing away. Once we clearly see the arising and passing away of hardness, we proceed to the next stage as follows:

We determine that "the arising and passing away of materiality is impermanence." This determining is mind-door adverting. After mind-door adverting, javana arises seven times. As the object of mind-door adverting and javana in this case is materiality, we see materiality arising and passing away in mind-door adverting and javana. When this becomes clear, we take the consciousness that knows materiality to be impermanent as object. In this way, the object changes from materiality to consciousness.

We see that specific consciousness arising and passing away. Afterward we determine that the consciousness is also impermanent. Then mind-door adverting and javanas that take the "consciousness seeing consciousness as impermanent" as object arise. The consciousness that knows it as impermanent arises and passes away. Again we determine that the consciousness that knows it as impermanent is itself impermanent. We practice vipassanā by taking that consciousness as object.

In this way we continue to practice vipassanā by taking the preceding consciousnesses as objects. In my case, when I practiced this, there was only the continuous passing away of consciousness.

Impermanence is arising and passing away, and the impermanence of materiality and mentality is suffering. Nonself is the truth that there are no materialities or mentalities that we can control. By clearly knowing moment-to-moment the fact that the ultimate realities of materiality, consciousness, mental factors, and dependent origination have the properties of impermanence, suffering, and nonself, we escape from thoughts of the permanence, pleasure, and self of dhammas that oppose impermanence, suffering, and nonself.

It is the same when we take dependent origination as object. We see the impermanence, suffering, and nonself of materiality and mentality that arises in dependent origination, and we see the impermanence, suffering, and nonself of the consciousness that discerns them as such. In this way we experience vipassanā on materiality and mentality. Once our insight into materiality and mentality deepens, we can experience nibbāna.

The Reason Why Vipassanā Meditation Is Helpful in Our Daily Lives

Vipassanā meditation is knowing the properties of things as they are. Among these things, the most important are the body and mind that make up our existence. When we practice vipassanā meditation, we will be able to know the body and the mind as they are, or in other words we will know our existence as it is.

We practice vipassanā meditation by taking as object the fundamental elements that constitute our body and mind. The body is made up of ultimate materiality and the mind is made up of the ultimate mentalities of consciousness and mental factors. Once we observe that our body and mind are made up of ultimate materiality and ultimate mentality through vipassanā meditation, we will know that ultimate materiality and ultimate mentality arise and pass away moment-by-moment. Since we see the properties of ultimate materiality and ultimate mentality this way, we will, with the maturing of vipassanā insight knowledge, be able to dispel all of our ignorance and defilements step by step.

"Suffering" is only being able to helplessly watch materiality and mentality arising and passing away quickly, and "nonself" is not being able to control anything pertaining to the body and mind. The mind and body move according to their own laws of cause and effect. There is no room for our thoughts or wishes to interrupt that. Since the situation is like this, suffering is inevitable, and we inevitably experience that suffering. If we resist this, we will only suffer more. The best thing we can do is to try and make it so that only inevitable suffering exists. Even modern Western psychotherapy distinguishes inevitable suffering and self-induced suffering, and focuses on reducing the latter.

We do certain things thinking that they will help us because we don't know clearly. We try to find things to do that will help us on the basis of ignorance. Therefore, since the foundation of our decisions is poor, the result can only be unpleasant. Once we see the fundamental nature of the mind and body and understand which way of living is best for us through vipassanā meditation, we become one with nature. When I look at arahants who stand at the pinnacle of Buddhist practice, it feels like they are one with nature. For instance, Sāriputta is considered to be the wisest after the Buddha. Once, someone struck his back very hard while he was walking, in order to make him angry. However, Sāriputta kept walking without being agitated at all. I wonder if Sāriputta continued walking thinking that there was a particular reason why someone struck him.

Once we know the properties of the body and the mind through vipassanā meditation, we will treat the body and mind as we see fit. We won't get very agitated once we know that the body continuously changes, that it doesn't listen to us, and that suffering is inevitable. Then, the mind won't suffer even if the body suffers. The same goes for the mind. It's important to try and make it so that the mind isn't in pain when the body is in pain, and to make sure the mind doesn't suffer more when it is in pain. We have to prevent vicious cycles that arise from our misunderstandings.

Knowing through vipassanā meditation that everything changes according to its conditions helps us in living our lives. Once we are able to know—even in the moments that we suffer—that suffering also disappears as time passes, we will change the way we look at suffering. Suffering itself will not give us such a hard time. The same goes for happiness. Once we know that happiness also disappears as time passes, we will change the way we look at happiness. Normally when something pleasant disappears we suffer and are afflicted by its aftermath. Once we know that happiness also disappears when the conditions change, we will be able to experience less suffering than when we are clinging to happiness.

Altogether, the way we live our lives will change once we know that everything changes according to the law of cause and effect. Regardless of what phenomena we see, we will see that they occur because they were meant to, and we will accept them. We will also make the best decisions in those situations with a calm and stable mind. We will live calmly without being agitated. This is how vipassanā helps us. Meditation is extremely important not only in terms of religion or spirituality but also in terms of our daily lives.

Conclusion

In returning to my job as a psychiatrist, I am no longer a formal practitioner focused on meditation, but rather I live the life of a householder in society while seeing patients. Although the experiences I had through the practice of samatha were so powerful that they remain vividly in my mind, they too can fade away, as they are affected by conditions. It is up to me whether this happens.

What I understood about the body and mind before this practice is something that anyone can know as long as they observe the body and mind moment-to-moment. These are also things that we can know by thinking logically. Therefore it isn't really difficult for me to convey these experiences to my patients or ordinary people.

However, the things I experienced by practicing meditation on materiality, mentality, and dependent origination, as well as vipassanā meditation based on the practice of samatha, are the ultimate realities of materiality and mentality that I saw only through samatha and are therefore not easy to convey to normal people. Of course I am not the only one who has had these experiences. These are universal experiences that countless practitioners including the Buddha have experienced. How can I share these with other people? Although I have woven together an account in this book, I am sure there are limitations to my effort. In the future I hope I can discover a better way of sharing my experiences. It would be quite rewarding for me if someone reads my book and thinks, "I also want to experience this."

If there is anyone who wants to experience this practice, I hope that person does so wisely by carefully considering his or her own circumstances and the effects this practice has on his or her surroundings. This is because this practice is not only difficult, it also greatly affects one's family, job, and environment.

The reason I was able to accomplish this practice in a relatively short amount of time was because I focused on the present moment and my breath in my normal life. Thanks to the accumulation of these things, I was able to enter jhāna and subsequently practice meditation relatively early when I had the time solely for the sake of practice.

In my period of most-intensive practice, I thought a lot about how my wisdom is lacking.

This is because there were times where I wasn't sure how to understand or accept the worlds I was experiencing. For example, in meditation on the four brahmavihāras, I didn't fully understand when beings of various realms including heavenly beings appeared. I also realized my lack of wisdom when I experienced things for the first time that I hadn't experienced during my life of nearly sixty years. This is also something that I must resolve in the future.

I would also like to address the role of faith concerning this process. Faith is not *knowing* the object of faith. If we clearly knew, there would be no need to have faith. But although we don't know, since we have faith we feel like we will be able to give it a shot. We can always live according to that belief. Embarking on this difficult path of meditation was possible for me because I had faith in the Buddha and faith in Pa-Auk meditation. If I hadn't had any faith, I would not have embarked on the path of confirming the object of my belief and making it my own—obviously there would have been no reason to accept that object, and it would have been impossible to live accordingly.

The practice of meditation has left me with many experiences and tasks to do. In order to complete these tasks, I will make continuous effort until the last moment of my present life.

7. Twenty-Four Pa-Auk Meditation Practices

Method of Practice		object of meditation
Mindfulness of Breathing (ānāpānasati)		breath, nimitta
Meditation on the Thirty-Two Constituent Parts of the Body		head hairs, body hairs, nails, teeth, skin, flesh, sinews, bones, bone marrow, kidneys, heart, liver, membrane, spleen, lungs, intestines, mesentery, contents of the stomach, feces, brain, bile, phlegm, pus, blood, sweat, fat, tears, grease, spittle, snot, oil of the joints, urine
Ten Kasiṇa Meditations		earth kasiṇa, water kasiṇa, fire kasiṇa, wind kasiṇa, black kasiṇa, yellow kasiṇa, red kasiṇa, white kasiṇa, kasiṇa of light, kasiṇa of enclosed space
Four Immaterial States		boundless space, boundless consciousness, nothingness, neither-perception-nor-nonperception
Four Sublime Abidings (Four Brahmavihāras, Four Immeasurables)	loving-kindness	"May beings be free from danger," "May beings be free from mental suffering," "May beings be free from physical suffering," "May beings be well and happy."
	compassion	"May beings be free from all suffering."
	sympathetic joy	"May beings not lose what they have gained."
	equanimity	"We are the owner of our kamma. This person must live according to his/her kamma."

Method of Practice		object of meditation
Meditation on Foulness		A dead person that we have seen while living our lives (except an image of a dead person of the opposite sex or a person that we might be attracted to sexually)
Recollection of Death		"I too will die."
Recollection of the Buddha		One of the 9 qualities of the Buddha—worthy one, perfectly enlightened, perfected in knowledge and conduct, well-gone, knower of the worlds, the unsurpassed and tamer of men fit to be tamed, the teacher of devas and human beings, the enlightened one, the blessed one—or other virtues of the Buddha
Four Elements Meditation	earth element	hardness, roughness, heaviness, softness, smoothness, lightness
	water element	cohesion, flowing
	fire element	heat, cold
	wind element	pushing, supporting

Bibliography

Bodhi, Bhikkhu. *A Comprehensive Manual of Abhidhamma: The Abhidhammattha Sanagha.* Onalaska, WA: BPS Parayatti Editions, 2000.

———. *The Connected Discourses of the Buddha: A Translation of the Saṃyutta Nikāya.* Boston: Wisdom Publications, 2016.

———. *The Numerical Discourses of the Buddha: A Complete Translation of the Aṅguttara Nikāya.* Boston: Wisdom Publications, 2012.

Ñāṇamoli, Bhikkhu. *The Path of Purification: Visuddhimagga.* Buddhist Publication Society, 2010.

Ñāṇamoli, Bhikkhu, and Bhikkhu Bodhi. *The Middle Length Discourses of the Buddha: A Translation of the Majjhima Nikāya.* Boston: Wisdom Publications, 2015.

Pe Maung Tin, trans. *The Path of Purity: A Translation of Buddhagosa's Visuddhimagga.* 3 vols. Pali Text Society, 1975.

Sayadaw, Pa-Auk. *Knowing and Seeing.* Singapore: Pa-Auk Meditation Centre, 2010.

Walshe, Maurice. *The Long Discourses of the Buddha: A Translation of the Dīgha Nikāya.* Boston: Wisdom Publications, 2013.

Glossary

absorption concentration. *See* jhāna.

access concentration (upacārasamādhi). Nonabsorptive concentration on the threshold of jhāna.

adverting. Turning attention toward an object. *See* mind-door adverting and five-door adverting.

aggregates. *See* five aggregates of clinging (*pañcaupādānakkhandha*).

ānāpānasati. Mindfulness of breathing.

arahant. Perfected one, fully enlightened being.

bhavaṅga. Life-continuum, the consciousness by which continuity is maintained within a lifespan.

bhikkhu. A monk.

boundless consciousness. The second of the four immaterial jhānas, the consciousness that knows only boundless space. *See also* four immaterial jhānas (*arūpajhāna*).

boundless space. The first of the four immaterial jhānas, a state of infinite space with no materiality. *See also* four immaterial jhānas (*arūpajhāna*).

brahma realm. A high divine realm of existence; brahmas are the heavenly beings of that realm.

brahmavihāras. Refers to four qualities or boundless states. *See* four brahmavihāras / four immeasurables.

bringing the mind together. Mental unification, the purpose of samatha meditation practices.

cognitive process of jhāna. The cognitive process that arises at the mind door in association with any of the jhānas; it consists of a series of cognitive moments: preparation (*parikamma*), access (*upacāra*), conformity (*anuloma*), change-of-lineage (*gotrabhū*), and *javana.*

consciousness + mental factors. Combination used to indicate the sum of both consciousness and mental factors that can be discerned in various cognitive processes.

counterpart sign. See paṭibhāga-nimitta.

dependent origination (paṭiccasamuppāda). The arising of phenomena in accordance with cause and effect. *See also* twelve links of dependent origination.

determining. The moment in a five-door cognitive process when the sense consciousness identifies the sense object.

deva. Heavenly being (males are devas, females are devis).

Dhamma. 1. The Teaching of the Buddha. 2. Phenomenon, state, mental object.

ethically variable factors (aññasamānacetasika). The universal and occasional mental factors taken all together, since they all assume the same quality as whatever consciousness they are combined with. *See* seven mental factors present in every consciousness *and* six mental factors that occasionally arise with consciousness.

eye of wisdom. The ability to see the ultimate realities, which are not perceptible to the naked eye.

five-door adverting. The moment in a five-door cognitive process in which attention is turned toward the object of the sense door; for example, eye-door adverting is the moment in which, when visible form impinges on eye sensitivity, attention goes to the visible form in order to see it.

five-door cognitive process. A cognitive process that arises by taking visible form, sound, smell, taste, and touch as objects from the eye, ear, nose, tongue, and body. Consists of a specific series of cognitive moments: *bhavaṅga*, adverting, consciousness, receiving, investigation, determining, *javana*, and registration. This is usually followed by the mind-door process, unless the object or the power of the mind is weak.

heart base. A form of concrete materiality that is the support for mental processes.

investigation. The moment in a five-door cognitive process when a sensory object is examined in the mind-door.

javana. Impulsion consciousness, a stage of the cognitive process in which consciousness experiences an object most vividly. Also the point at which wholesome or unwholesome consciousnesses arise and thus have an effect on present and future lives.

jhāna. Absorption consciousness, in which the mind is "brought together as one." There are four material jhānas and four immaterial jhānas.

jhānic factors. The wholesome factors that appear in the state of jhāna, as the

hindrances and suffering disappear. Each jhāna has a specific number of these factors. *See* five factors of jhāna.

kalāpa. The smallest unit of mass in which materiality can exist.

kamma. Action (wholesome or unwholesome) that leads to results.

kamma-consciousness. Nonresultant consciousness that causes new states of existence to arise.

kasiṇa. Literally means "complete" or "whole." Used to refer to ten specific concentration subjects (four colors and six elements).

life faculty. The factor responsible for maintaining the existence of other material elements and mental factors.

materiality. Form or matter. *See also* ultimate materiality *and* ultimate realities.

mentality. Mental phenomena, both consciousness and mental factors. *See also* ultimate mentality *and* ultimate realities.

mind-door adverting. The moment in a mind-door cognitive process in which attention is initially turned toward a mental object.

mind-door cognitive process. A cognitive process that arises by the mind taking a mental formation as object. Can arise following a five-door cognitive process, or without association with a five-door cognitive process (either as a cognitive process of jhāna or a cognitive process that arises taking dhamma as object). Consists of a specific series of cognitive moments: *bhavaṅga,* mind-door adverting, *javana,* and registration.

neither-perception-nor-nonperception. The fourth of the four immaterial jhānas, a state in which consciousness and mental factors are neither present nor absent. *See also* four immaterial jhānas (*arūpajhāna*).

nibbāna. The unconditioned, deathless, cessation.

nimitta. Sign of concentration.

nothingness. The third of the four immaterial jhanas, the absence of boundless space and its consciousness. *See also* four immaterial jhānas (*arūpajhāna*).

occasionals. See six mental factors that occasionally arise with consciousness (*pakiṇṇaka*).

paṭibhāga-nimitta. The counterpart sign of concentration, a pure or refined object.

rebirth-linking. The process that generates a new life in the unfolding of multiple lives.

receiving. The moment in the five-door cognitive process when a sensory object is received in the mind door.

registration (*tadārammaṇa*). The concluding moments of a cognitive process, which arise after *javana.*

rūpa. Materiality (or material form, matter), one of the five aggregates.

samādhi. Meditative concentration, a state in which the mind has been "brought together."

samatha. The practice of cultivating the jhānas and samādhi.

saṃsāra. The cycle of rebirth.

saṅkhāra. Formation, mental formation (one of the five aggregates), kammic formation, prompting.

saññā. Perception, one of the five aggregates.

sense doors. See six sense doors.

sensitive materiality. Five types of matter located in each of the five sense organs. They receive sense objects. *See also* five sensitive materialities.

sutta. Buddhist scripture.

ultimate materiality. The irreducible reality of material form. *See also* ultimate realities.

ultimate mentality. The irreducible reality of mental phenomena. *See also* ultimate realities.

ultimate realities (paramattha). Phenomena that are irreducible, contemplated so as to have a basis for insight meditation. There are four ultimate realities: (1) of materiality; of mentality, which includes both (2) consciousness and (3) mental factors; and (4) of nibbāna (the unconditioned).

universals. See seven mental factors present in every consciousness (*sabbacittasādhāraṇa*).

vedanā. Feeling, one of the five aggregates.

viññāṇa. Consciousness, one of the five aggregates.

vipassanā. Insight, the observation of materiality, mentality, and dependent origination to see the characteristics of impermanence, suffering, and nonself.

wise attention. Seeing ultimate materiality and ultimate mentality when coming into contact with objects through the six sense doors, and seeing their properties of impermanence, suffering, nonself, and impurity.

ENUMERATIONS

two groups of consciousnesses. (1) Rebirth-linking, *bhavaṅga*, and the consciousness of death are consciousnesses that have transcended the cognitive process, and (2) consciousness of the five-door cognitive process and consciousness of the mind-door cognitive process are consciousnesses of the cognitive process.

two kinds of existence. Existence as kamma (*kamma bhava*) and the resultant process of existence (*upapattibhava*).

two kinds of unwholesome consciousness rooted in ignorance. Permutations of unwholesome consciousnesses rooted in ignorance, depending on whether ignorance is associated with restlessness or with doubt. *See* table 6.

two types of nimitta. The acquired sign (*uggaha-nimitta*) and the counterpart sign (*paṭibhāga-nimitta*).

three abstinences (virati). Right speech, right action, and right livelihood.

three kinds of cognitive processes. (1) The cognitive process that arises in the eye, ear, nose, tongue, and body (the five doors) and then continues to the mind door; (2) the cognitive process that only arises in the mind door; and (3) the cognitive process of jhāna, which is a kind of mind-door cognitive process but assumes a distinctive character and is therefore classified separately.

three kinds of materiality that form during rebirth-linking. Kalāpas that have the heart base, kalāpas that have body sensitivity, and kalāpas that have materiality of sex.

three marks of existence. Impermanence (*anicca*), suffering (*dukkha*), and nonself (*anattā*).

three realms in which beings can dwell. The desire realm (*kāmāvacara*), the material realm (*rūpāvacara*), and the immaterial realm (*arūpāvacara*).

three trainings. Morality (*sīla*), concentration (*samādhi*), and wisdom (*paññā*).

three types of kalāpas. (1) From eight kinds of materiality gathered together, (2) from nine kinds of materiality gathered together, and (3) from ten kinds of materiality gathered together.

four aspects of dependent origination, materiality, and mentality. Characteristic, function, manifestation, and proximate cause.

four brahmavihāras / four immeasurables. Loving-kindness (*mettā*), compassion (*karuṇā*), sympathetic joy (*muditā*), and equanimity (*upekkhā*).

four great elements. The earth element (*paṭhavīdhātu*), the water element (*āpodhātu*), the fire element (*tejodhātu*), and the wind element (*vāyodhātu*).

four immaterial jhānas (arūpajhāna). Boundless space (*ākāsānañcāyatana*), boundless consciousness (*viññāṇañcāyatana*), nothingness (*ākiñcaññāyatana*), and neither-perception-nor-nonperception (*nevasaññānāsaññāyatana*).

four material jhānas. The first, second, third, and fourth.

four noble truths (cattāri ariyasaccāni). The noble truth of suffering (*dukkha ariyasacca*), the noble truth of origin (*samudaya ariyasacca*), the noble truth of cessation (*nirodha ariyasacca*), and the noble truth of the path (*magga ariyasacca*).

four parts of the body marked by the fire element. Heat that warms the body, heat that causes maturing and aging, heat of fever, and digestive heat.

four preliminary javanas of access concentration. Preparation, access, conformity, and change-of-lineage.

four protective meditations (caturārakkha bhāvanā). Loving-kindness meditation from the four brahmavihāras, recollection of the Buddha, meditation on foulness, and recollection of death.

four stages of focusing on the breath. The first stage is knowing that the breath is long if it is long; the second stage is knowing the breath is short if it is short; the third stage is knowing the whole body of breath, not missing a single breath; the fourth is experiencing the subtle breath.

four sublime abidings. See four brahmavihāras / four immeasurables.

four unwholesome universals. See fourteen unwholesome mental factors.

five aggregates (pañca-kkhandha). The five factors that constitute sentient beings: the aggregate of *rūpa* (materiality), the aggregate of *vedanā* (feeling), the aggregate of *saññā* (perception), the aggregate of *saṅkhāra* (intention or mental formations excluding the other mental aggregates), and the aggregate of *viññāṇa* (consciousness).

five consciousnesses. Eye consciousness, ear consciousness, nose consciousness, tongue consciousness, and body consciousness.

five factors of jhāna. Initial application (*vitakka*), sustained application (*vicāra*), joy (*pīti*), happiness (*sukha*), and concentration (*ekaggata*); each of the four material jhānas has some or all of these; *see* table 2.

five hindrances (pañca nīvaraṇāni). Sensual desire (*kāmacchanda*), ill will (*vyāpāda*), sloth and torpor (*thīna-middha*), restlessness and remorse (*uddhacca-kukkucca*), and doubt (*vicikicchā*).

five masteries of jhāna. The ability to (1) enter jhāna whenever we want, (2) stay in jhāna as long as we want, (3) exit jhāna whenever we want, (4) turn our mind to the factors of jhāna, (5) examine the factors of jhāna.

five past causes and *five present effects.* Past ignorance, craving, clinging, formations, and kamma, and present consciousness, mentality-materiality, the six sense bases, contact, and feeling.

five present causes and *five future effects.* Present ignorance, craving, clinging, formations, and kamma, and future consciousness, mentality-materiality, six sense bases, contact, and feeling.

five sensitive materialities. Eye, ear, nose, tongue, and body sensitivity, located within the sense organs; doors to the five consciousnesses.

five types of feeling. Physical pleasure, physical suffering, mental pleasure, mental suffering, and equanimity.

six categories of dhammas that give rise only to the mind-door process. Sensitive materiality (*pasādarūpa*; eye-, ear-, nose-, tongue-, and body-sensitive materiality), subtle matter (*sukhumarūpa*; sixteen kinds), consciousness (*citta*), mental factors (*cetasika*), *nibbāna*, and concepts.

six kinds of contact. Contact of the eye, contact of the ear, contact of the nose, contact of the tongue, contact of the body, and contact of the mind.

six mental factors that occasionally arise with consciousness (*pakiṇṇaka*). Also known as the "six occasionals." Initial application (*vitakka*), sustained application (*vicāra*), decision (*adhimokkha*), energy (*viriya*), joy (*pīti*), and desire (*chanda*).

six parts of the body marked by the wind element. Wind that rises, wind that falls, wind in the abdomen, wind in the intestines, wind in the entire body, and the in-breath and out-breath.

six properties of the earth element. *See* twelve properties of the four great elements.

six sense bases. *See* twelve sense bases.

six sense doors. Eye, ear, nose, tongue, body, and mind doors.

seven mental factors present in every consciousness (*sabbacittasādhāraṇa*). Also known as the "seven universals." Contact (*phassa*), feeling (*vedanā*), perception (*saññā*), volition (*cetanā*), concentration (*ekaggatā*), life faculty (*jīvitindriya*), and attention (*manasikāra*).

eight kinds of basic materiality. The earth element, the water element, the fire element, the wind element, color, smell, taste, and nutriment (a subset of eighteen kinds of concrete materiality).

eight kinds of suffering. Birth, aging, sickness, death, separating from loved ones, uniting with enemies, not getting what we desire, and the five aggregates of clinging.

eight kinds of unwholesome consciousness rooted in greed. Permutations of unwholesome consciousnesses rooted in greed, depending on whether or not they are prompted, accompanied by joy or equanimity, and/or associated with greed and wrong view. *See* table 6.

eight kinds of unwholesome consciousness rooted in hatred. Permutations of unwholesome consciousnesses rooted in hatred, depending on whether or not they are prompted and/or associated with hatred, envy, avarice, and remorse. *See* table 6.

eight kinds of wholesome sense-sphere consciousness. Permutations of wholesome sense-sphere consciousnesses depending on whether or not they are prompted, accompanied by joy or equanimity, and/or associated with knowledge. *See* table 6.

eightfold path, noble. Right view (*sammā-diṭṭhi*), right thought (*sammā-saṅkappa*),

right speech (*sammā-vācā*), right action (*sammā-kammanta*), right livelihood (*sammā-ājīva*), right effort (*sammā-vāyāma*), right mindfulness (*sammā-sati*), and right concentration (*sammā-samādhi*).

ten directions. North, west, south, east, northwest, northeast, southwest, southeast, below, and above.

ten fetters. Mental chains keeping us in saṃsāra. Belief in a self (*sakkāya-diṭṭhi*), attachment to rituals (*sīlabbata-parāmāsa*), doubt or uncertainty (*vicikicchā*), sensual desire (*kāmacchanda*), ill will (*vyāpāda*), lust for material existence (*rūparāga*), lust for immaterial existence (*arūparāga*), conceit (*māna*), restlessness (*uddhacca*), and ignorance (*avijjā*).

ten kasiṇas. The earth *kasiṇa*, the water *kasiṇa*, the fire *kasiṇa*, the wind *kasiṇa*, the black *kasiṇa*, the yellow *kasiṇa*, the red *kasiṇa*, the white *kasiṇa*, the *kasiṇa* of light, and the *kasiṇa* of enclosed space.

ten nonconcrete materialities. Element of space, bodily intimation, verbal intimation, lightness, malleability, wieldiness, production, continuity, decay, and impermanence.

ten objects of foulness. The swollen corpse, the discolored corpse, the festering corpse, the fissured corpse, the gnawed corpse, the dismembered corpse, the scattered corpse, the bleeding corpse, the worm-eaten corpse, and the skeleton.

ten qualities (or epithets) of the Buddha. Worthy one (*arahaṃ*), perfectly enlightened (*sammāsambuddho*), perfected in knowledge and conduct (*vijjā-caraṇasampanno*), well-gone (*sugato*), knower of the worlds (*lokavidū*), the unsurpassed (*anuttaro*), the tamer of men fit to be tamed (*purisadammasārathī*), the teacher of devas and human beings (*satthādevamanussānaṃ*), the enlightened one (*buddho*), the blessed one (*bhagavā*).

ten recollections. Recollection of the Buddha, recollection of the Dhamma, recollection of the Sangha, recollection of morality (*sīla*), recollection of liberality (*cāga*), recollection of the attributes of heavenly beings (*deva*), mindfulness of the body (*kāya*), recollection of death, mindfulness of breathing, and recollection of peace.

ten unwholesome occasionals. *See* fourteen unwholesome mental factors.

twelve links of dependent origination. Formations arising dependent on ignorance (*avijjāpaccayā saṅkhāra*), consciousness arising dependent on formations (*saṅkhārapaccayā viññāṇam*), mentality-materiality arising dependent on consciousness (*viññāṇapaccayā nāmarūpam*), the six sense bases arising dependent on mentality-materiality (*nāmarūpapaccayā saḷāyatanam*), contact arising dependent on the six sense bases (*saḷāyatanapaccayā phasso*), feeling arising

dependent on contact (*phassapaccayā vedanā*), craving arising dependent on feeling (*vedanāpaccayā taṇhā*), clinging arising dependent on craving (*taṇhāpaccayā upādānam*), existence arising dependent on clinging (*upādānapaccayā bhavo*), birth arising dependent on existence (*bhavapaccayā jāti*), and old age, death, sorrow, lamentation, pain, dissatisfaction, and despair arising dependent on birth (*jātipaccayā jarāmaraṇaṃsokaparidevadukkhadomanassūpāyāsā*).

twelve parts of the body marked by the water element. Bile, phlegm, pus, blood, sweat, fat, tears, grease, spittle, snot, oil of the joints, and urine.

twelve properties of the four great elements. Comprising (1) six properties of the earth element (hardness, roughness, and heaviness; softness, smoothness, and lightness), (2) two properties of the water element (flowing and cohesion), (3) two properties of the fire element (heat and coldness), and (4) two properties of the wind element (supporting and pushing).

twelve sense bases. Six internal sense bases (eye, ear, nose, tongue, body sensitivity, and mind base) and six external sense bases (visible form, sound, smell, taste, touch, and dhamma); all consciousnesses are called the mind base.

twelve types of beings. Beings (*sattā*), breathing things (*pāṇā*), creatures (*bhūtā*), people (*puggalā*), individuals (*attabhāvapariyāpannā*), women (*itthiyo*), men (*purisā*), enlightened beings (*ariyā*), unenlightened beings (*anariyā*), heavenly beings (*devā*), human beings (*manussā*), and beings in the lower realms (*vinipātikā*).

thirteen ethically variable mental factors. A combination of the seven universal and six occasional mental factors. *See* seven mental factors present in every consciousness *and* six mental factors that occasionally arise with consciousness.

fourteen unwholesome mental factors. Four "unwholesome universals": delusion (*moha*), shamelessness of wrongdoing (*ahirika*), fearlessness of wrongdoing (*anottappa*), and restlessness (*uddhacca*); ten "unwholesome occasionals": greed (*lobha*), wrong view (*diṭṭhi*), conceit (*māna*), hatred (*dosa*), envy (*issā*), avarice (*macchariya*), remorse (*kukkucca*), sloth (*thīna*), torpor (*middha*), and doubt (*vicikicchā*).

sixteen kinds of subtle materiality. The water element, nutriment, the heart base, femininity, masculinity, life faculty, the space element, bodily intimation, verbal intimation, lightness of materiality, malleability of materiality, wieldiness of materiality, the characteristics of production, continuity, and decay of materiality, and impermanence.

eighteen concrete materialities. The earth element, the water element, the fire element, the wind element, color (visible form), sound, smell, taste, nutriment, eye

sensitivity, ear sensitivity, nose sensitivity, tongue sensitivity, body sensitivity, the heart base, femininity, masculinity, and life faculty.

eighteen unwholesome conciousnesses. Comprising the eight kinds of unwholesome consciousness rooted in greed, the eight kinds of unwholesome consciousness rooted in hatred, and the two kinds of unwholesome consciousness rooted in ignorance.

nineteen universal beautiful mental factors. Faith (*saddhā*), mindfulness (*sati*), shame of wrongdoing (*hiri*), fear of wrongdoing (*ottappa*), nongreed (*alobha*), nonhatred (*adosa*), neutrality of mind (*tatramajjhattatā*), tranquility of the mental body (*kāyapassaddhi*), tranquility of consciousness (*cittapassaddhi*), lightness of the mental body (*kāyalahutā*), lightness of consciousness (*cittalahutā*), malleability of the mental body (*kāyamudutā*), malleability of consciousness (*cittamudutā*), wieldiness of the mental body (*kāyakammaññatā*), wieldiness of consciousness (*cittakammaññatā)*, proficiency of the mental body (*kāyapāguññatā*), proficiency of consciousness (*cittapāguññatā*), rectitude of the mental body (*kāyujjukatā*), and rectitude of consciousness (*cittujjukatā*).

twenty parts of the body marked by the earth element. Head hairs, body hairs, nails, teeth, skin, flesh, sinews, bones, bone marrow, kidneys, heart, liver, membrane, spleen, lungs, intestines, mesentery, contents of the stomach, feces, and the brain.

twenty-five beautiful mental factors. The nineteen universal beautiful mental factors, the three abstinences, the two illimitables, and wisdom.

twenty-eight kinds of materiality. The earth element, the water element, the fire element, the wind element, visible form, sound, smell, taste, nutriment, eye sensitivity, ear sensitivity, nose sensitivity, tongue sensitivity, body sensitivity, the heart base, femininity, masculinity, life faculty, the element of space, bodily intimation, verbal intimation, the lightness of materiality, the malleability of materiality, the wieldiness of materiality, the production of concrete materiality, the continuity of concrete materiality, the decay of concrete materiality, and the impermanence of concrete materiality.

thirty-two constituent parts of the body. Head hairs, body hairs, nails, teeth, skin, flesh, sinews, bones, bone marrow, kidneys, heart, liver, membrane, spleen, lungs, intestines, mesentery, contents of the stomach, feces, brain, bile, phlegm, pus, blood, sweat, fat, tears, grease, spittle, snot, oil of the joints, and urine.

forty methods of cultivating samatha. The ten *kasiṇas*, the ten subjects of foulness, the ten recollections, the four sublime abidings (*brahmavihāra*), the four immaterial states (*arūpajhāna*), one perception, and one analysis.

forty-two constituents of the body. See thirty-two constituent parts of the body,

plus four parts of the body marked by the fire element *and* six parts of the body marked by the wind element.

fifty-two mental factors. Comprising the thirteen ethically variable mental factors, the twenty-five beautiful mental factors, and the fourteen unwholesome mental factors. *See* table 4.

About the Author

Born 1956 in Pusan, Hyunsoo Jeon became a psychiatrist and a psychotherapy specialist after graduating from Kyung-nam High School and Pusan National University School of Medicine, and receiving neuropsychiatry training at the Soonchunhyang University Hospital. He attended Hanyang University Medical School where he obtained his master's and doctoral degrees. He was introduced to Buddhist teachings two years after becoming a neuropsychiatry resident. After that, he met with patients and studied Buddhism concurrently, using Buddhist wisdom to aid him in treating his patients. The use of Buddhist wisdom was so effective that he detailed his experiences in his other books.

In 1990, he opened Hyunsoo Jeon Psychiatry Clinic. In 2003, he took a month off from his clinic to go to Burma to partake in vipassanā training. Later that year, he gathered specialists in Buddhism, psychology, and psychiatry to study together and hold discussions. This gathering developed into the Korean Association of Buddhism and Psychotherapy in 2007. In March 2009, he took a year off from therapy to practice Buddhism, travel, and write books. In March 2010, he reopened his clinic and returned to helping patients. He also spent two years practicing samatha and vipassanā in Myanmar and Korea.

Dr. Jeon has authored the following books in Korean: *Cry When You Want to Cry* and *A Psychiatrist's Wisdom from the Buddha: Stories of Healing the*

Mind, A Psychiatrist's "Guidebook for the Mind," and collaborated in writing *Value of Labor: A Buddhist Perspective,* as well as translating Mark Epstein's book *Thoughts without a Thinker* into Korean.

ABOUT THE TRANSLATOR

Born in the United States, HaNul Jun graduated from the University of Michigan in 2017 with a master of arts in Asian Languages and Cultures focusing on Buddhist thought and practice.

During a period of more than ten years Jun has had various experiences with Buddhism and meditative practice. Having first ordained temporarily as a novice monk in Myanmar in 2002, he also underwent temporary ordination as a Korean novice at Woljeong temple in Kangwon Province in 2006, and became a fully-ordained bhikkhu in Myanmar in 2013. He also traveled to Dharamsala, India, in 2007 and 2011 to study Tibetan Buddhism. He has studied vipassanā meditation under several Burmese meditation teachers. He also practiced Korean Ganhwa Seon at a retreat at Baekdamsa Temple.

Jun is currently working at Google in Austin, Texas. Despite his departure from Buddhism academically, he remains engaged and interested in Buddhist meditation.

What to Read Next
from Wisdom Publications

Focused and Fearless
A Meditator's Guide to States of Deep Joy, Calm, and Clarity
Shaila Catherine

"A wonderful book. Shaila Catherine describes the paths of deep concentration and transforming insight in a way that both inspires and enriches our practice. Her prose and her understanding are exceptionally lucid. This book is a treat to read."—Joseph Goldstein, author of *A Heart Full of Peace*

Wisdom Wide and Deep
A Practical Handbook for Mastering Jhāna and Vipassanā
Shaila Catherine
Foreword by Pa-Auk Sayadaw

"If you are interested in Dharma study, then Shaila's book belongs in your library."—Phillip Moffitt

Stilling the Mind
Shamatha Teachings from Dudjom Lingpa's Vajra Essence
B. Alan Wallace

"A much needed, very welcome book."—Jetsun Khandro Rinpoche

About Wisdom Publications

Wisdom Publications is the leading publisher of classic and contemporary Buddhist books and practical works on mindfulness. To learn more about us or to explore our other books, please visit our website at wisdompubs.org or contact us at the address below.

Wisdom Publications
199 Elm Street
Somerville, MA 02144 USA

We are a 501(c)(3) organization, and donations in support of our mission are tax deductible.

Wisdom Publications is affiliated with the Foundation for the Preservation of the Mahayana Tradition (FPMT).